CENTS &
SENSIBILITY

How Couples Can Agree About Money

BETHANY & SCOTT
PALMER

 LIFE JOURNEY®

Bringing Home the Message for Life

COOK COMMUNICATIONS MINISTRIES
Colorado Springs, Colorado • Paris, Ontario
KINGSWAY COMMUNICATIONS LTD
Eastbourne, England

Life Journey® is an imprint of
Cook Communications Ministries, Colorado Springs, CO 80918
Cook Communications, Paris, Ontario
Kingsway Communications, Eastbourne, England

CENTS AND SENSIBILITY
© 2005 by Bethany and Scott Palmer

First Printing, 2005
Printed in the United States of America
1 2 3 4 5 6 7 8 9 10 Printing/Year 09 08 07 06 05

ISBN: 078144148X

We dedicate this book to our parents:
Chuck, Sue, Bruce, and Judy.
Thank you for your unyielding support and prayers.

CONTENTS

Part Three: Checks and Balances

Building Financial Compatibility and Cooperation

Part Four: Developing a Positive, Prosperous Partnership

Five Hot Buttons on Which Couples Need Compatible
    Perspectives

ACKNOWLEDGMENTS

We would like to thank the many people who made this book possible and helped make our dream come true.

Thank you to our wonderful staff at Envoy Financial for your support. Other professionals we would like to thank include Keith Wall, Mary McNeil, Dan Benson, Sarano Kelley, and Jackie Johnson.

We also want to thank our fathers for introducing us to the financial industry. Without your knowledge and guidance, this book would have never been possible.

Next we want to thank Grams, Brent, Steve, TL, Dean, Cher, Shelly, Chris, Amy, Sandy, Bruce, Val, Larry, Tom, Deb, Ann, Jim, and Bob.

Finally, we want to thank our boys, Cole and Cade, for all the joy you bring to our lives.

THE CLASH OVER CASH

How You and Your Partner Approach Money
Can Cause Your Relationship to Sink or Soar

When we began telling friends, clients, and acquaintances that we were writing a book on how couples can agree about money, we nearly always received one of two responses. Some people would tell us, "Hurry up and get it done. My wife and I need help—lots of help—in that area." Others would say, "Oh, you can interview my husband and me for your book." Then they would quickly add, "We're a perfect example of what *not* to do when it comes to dealing with money in marriage."

What we almost never heard was this: "A book about financial compatibility in relationships? Nah, we don't need it. That's not a problem for us."

It's true. The vast majority of couples—even Christian couples—struggle to some degree with money management, budgeting, debt, investments, and everything else related to finances. Indeed, issues surrounding money are one of the primary reasons couples argue. This is not merely conjecture—numerous research studies show that money and marriage are often a toxic blend. For example, Drs. Scott Stanley and Howard Markman, two of the nation's leading researchers on relationship issues, conducted a large-scale study to determine what causes couples the most trouble. Their finding? Money is the number one issue people say they argue about most in marriage.[1]

We could fill pages with similar research findings, but chances are you don't need to be convinced. You know that for most couples, money is a contentious subject. Sometimes the disagreements are relatively mild, generating tension rather than tantrums, tussles rather than tirades. For many other couples, however, financial disputes represent a major issue that causes ongoing strain, division, and heated arguments.

If left unaddressed, money conflicts can undermine the foundation of a marriage. Sometimes what begins as a little wrangling about saving and spending can lead to all-out warfare, with disastrous consequences. One study found that 56 percent of all divorces are a result of financial tension in the home.[2]

Why is money so often at the heart of relationship conflict? Because spouses frequently approach financial matters differently—sometimes *extremely* differently. In many cases, one spouse is a saver, while the other is a spender. Or it might be that one partner is a risk-taker, while the other is a security-seeker. Other times, one person will get exceedingly stressed about mounting debt, while his or her partner shrugs it off as no big deal.

All of us develop a "money personality"—a framework or context from which we approach finances. And many influences shape this personality: family background, spiritual beliefs, past experiences, and so on. For instance, if you grew up in an affluent family and married someone from a poor family, you're bound to run into money-management differences. If you derive great satisfaction from giving lots of money to your church or favorite charity, while your partner obsessively squirrels away funds in IRAs and 401(k)s, some sparks are going to fly in your relationship.

No doubt about it, differing behaviors and beliefs about finances create conflicts and clashes. At the intersection of marriage and money, lots of nasty collisions occur. Olivia Mellan, a psychotherapist specializing in financial issues, said,

> Most people relate to money much as they relate to another person—in an ongoing and complex way that taps deep-seated emotions. When two individuals form an enduring relationship with each other, money is always a partner, too.... Many individuals have a troubled relationship with money. Then, when they get into a couple relationship, money matters get explosive. Other people may have no problem with money individually; the trouble starts after they're in a relationship.
>
> I have observed that couples usually polarize around money. Partners tend to assume defensive styles, or personalities, in relation to money that are direct opposites of each other.[3]

We couldn't agree more. In our work as financial professionals over the past fifteen years, we have counseled scores of couples for whom financial disagreements undermined the quality of their relationships—and the quality of their lives. We have listened to countless stories of shattered lives and broken families. Some managed to resolve their differences and restore their relationships; many did not.

If you are currently married or planning to get married sometime soon, you don't want to let money be a constant source of stress and strife in your relationship. Whether you and your partner collide because of differing money personalities or other issues, you want things to be better. You're tired of the tension and frustration. You've tried to talk about it (or tried *not* to talk about it), but whatever you've done has not worked. You don't want to fight, and you certainly don't want to be another statistic—a couple that separated or divorced because they couldn't resolve problems.

Just as couples have diverse perspectives about saving, spending, and planning for the future, they also have different styles of communication, problem solving, and conflict resolution. How do you handle things when you disagree? Do you argue or withdraw? Do you insist on hammering home your point, or do you erect an emotional wall of silence? Misunderstandings and miscommunication inevitably lead to arguing, blaming, or distancing.

It's time for change. *Cents and Sensibility* is a relational guidebook designed to help married and engaged couples build (or rebuild) their relationship by working *together* on financial issues. With sound principles, open-mindedness, and a clear-eyed perspective, you and your partner can make radical changes for the better. By learning to understand your spouse, respect each other, and communicate more effectively, you can begin your journey toward healing and happiness.

Here's a big bonus: we've learned that when couples agree on money—when they accept differences, stop blaming each other, and establish mutual goals—they usually move rapidly toward financial success. Two partners who link arms and cheer each other on take giant strides toward their goals and dreams. Of course, the reverse is also true. People working at cross-purposes encounter one roadblock after another. They expend so much energy hassling and haranguing each other that they undermine whatever financial goals they might have.

Money *can* be a great source of joy and delight for every individual and couple. It can provide a sense of excitement about the future rather than trepidation and dread. It can provide peace of mind rather than high blood pressure. It can foster unity and intimacy in a relationship rather than division and discord. Our desire is to help you and your partner experience the joy that comes from addressing personal stewardship issues in a positive, productive way.

We recently read a fascinating article titled "Marriage and Money Most Closely Linked to Quality of Life," which described a study conducted by Dr. William Fleeson, professor of psychology at Wake Forest University. Dr. Fleeson analyzed national survey data to determine Americans' overall quality of life and assess the reasons people experience either satisfaction or dissatisfaction, contentment or discontentment. The number one reason people enjoy high quality of life is a happy marriage. The second-rated reason is financial stability. (Other factors, lower on the list, include good health, child rearing, fulfilling work, and a gratifying sex life.) Clearly, marriage and money are vital to our sense of satisfaction and fulfillment.

As Dr. Fleeson concluded, "We often have to make decisions in our lives about where to invest our energy, be it family, career, or health. This study suggests that individuals' investment in maintaining their relationships and their financial stability is more richly rewarded than are efforts in other domains."[4]

If marital harmony and financial security are crucial *individual* factors for happiness and well-being, imagine their influence when working in tandem. In other words, what if you could achieve both a happy marriage *and* financial stability? Your quality of life would soar to new heights.

We want to help that to happen in your relationship. This book provides time-honored and practical principles that will enable you to understand each other's approach to money. It also includes useful ways to resolve conflict caused by financial issues and experience joy when you wisely and intentionally manage all of your God-given resources. When you interact and relate in a way that's constructive rather than destructive, you'll achieve those two key components—a happy marriage and financial stability.

This book is different from most financial self-help volumes that fill bookstore shelves. It's not a financial-planning book with a lot of

charts and graphs you don't understand. Nor does it contain complicated tools you'll never use. *Cents and Sensibility* is a book about
understanding yourself and your partner better, improving your
communication about money, realizing how basic financial strategies
can enrich your relationship, and identifying mutual goals and working toward them. It's practical, understandable, and applicable. Best
of all, it's empowering! We know that guilt trips, regrets, and fear
only serve to keep people stuck. And we know that you're reading
this book because you want to get *unstuck*. It is our hope that we can
help you to move forward and look ahead with optimism, enthusiasm, and confidence.

As a married couple, we've had to deal with these issues in our own
relationship (we'll tell you some of our stories in the pages that follow).
Like many spouses, we have experienced the collision brought on by
differing money personalities. We have gotten ourselves into (and out
of) a serious debt problem, and we struggled through times of tension
and squabbling over our dissimilar spending habits. All of which is to
say that the guidance offered in this book is far from theoretical. We've
been there! Thankfully, we've learned quite a bit over the years about
communicating well as a couple.

Much of the information in the following chapters comes out of our
many years of experience as financial professionals. Between us, we have
worked with nearly three thousand individuals and couples, and our
company, Envoy Financial, currently serves eight thousand people in
businesses, organizations, and ministries. We have both sat down with
hundreds of couples, and we've often been saddened by what we've
observed—hurt, discord, and brokenness because of misunderstandings
about money. We've learned a lot from the people we've served, and we
look forward to sharing stories and positive strategies with you.

Here is the kind of help you'll find in the pages ahead.

In part 1, we'll explore the five most common financial dilemmas
couples face. Sometimes opposing approaches to money present problems for partners. Other times, self-inflicted troubles, such as debt or
disorganization, are the source of difficulties. Chances are that you will
see yourself described somewhere in this section.

Part 2 examines precisely how each of us develops his or her money
personality. We'll help you understand your psychological relationship
with money to determine how and why you make decisions. Once you

begin to understand yourself and your spouse, you can blend your styles and strengths in a complementary way.

In part 3, we'll offer guidance for overcoming obstacles and working together. We'll help you develop healthy, productive ways to communicate about money and resolve differences so you can achieve unity. We'll also give you some ideas about setting goals and dreaming big together.

Part 4 features the five key financial issues couples need to agree on in order to develop unity and harmony in their relationship. We'll talk about investments, retirement planning, budgeting, and other important areas. We've learned that financial matters can be as simple or complex as you choose to make them, and we know that most people prefer a simple and straightforward approach. Therefore, the information in this section is uncomplicated and easy to understand.

Throughout this book, you'll read many real-life stories about couples who have mastered money management—as well as those who have messed up and learned valuable lessons as a result. We sent a questionnaire to hundreds of people, and most of them were eager to share their stories. You'll also find discussion questions at the end of the book to stimulate dialogue between you and your partner. These will help you apply the information to your specific situation.

There's no reason to let misunderstandings about money drain the joy from your relationship. By employing the principles in this book and working through the practical steps, you can have a closer partnership, a brighter future, and a happier life.

PART ONE

THE STATE OF YOUR UNION

*The Five Most Common Ways
Couples Disagree About Money*

CHAPTER ONE

SAVERS VERSUS SPENDERS

S cott cracked open the front door and peeked in. Wearing a wide smile, he glanced around the entryway and toward the living room beyond. Empty.

"Hello! I'm home!" he called. "Bethany? I've got a surprise!"

Bethany strolled in from the back room. "Did you say a surprise? What surprise? What is it?"

"You're going to love it."

How exciting, Bethany thought. *What's he got? A bouquet of flowers? Symphony tickets? Or maybe that expensive necklace I've been drooling over.* Scott knew she had been eyeing it for months. Could he have bought it as an early anniversary gift?

"Okay, close your eyes," he said.

Bethany pushed up the sleeves of her sweatshirt and covered her eyes with her hand. Scott darted outside for a moment. With a grunt, he lugged two large stereo speakers inside the door, one at a time. Actually, *large* is an understatement—they looked like they could have damaged eardrums at a Rolling Stones concert at Yankee Stadium.

Now wearing a wide grin of her own, Bethany said, "Can I open my eyes now?"

"Just a sec," Scott said. He hauled in from the porch six boxes of stereo equipment—an equalizer, subwoofers, an amplifier, and all the rest. He positioned the speakers in front of his wife, then spread out his arms in a motion that said *Ta-da!* "Okay, go ahead."

Bethany's eyes popped open, and it all took a moment to register. *What is this stuff?* she thought. A half-second later, her eyes narrowed and her smile dissolved into a semi-scowl, but she quickly tried to mask her disappointment. "Oh. Speakers. Wow. They're so ... big. And look at all those boxes."

"Yeah, isn't it great?" Scott gushed. "This system is going to be so cool. It'll blow you away. My Coltrane CDs are going to sound incredible. And wait till we watch movies with surround sound."

He started to drag one of the speakers toward the living-room entertainment center. His excitement was palpable; he was like a kid ready to try out a new toy on Christmas morning.

"Uh, wait a minute," Bethany said. "I don't mean to rain on the parade, but how much did this stuff cost? I mean, look at those speakers—they're *huge.*"

Scott straightened up and rubbed his hands on his jeans. "Let me tell you, honey, I got a sweet deal. Sure, I had to buy more equipment than I originally thought, but it was a good deal. Really."

"Where'd you get all this?" Bethany asked, momentarily leaving behind the question of cost.

"Well, it was an amazing thing," he replied. "I went over to Sound Station, the electronics store we were shopping at last week, remember? So anyway, once I was in the store I found a salesman and he got me the deal of a lifetime—cheap. Turns out he didn't just have speakers, but an entire surround-sound system that would take care of all our needs. And it was much cheaper than similar setups I saw for sale at other stores."

"You bought an entire surround-sound stereo system?" Bethany asked. "I can't wait to read the return policy and warranty agreement. Okay, so how much?"

Scott swallowed hard. He'd hoped that question had been forgotten. He did one of those hokey sitcom maneuvers where a guilty character rubs his hand across his mouth at the same moment he speaks. He mumbled his reply and gave a melodramatic shrug. He knew he was caught.

Bethany just waited, her hands now planted on her hips.

"Oh, all right," Scott mumbled. "It was, uh, five times the amount we talked about."

"Five times?" Bethany blurted. "Five times the amount?" She could envision him at the check-out counter, salesman and boxes in tow, holding the Visa card. She plopped onto the couch and sighed.

Scott knew where this discussion would go next and decided to beat Bethany to the punch. "Yes, yes, I know. I overshot the budget. I did pay more than we agreed to spend. I admit it. But what a deal. I mean, *what* a deal! And this system will last us, well, *forever*. In the long run, it's a much better deal than those systems we saw at the other stores."

Bethany tried hard not to roll her eyes, but she couldn't stifle the groan that slipped out of her mouth. "Scott, you overshot the budget by *five times the amount*! We agreed on a specific amount. I think we better talk about this."

What followed was a lengthy—and intense—discussion about the effort they had been making to pay off credit-card debt. They had squeezed their budget, refusing to go out to eat, skipping morning lattes, and making their date nights much cheaper. Their conversation was peppered with words such as *accountability, responsibility*, and *reliability*. Bethany concluded by saying, "The bottom line is, we had an agreement. We talked it all through ahead of time, and we determined together what we could afford. You spent five times as much as you said you would."

Although he felt chastened and rebuked, Scott could only admit that, yes, he'd blown it. He hadn't realized that surround-sound speakers required other equipment to enable them to work. And once he started buying, he went full speed ahead. Despite the unexpected expense and the ensuing conflict over it, the stereo spending spree did have an upside: Scott and Bethany decided then and there that they would never make a purchase over $100 without checking with each other first. Since then, there has never been a surprise purchase of that size—or anything close to it.

Going to Extremes

As you've probably guessed by now, *we* are the Scott and Bethany featured in this vignette. And that is a true incident that happened several years ago. We didn't need the extra outlay of cash for those super-sized speakers and the other paraphernalia. On the road to financial freedom, we had taken an abrupt U-turn. But, of course, the real issues were a lack of restraint, uncontrolled spending, and most of all, a broken agreement.

Does all of this sound familiar to you? Can you see yourself in our squabble? As we mentioned in the introduction, we sent out questionnaires to hundreds of people as part of our research, and that feedback revealed that the saver-versus-spender conflict is probably the most common of all. But even if this is not your primary trouble spot, it's

DIFFERENCES THAT LEAD TO DIVISIONS

When partners approach saving and spending from different angles, they're bound to run into problems. As psychologist Olivia Mellan commented, "The failure of people to explore their money personalities leads to deep misunderstanding and hurt. Take the case of a man who views money as security. He does not believe in spending a great deal on gifts; he believes in saving. He's married to a woman who believes that money brings both love and happiness; she's a spender. They are about to celebrate a major anniversary. He spends days in record stores searching for the song they danced to when they were dating in the '60s—their song. When she gets his gift, she thinks he's chintzy and is insulted. He's inconsolably hurt. She, meanwhile, has bought him an expensive gift."[1]

highly likely that you've encountered this conundrum somewhere along the line.

If you are a saver, you've probably found yourself saying to your spouse, "Why did you buy *that?*" Or, "You paid *how much?*" Or perhaps, "We're already in debt! Quit spending!" Of course, if you are someone who likes to spend, you've probably said something like this: "I work hard to earn a paycheck, and I'm going to enjoy it." Or, "I prefer to savor life now and live in the present. What's the point of having money if you don't use it to pamper yourself a little?"

Savers and spenders simply come at the money issue from different philosophical approaches. One looks at the wallet as half empty; the other sees it as half full. One looks at the amount in the savings account and says, "That's pretty bad. We'd better tighten the belt and redouble our effort to save." The other looks at that same amount and says, "Hey, that's pretty good. Let's go out to dinner to celebrate. And afterward, we can swing by the mall." It's not hard to see how these differing approaches cause conflicts.

We agree with the psychologist Betsy Stone, who said,

> I believe that the ways we discuss money and its attendant issues are of paramount importance in any marriage. Whether we have too little money or just enough (we so rarely feel that we have too much!), all of us have strong emotional responses to money, saving, and expenditures.... We have strong opinions on how money is used, whether it is saved, invested, or spent indulgently. In fact, one person's

> extravagance is another person's essential expenditure. When these differences exist, they can have severe consequences within a marriage.[2]

So true, and it happens in households across America. One spouse scrimps and scrapes to put a few dollars away each week, while the other person spends like there's no tomorrow. Imagine how it unfolds: Larry pulls his sweater tighter around him as he furtively turns down the thermostat—even though it's twenty degrees outside and pretty nippy inside. He knows the utility bill this month is going to be a doozy, and here's a chance to lessen the damage. About this time, his wife, Janet, arrives home carrying several overstuffed Neiman Marcus bags. They exchange glances, and even though they don't say a word, loaded messages pass between them. They've discussed all this before. What more needs to be said? Larry feels his blood pressure rising and his fists clenching. Here he is trying to be fiscally responsible, trying to stick to the budget when—

"Why is it so cold in here?" Janet says. "C'mon, Larry, it's like an icebox."

As she moves to turn up the thermostat, he sneaks a peak inside her bags and emits a disgusted sigh. They retreat to different parts of the house in chilly silence (literally and figuratively). Maybe their unspoken strain will subside by dinnertime. But maybe not.

Or perhaps it happens like this. Carol is a devoted coupon cutter. In fact, her friends have dubbed her the Coupon Queen, and they pass along their own clip-and-save circulars that come stuffed into the Sunday paper. Carol has them all organized in a file box, which she proudly carries to the grocery store each Wednesday afternoon (when the weekly specials are announced).

When Carol arrives home from the store with the trunk of her well-used '86 Toyota Corolla stuffed with grocery bags, she will present her receipt to her husband, Phil. Wearing a triumphant expression, she will announce, "How 'bout that? I saved $29.52. Certainly not my best outing, but not bad—especially if you multiply that by four weeks in every month and twelve months in every year and ..." Phil hears this multiplication routine almost every week, but he knows better than to interrupt.

Phil also knows now would not be the best time to reveal that he just upgraded the cable TV package from basic to premium. Oh, and he

MAKING CENTS ¢

Who wins, spenders or savers? More people enjoy making money than spending it (40 percent to 22 percent). Just 39 percent are balanced, experiencing equal joy from taking in and giving out money.

What does money mean to you? For 60 percent of people, it means security and independence. Thirty-seven percent consider it a tool to accomplish some of life's goals. Two percent equate it with power, while less than 1 percent associate it with attaining happiness.[3]

also ordered the NFL Season Ticket deal, so he can now get all the games every weekend. As Phil stares at Carol's receipt, he executes a quick calculation. He just upped their monthly expenses by the same amount Carol saves with two or three weeks' worth of coupons. Then he gulps. He knows *she* pays the monthly bills, and *she* will not be pleased when she opens the invoice from the cable company. Normally an easygoing person, Carol gets downright fierce when someone—namely Phil—undermines her efforts to save.

These two scenarios are relatively minor examples of saver-spender conflicts. Sometimes, however, the stakes are much higher and the expenses much greater. Not long ago, a woman told us about the time her husband pulled into their driveway in a brand-new Lexus SUV with all the bells and whistles. He hadn't even mentioned the possibility of replacing their old vehicle—probably because it didn't need replacing. How did he pay for the Lexus? He raided their retirement account.

"I fumed for two weeks," the woman said. "I was astonished that he could be so irresponsible and inconsiderate about my needs and wishes."

Then there's the email we received from a man who wrote,

> After five years of being in debt, my wife and I finally paid off all our credit cards. It took a lot of work and a lot of sacrifices. But we celebrated when we saw a zero balance on our last Visa statement. Over the next couple of months, however, my wife went wild with spending. She accumulated $10,000 in new credit-card debt—without my knowing it. When I did find out, I was shocked and horrified. In fact, I felt so betrayed that it was like she'd had an affair. Our trust was severely wounded. We're still paying off those debts, and we're still repairing the damage done to our relationship. Now we have another expense: weekly marriage counseling fees.

Sometimes spender-saver discrepancies cause headaches and aggravation. Other times, they cause heartache and anguish.

Dealing with Differences

Psychologists tell us that a natural attraction usually occurs between people with opposite personality types—hence the saying, "opposites attract." This may not be true in many relationships, but it certainly seems to be the case when it comes to savers and spenders. When Mr. Tightwad marries Ms. Spendthrift, the two are headed for a battle over the bank account.

If this is the situation in your household, you each need to understand yourself as well as your partner, respect each other, and accept responsibility. Maybe you enjoy spending money. That's okay so long as you realize that your behavior affects your partner. You need to be willing to respect your partner's need to save some and negotiate compromises. Maybe you feel more secure saving. That's okay, too. But you need to be willing to allow your partner to be him- or herself and enjoy spending some money. If you always look down on your partner because he or she is not like you, you'll poison your relationship.

Even if you are both frugal compared to most people, when you're just comparing the two of you, one of you will likely feel better about spending, the other about saving. One tends to think more about today, the other more about tomorrow. How much trouble these differences create usually is determined by how much space separates a couple on the spender-saver continuum. Suppose there's a scale from zero to a hundred, with zero being the person who won't spend a dime on anything and a hundred representing the compulsive spender with a chronic problem. If a couple consists of one person who is a forty

¢ **WHAT'S THE DIFFERENCE BETWEEN A SPENDER AND A SAVER?**

A saver's motto is "A penny saved is a penny earned." A spender's motto is "You only live once, so shop till you drop."

A spender will buy an extravagant birthday gift for a friend—a crystal vase or a cashmere sweater. A saver insists that a birthday card will do. After all, it's the thought that counts.

A saver's favorite Bible verse is Proverbs 13:11: "Dishonest money dwindles away, but he who gathers money little by little makes it grow." A spender's favorite is "There is nothing better for a man than to be happy and to enjoy himself as long as he can ... that he should eat and drink and enjoy the fruits of his labors" (Eccl. 3:12–13 TLB).

Celebrate Diversity

Spenders and savers can learn to live in harmony by respecting differences and appreciating what the other has to offer. In fact, both types of people have several potential advantages and disadvantages.

The Upside of Savers

• They model frugality, restraint, and self-discipline for their children and others. In a society driven by consumerism and self-indulgence, people who save act as healthy role models.

• They employ long-range thinking, which will serve them well later on. Come time to retire, their prudence and discretion will be rewarded.

• They are not wasteful and careless. We all know our society has a deplorable amount of waste, and our landfills overflow with junk that was purchased but never used. Savers tend to buy only what they need and use it until it wears out.

The Downside of Savers

• They can be so tightfisted that they miss out on fun and enjoyment. Some people are so zealously committed to saving that they rob themselves and their loved ones of the things God intended to enrich their lives.

• They can hurt relationships with their negativity and lack of enthusiasm for things their loved ones cherish.

and another who is a fifty, they will likely run into the occasional skirmish but nothing catastrophic. If there's a couple in which one spouse is a five and other a ninety-five, the clashes will be frequent and fierce.

Where might you and your partner fall on such a scale? If a significant distance spans between your saver-spender rating and your partner's, you'll likely have to work harder to negotiate, compromise, and cooperate. The greater distance, the more resistance. Take some time to determine your spender-saver ratio. But beware: most of us are notoriously unrealistic and self-deceptive when it comes to our spending habits. Specifically, most of us spend more and save less than we'd like to admit.

If you want to overcome saver-spender conflicts in your relationship, begin by taking a realistic look at your propensity to spend or save. It will also help to explore *why* you either spend or save. (We'll discuss how our money personalities are formed in part 2.)

Variations on a Theme

Although the most prevalent predicament involves one person who is a dedicated saver and a partner who is equally dedicated to spending, two subcategories are worth mentioning. As we said earlier, sometimes two spouses have similar orientations toward money use, but they have different degrees or methods of spending or saving. One partner may be inclined to save, while the other feels compelled to save *a whole lot more.* Or there may be two spenders, but one limits spending to $50 a week, while the other can easily go through several hundred dollars. Let's take a look.

Spender versus Spender Couple

Doug and Anna have been married for three years, yet neither of them has ever been able to stick to a budget. They hang out at the outlet mall as often as they can. Doug spends only the cash left over from his paycheck (after paying bills), while Anna spends what she has and then starts whipping out credit cards. She doesn't think twice about plopping the plastic on a store counter to pay for household goods and clothes. Now Doug and Anna have more than $15,000 in credit-card debt and no savings. Guilt and feelings of desperation are beginning to overwhelm them. And their fights are growing more frequent. Doug tries to talk to his wife about her excessive spending, but Anna retorts, "Who are you to talk? It's not just me. You spend plenty of money, too."

Saver versus Saver Couple

Tyrone and Alesha are both cautious with their money, and they never pay credit-card late fees or finance charges. They considered

• They can come to trust in their bank account instead of the Creator. Some people look to money for security and safety rather than to God's provision and care.

The Upside of Spenders

• They're not afraid to pay for experiences and memory-making events, which are often the most meaningful things in life.
• They are usually a spur-of-the-moment kind of people who are fun to be around.
• They are often generous, sharing their resources to enrich the lives of others. Frequently, they enjoy spending money on others just as they do on themselves.

The Downside of Spenders

• They can rack up debts in a hurry. Money has to come from somewhere, and that "somewhere" is frequently credit cards, home loans, and other debt-inducing sources.
• They can lack self-discipline and restraint. Some people just don't know when to say no, and if they do, they lack the willpower to follow through.
• They may be avoiding real issues. Many spenders buy things to make themselves feel better, assuage depression or anxiety, and fill an empty spot deep down inside. The temporary good feeling that comes from a purchase masks a significant emotional or spiritual issue that should addressed.

adding on to their tiny house, but neither could stomach the idea of a second mortgage to pay for it. So they agreed to wait until they can pay up front, which could take many years.

While Alesha likes to find good deals on eBay and at thrift stores, she also enjoys going out for a nice dinner every once in a while. She figures they deserve an occasional treat. Not so for Tyrone. He wants to save every penny they make. He believes dining out is a big waste of money. What's more, he only rarely goes to a movie at the local cineplex. Tickets cost too much, and there's always the temptation to get popcorn and sodas (Alesha likes popcorn with her movies). Tyrone would much rather rent a video and watch it at home—or better yet, check one out from the library for free. Both Tyrone and Alesha are savers, but a wedge is starting to build between them because of their differences. He says, "I'm being frugal and wise." She says, "No, you're being cheap and stingy."

Who's Right; Who's Wrong?

The entire point of this book is to help bring clarity and understanding to your relationship in the area of finances—not to label either partner as right or wrong, good or bad. In the previous examples, it's easy to paint the spender as the bad guy. As we've learned from our financial counseling business, however, these issues are rarely as cut-and-dry, black-and-white as they appear at first glance.

We believe the keys to resolving saver-spender issues are balance and compromise. The person who buys things he doesn't need or spends money she doesn't have is clearly out of balance. That individual obviously should concentrate on saving more and spending less. Also unbalanced is the saver who is so miserly that he deprives his spouse and children of joy. Hoarding money so insatiably that it isn't used to enrich the lives of others is not noble.

Compromise becomes an ally when partners with different spending habits agree on a reasonable and sensible plan they can both abide by. They can negotiate a plan that helps them both—one that reins in the spender and loosens up the saver. Working as a team, they can both agree to make sacrifices for the sake of the relationship.

CHAPTER TWO

DUELING OVER DEBT

Suppose you and your partner were invited to appear on an updated version of "The Newlywed Game" for the upcoming television season. Remember how the show works? All the male contestants go backstage while their wives remain seated in front of a studio audience. The host—with gleaming white teeth, perfect hair, and a corny sense of humor—asks a series of questions that the women answer about their husbands' preferences, opinions, and experiences.

The host might ask, "What kind of vehicle would your husband say he is—a Corvette, Humvee, minivan, or garbage truck?" Or, "If he were stranded on a desert island, who besides yourself would your husband want with him?" These days the questions would be much more risqué, but you get the idea.

The men return, and their responses are compared to the ones given by their wives. Amid much finger-pointing, eye rolling, and melodramatic reactions, the couples scoff at each other while the audience laughs uproariously (boosted by a laugh track, of course). Then the husbands get a chance for revenge when the women retreat to the soundproof room. On it goes.

Now it's your turn. After a few questions related to your partner's favorite kinds of food, preference about pajamas, and pet peeves, the host says, "Next question: How does your partner feel about going into debt?" You're given four choices.

"He absolutely hates going into debt and avoids it like a shopping trip."

"He's willing to go into debt sometimes but pays it off as soon as possible."

"Debt doesn't bother him—and we've got plenty of it."

"Debt *does* bother him—and we've got plenty of it."

What would your answer be? How does your partner approach

When Is Debt a Good Choice? ¢

We usually advise couples to avoid debt if at all possible, simply because most people can't pay it off quickly. There are, however, a few situations in which borrowing money may pay off in the long run:

1. *Education or additional training.* Furthering your education is a way to increase the value of your biggest asset—you. In most cases, the net gain will far outweigh the debt incurred over time. Research indicates that training and education do pay off in the long run because your earning power rises, your chances for advancement are greater, and your competitive edge in the marketplace improves.

2. *Home mortgages.* If you purchase real estate wisely (avoid overpaying, buy in an economically stable area, and so on), it may be one of the best investments you'll ever make. Numerous studies confirm that real estate—a primary residence, rentals, commercial space, property—have helped families increase their assets. For this reason, when we counsel couples, we do not consider mortgages part of their "debt load."

debt? Does he or she despise it, tolerate it, or accept it as a fact of life? Now imagine that the question is reversed, and your spouse is asked about *your* attitude toward debt. Which of the four responses would be true of you?

Let's step out of the world of make-believe and back into reality. That question posed by our fictitious host is apropos to every couple that wants to achieve peace and harmony regarding finances. Debt is such an enormous problem in our culture that it often places strain on relationships and can even divide spouses.

The vast majority of couples today realize that debt is not a good thing. It costs extra money in interest, finance charges, and late fees. Worse, it locks you into long-term payments. Only in a few isolated situations—such as home purchases, vocational training, and education—is debt worth the cost and anxiety it produces (see sidebar). The point we want to make here is that debt is not only a drain on a couple's financial well-being, but it is also a drain on their relational well-being. Indeed, this was a recurring theme in our interviews and questionnaires as we examined the most common financial stresses for couples. Here are a few responses we received:

Jenny, age 34, Anaheim, California: "My husband, Steve, and I have been married for eight years, and we have carried at least $10,000 in credit-card debt that entire time. About every six months, we sit down and have a serious talk about paying off the cards. We stick to our plan for a month or two, then one of us will blow it and charge something—gifts or household items or groceries. Then it starts all over as we charge more and more stuff. We're caught in this cycle, and we feel trapped. Recently, this has caused a lot of fights between us. We end up blaming each other, but the truth is, we're both at fault."

Micah, age 26, Boston: "Tammy and I met in college and got married right after graduation. Since we attended the same expensive Ivy League school, we entered marriage owing more than $200,000 in student loans. We both appreciate our good education, but we sure don't appreciate those huge loans. What a way to start a marriage! We've barely begun our lives together, and we already feel buried under that load. It's like we're in a deep pit and trying to claw our way out. We feel the stress every day."

Paul and Lynn, ages 41 and 38, Lincoln, Nebraska: "When I (Paul) was laid off from my job at the hospital, the only way we could survive was to borrow against the equity in our house. We took out a home equity loan to cover everyday expenses like utilities, food, and clothes for the kids. We're sinking fast—financially and emotionally. We're both very depressed, and our kids are picking up on our anxiety. For years, we worked hard to stay out of debt, but here we are, going deeper all the time."

Can you relate to any of these people? Every couple has its own unique circumstances, but the underlying problems are often the same: we don't like debt, but we've got it. Why did we go in the hole in the first place? How could we be so foolish as to get into this dilemma? Most important, how can we get out of this mess?

> Only in a few isolated situations—such as home purchases, vocational training, and education—is debt worth the cost and anxiety it produces.

We've heard hundreds of stories like the ones cited above—and each tale is laced with pain and strain. Sometimes a debt problem is self-inflicted through overspending, unwise investments, or poor planning. Other times, it's a result of unforeseen or unavoidable circumstances, such as a health crisis, job loss, or even a natural disaster. However the debt came to be, the result is always the same: a dark cloud hanging over your head.

Dwelling in a Debt Culture

The nineteenth-century writer Artemus Ward once said, "Let us all be happy and live within our means, even if we have to borrow the money to do it." That incongruous statement could be the motto for the current generation of Americans. We *want* to be happy, and we'd *prefer* to live within our means—but we'll go into debt if we can't straddle the fence between those two desires.

For most of recorded history, people had no choice. Either they paid as they went, or they went without. Just two generations ago, if someone wanted a new car, he had to pay for it with cash up front. Same for groceries, household goods, vacations, and everything else. You may have heard your parents or grandparents talk about "layaway plans" in which an item was put aside until they could pay for it. We don't imagine those people *enjoyed* having to wait until they had enough money for those things, but it sure did help them avoid headaches and heartaches over the long haul.

Now, of course, we can get what we want when we want it. We have a different kind of layaway plan: we acquire whatever item we want immediately, and we "lay away" the expense for a month until it shows up our credit-card statement. You're still going to pay—and maybe with interest—just a little later.

If you ever wonder how much credit pervades our culture, you need to go only as far as your mailbox. You know exactly what we mean. Like us, you probably receive an endless stream of credit-card applications with enticing features, such as low introductory rates, rewards programs, or no-fee balance transfers. These direct-marketing pieces show up almost daily. In fact, we once kept track of all such mailings we received in a month, and the total came to thirty-two.

How widespread are these credit-card pitches getting? We read about a three-year-old from Rochester, New York, who received an application for a platinum Visa card in the mail. This so amused Allesandra Scalise's mother that she filled it out, listing her daughter's occupation as "toddler" and leaving the income line blank. She also wrote on the application, "I'd like to have a credit card to buy some toys, but I'm only three and my mommy says no." Allesandra's credit card arrived a few weeks later.[1]

It's common today for high school and college students to possess their own plastic. One in three high school seniors uses credit cards, and half of those have cards in their own names.[2] Seventy-eight percent of college students have credit cards, according to student loan maker Nellie Mae, and the typical student carries a balance of $2,800. One of ten college students carries a balance of more than $7,800. In 2001, nearly ninety-four thousand people under age twenty-five filed for bankruptcy.[3]

What's the debt picture look like for families? Here's a snapshot.[4]
- Average debt for US families with at least one credit card: $9,205
- Number of annual personal bankruptcy filings: 1.6 million
- Percentage of Americans who believe they will always be in debt: 30
- Percent of the average person's take-home pay that is already committed to payment of existing debt: 23

We don't include these grim statistics to heap guilt and shame upon anyone. If you're in debt, you feel bad enough as it is. We want to point out how pervasive this problem is and show that you are not alone. Countless couples are struggling to balance their books—and their relationships are often struggling as a result. Many spouses feel as if they're stuck in quicksand because they are barely keeping up with their debt payments. Does that confined and constricted feeling add stress to a relationship? You bet it does.

Till Debt Do Us Part?

Two primary issues related to debt cause stress and strain for couples. The first is when partners have differing perspectives about borrowing money. This is similar to the spender-versus-saver conflict we discussed in the previous chapter. When approaches to money management differ, friction is inevitable. So if a husband freely and blithely

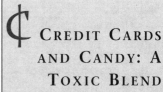

CREDIT CARDS AND CANDY: A TOXIC BLEND

I (Scott) got my first credit card at my college student union. I was enticed by the free one-pound bag of M&M's that came with a signed application. Well, after quickly racking up $1,200 in debt, that bag of M&M's didn't feel quite so free. I spent the entire summer paying off the credit card so my dad wouldn't discover my foolishness.

FIVE WAYS TO GET OUT ¢ OF DEBT FASTER

1. Stop going further into debt! Someone once said if you want to get out of a hole, the first step is to stop digging. If you're serious about eliminating debt, pay for everything as you go, and refuse to use your credit cards (unless it's an emergency).

2. Be ruthless about cutting out all luxuries and nonessential expenses. Skip the pricey bistro, and take a picnic to the park instead. Cancel cable. Iron your own clothes instead of using a dry cleaner. Apply all the money saved directly to debt repayment.

3. If you have more than one credit card, consolidate them onto one low-interest (or better yet, *zero* interest) card. This reduces the possibility of losing track of due dates and incurring late fees. It also helps to provide a reality check: if you have five credit cards with a $2,000 balance on each, you might fool yourself into thinking each of those is not so bad. Put them together, however, and you'll see what you really owe.

4. Pay off the card with the highest interest rate first. Some couples say, "Let's pay off the card with the small balance first." Others say, "Let's take on the biggest challenge first and focus on the card with the largest balance." We advise couples to pay off the account with the highest interest rate first—after all, it's the interest that is the real killer.

5. Once debt is paid off, resolve to use your credit card for emergencies only. To make sure you can't easily access the card, store it in a place that's hard to get to: freeze it in a block of ice, or give it to a trusted friend with strict instructions to give it back only under dire circumstances.

goes into debt while his wife can't stand owing money to anyone, they'll feel the tension rise every time a bill comes due. Imagine the scene.

"Jim, I just opened the Visa bill and couldn't believe my eyes," Terrie says. She tries not to sound like a nag, but she's about had it. "When is this going to stop? The balance keeps going up, up, up. And we still owe your parents $8,000 for the addition. I can hardly look them in the eye when they come for dinner. Let's work together to resolve this."

"You're such a worrywart. Would you relax about it?" Jim responds with a shrug. "I'm due for a year-end bonus, and I'll put it all toward the credit card. I may even get a raise this year if I meet quota. Anyway, I don't see what the big deal is."

Sadly, conversations like this happen in households all across America.

Sometimes they happen in our office, and though we try to remain neutral when counseling couples, in this case Terrie's perspective makes a lot of sense. The point we're making is that Jim and Terrie have conflicting views about proper debt use. Terrie wants to plan ahead, pay as they go, and stay out of debt. Jim believes borrowing money is a means to acquiring things and achieving goals now, and he's confident they can catch up later. Unless Jim and Terrie strike an "economic accord," they're sure to continue squabbling.

The second negative impact for couples is that debt is a chronic burden, a heavy weight that hinders their forward progress. Even if spouses do not bicker about debt, pressure bears down on them constantly.

With debt comes a loss of freedom and flexibility. A thirty-two-year-old woman named Gina recently told us,

> When Bill and I had our baby, I wanted to stay home full time. I hated the idea of hiring a nanny or getting some other kind of child-care. I'd always dreamed of being at home with our child for five or six years—until he started school. Unfortunately, we had so many expenses and debt payments that we needed my salary. Because I pulled in almost half of our income, there was no way I could quit my job. If we didn't have debt, we could've swung it with a little belt-tightening. But no. Frankly, I feel angry and depressed every time I leave my son to go off to work. And almost every Friday night, the tension erupts into a fight between Bill and me.

¢ WHEN IS BANKRUPTCY AN OPTION?

We have seen couples who use bankruptcy as a first resort—a quick way to get out of a bad situation. We disagree with that approach; we believe bankruptcy should be a last resort. Here are some steps to take before proceeding to bankruptcy.

1. Seek help and advice from a financial professional.

2. Consolidate debts into a low-interest loan.

3. Call lenders to see if the debt and/or payments can be negotiated.

We have heard hundreds of stories like these and have seen hundreds of clients in similar situations. We have also witnessed the positive results when debt is reversed and couples start living a debt-free lifestyle. The first step is acknowledging that you have a debt problem and then resolving together to correct the situation.

Divulging Our Own Debt Debacle

It's not easy for financial professionals such as ourselves to admit they've fallen into the debt trap, but we have. We would rather be honest about our own struggles than pretend to have it all together, so let us tell you what happened.

Six years ago, we were preparing to relocate from Southern California to Colorado Springs. We had not been married long, and we were eager to establish ourselves in a new place and enjoy our first real adventure together—a big cross-country move. On a house-hunting trip, we found a charming three-bedroom, two-bath condo. It was in a nice neighborhood, close to where our offices would be, and it was in good condition. We loved it instantly, and we began dreaming about where we would place furniture and how we'd host friends and out-of-town guests. We made an offer, which was accepted.

As we flew back to California, we couldn't stop talking about how great it was going to be—our own beautiful home in a beautiful city. We were positively giddy, as most first-time homeowners are.

Although we wanted to move right away, we had business to wrap up and details to attend to. In fact, there was a three-month lag time before we could pack our belongings and move to the Rocky Mountains. Unbeknown to us, the seller kept several cats and dogs in the condo during those months. Essentially, he used our dream condo as a pet kennel—with predictable results. When we finally arrived and excitedly opened the front door, we received a rude welcome. Our new home—which we'd been fantasizing about for months—was a total and complete mess. It reeked of urine, the doors and cabinets were badly scratched, and the walls were clawed. We were horrified.

In retrospect, we should have taken the seller to small-claims court to recoup the cost of repairs. But as the saying goes, hindsight is 20/20. We were eager to begin our lives in Colorado, and we wanted to get settled in. Neither of us wanted our bubble burst by confrontations with the seller, meetings with lawyers, legal depositions, and that whole mess. We wanted everything to be perfect, so we decided to get the repairs done as quickly as possible and get on with our lives.

That's when the real trouble began. Our refurbishing plans started small but soon escalated. Initially, we had decided to replace the damaged kitchen cabinets and the soiled carpets, and to patch and replaster the scratched-up walls. One thing led to another, however, and we got caught in a vicious cycle without even realizing it. Our conversations went something like this.

We recommend that you sit down together when you're not under pressure and talk through a "debt policy" for your relationship. What are you and are you *not* willing to go into debt for? What is the limit you feel comfortable borrowing? What will be your guidelines for repaying debt? Determining parameters in advance will arm you against impulsive, emotion-driven decisions.

With debt looming large for most couples today, we know it can easily tarnish the quality of the relationship and compromise your goals. By addressing this issue honestly and openly, you can come to agreement about how to get out of debt and stay out. Your future will be brighter because of it.

Chapter Three

Risk–Takers versus Security–Seekers

R ob and Pam Johnson cradled coffee mugs in their hands as they sat in the breakfast nook of their San Antonio apartment. Outside, the sky was clear and the temperature warm. Inside, things were starting to feel chilly, and dark clouds were forming above the small, round table where the Johnsons had papers spread before them.

Both in their late thirties, Pam and Rob had sat down that morning to discuss a business opportunity he had been pondering. This was not unusual, since Rob had a new money-making plan about every six months. Over the course of their eleven-year marriage, Rob had been in and out of several business ventures—most of which flopped, a couple of which actually generated income.

Five years earlier, he had started a company called Better than Butlers, a sort of upscale errand-boy service. He paid college students— outfitted in suits and ties—to run errands for high-income clients too busy to get their car oil changed or pick up dry cleaning. It wasn't a bad concept; it just never caught on. Seems that even wealthy people hedge at paying someone $35 an hour to run their Mercedes over to Jiffy Lube.

After that, Rob bought into a business that sold grooming products for men—a Mary Kay knockoff for the masculine gender. He quickly discovered, however, that most guys are happy to pay $2.97 for styling gel at Wal-Mart rather than $11.99 for the ultra-luxury, miracle-working kind he sold. After that, Rob set up shop as a talent agent, then a Web designer, then a landscaper …

Through it all, Pam's steady income as a pediatric nurse kept them afloat while Rob waited for his ship to come in. Not that he wasn't a hard worker. He's always been dedicated to pulling his weight financially. For years, he's tutored high school kids in English at $25 an hour and stayed busy as a substitute teacher.

Now, as Rob explained his idea latest idea, Pam thought, *If this is another one of your surefire, get-rich-quick schemes, you can forget it. Your "surefire" plans usually go up in the smoke, and most them are more like get-poor-quick schemes.* But as she sipped her coffee, she forced herself to smile, nod, and exude an air of receptivity.

"So all it takes is five thousand dollars to buy in," Rob said. "That covers start-up costs, marketing materials, Web site support, and one demo for each of the five models available."

> Most couples are not similar when it comes to their individual risk tolerance and desire for security.

The *models* referred to were air purifiers, and Rob was sure these would be a hit. They were state-of-the-art and different from the kind you could buy at any old hardware store—though exactly *how* they were different he had trouble explaining to Pam.

"So tell me again why this is not a multilevel marketing plan," Pam said, trying hard not to sound pessimistic. "It seems similar to the nutritional-supplement business from a year ago. Heaven knows we have enough supplements in the garage to last a lifetime."

"Well, the parent company, Purity Plus Industries, arranged it so their associates are more like independent business owners than salespeople. I could choose to have down-line salespeople working for me if I want. That's where the multiplication of profits really kicks in. But I can be totally independent, too. And since I'm getting in on the ground floor, I'd have no one above me siphoning off percentages of sales."

Pam murmured to indicate she was listening.

"I'm telling you, honey, this is the real deal. Everyone is concerned about the air we breathe, especially parents of young children. And people who live with smokers. It's a major health hazard, so these air purifiers practically sell themselves. Besides, it's a service to the community. It's a way to help people live happier, healthier lives."

"That's exactly what you said about Nature's Nectar, but everyone thought the supplements were too expensive," she said. "You could buy practically the same thing at half the cost down at Whole Foods Market. Isn't it the same situation with these air purifiers?"

Pam watched as Rob's face reddened and the vein in his neck bulged out. Yep, he was getting steamed. She expected the response he gave every time she held up a caution sign: "Why do you always have to throw cold water on a hot idea?" Or, "You don't believe in me. You don't think I can pull it off."

To her surprise, Rob had worked up a new approach. He rummaged in the briefcase at his feet and pulled out a copy of *Rich Dad, Poor Dad*. "Look at this. Robert Kiyosaki says that if you want to get rich, you've got to start your own business. Working for other people gets you nowhere. There's a ceiling for how much you can make, but having your own business blows the lid off. That's why he encourages every American to own a business."

Pam took the book from Rob and read the subtitle on the jacket: "What the Rich Teach Their Kids About Money." Then she said, "Well, if every American owned a business, who would work at all those businesses? Besides, I'm a nurse—am I supposed to own a hospital?"

"See, this is the problem," Rob barked. "Your first reaction is always why something *won't* work. You see the dark cloud rather than the silver lining!" He was starting to rant. "I don't want us to tread water the rest of our lives. I don't want to be a poor dad! I want to be a rich dad! A rich dad!"

"But we don't even have children," she said, despite thinking better of it.

"That's not the point!" Rob shouted. He grabbed the packet of papers from the table and threw them into his briefcase. He slammed the lid shut and closed the latches forcefully. "Give me the book. It's obvious you won't be needing it."

Pam pushed it across the table and said softly, "Rob, honey, come on. Let's not spoil the whole day. We can talk about air purifiers later, when we're both feeling less emotional and more reasonable."

But she knew it was no use. His feelings were hurt, and he would sulk the rest of the day. Pam felt bad, too, though not bad enough to give in to another one of Rob's pie-in-the-sky schemes.

> When the aggressive and conservative partners learn to blend their styles, they can balance each other in a productive, prosperous way.

Who's Aggressive; Who's Conservative?

The incident above is true—only the names have been changed to protect the innocent—and the guilty. This couple told us about their struggles with his string of business ventures and her vexation at every one he pursued. He was always eager to try something new, and she was always eager to talk him out of it.

Their tale illustrates a third money conflict frequently encountered by couples: one partner is a risk-taker, while the other is a security-seeker. Another way to describe this difference is to say that one person has an aggressive, assertive, and active approach to money, while the other is more cautious, careful, and conservative. One person is ready to put a quarter in the big slot machine of life and pull the handle. The other prefers to put that quarter in a safe, secure piggy bank.

How about you and your partner? Do you differ in this area? As with nearly every aspect of money management, it may be that you and your spouse are not polar opposites on the risk-versus-security continuum. It might be that both of you are risk-takers, but one of you is willing to risk far more than the other. Or you both may be cautious with your money, but to varying degrees.

If both of you are very close on the risk-security ratio, this may be a relatively minor issue for you. Perhaps it comes up occasionally—when making a big purchase or deciding on a large investment—but otherwise you're fine in this area. Our experience has shown, however, that most couples are *not* similar when it comes to their risk tolerance and desire for security. One instinctively says, "Yes, let's go for it!" The other's first words are, "Slow down. Let's think this through."

As we have talked with hundreds of couples about their financial goals, we have noticed a pattern related to willingness to risk. Perhaps not surprisingly, it is usually men who take a more assertive, even chancy, approach to money, while women typically want to play it safe. Men want to "push the envelope," while women would just as soon keep the envelope locked up in a safe-deposit box. (Understand that we are speaking generally, and sometimes the roles are reversed. We've met plenty of women who were highly entrepreneurial, while their husbands were the cautious ones.)

In addition to our own experience, numerous studies confirm that men are more often the risk-takers. For example, researchers Sherman Hanna and Rui Yao studied more than twenty-four thousand adults' financial risk tolerance by analyzing six Survey of Consumer Finances data sets. They assessed people's money attitudes based on four categories: those who would be willing to take substantial risk, high risk, some risk, and no risk.

Their findings show (in descending order) the willingness of each group to take at least some financial risk.

- never-married men: 70 percent
- married men: 66 percent
- divorced men: 61 percent
- married women: 55 percent
- never-married women: 50 percent
- divorced women: 45 percent
- widowers: 38 percent
- widows: 27 percent

What's more, female respondents rated high in the "no risk" category and were less likely to take "some risk," "high risk," or "substantial risk" than males of the same marital status.[1]

Also relevant to this discussion is a recent study conducted by Yankelovich Partners, which found that men and women have similar life priorities and financial goals, but the means by which they achieve these goals differ greatly. A majority of both men and women (85 percent) cited "family" and "love/relationships" as their top two priorities in life. However, when asked about achieving financial goals, men's and women's money styles differed significantly. More women than men described themselves as "bargain hunters," while more men than women described themselves, in terms of money style, as "risk-takers." These results suggest that women set out to reach financial goals through practical methodologies, while men are more inclined to invest and take their chances in the hopes of hitting it big.[2]

We agree with financial consultant and author Dr. Judith Briles, who said,

MAKING CENTS

Do you expect to strike it rich? Optimism reigns. More than half of all college students expect to be millionaires by age forty. One in four expects to make his or her first million by age thirty. Just 29 percent don't ever expect to make a million.

If you suddenly inherited $10 million, how would your life change? Fifty-eight percent of people said they would continue living as they did before the windfall. Forty-five percent would move to a new home nearby, and 22 percent said they would move far away. Forty-eight percent would buy a second or even a third home.[3]

Losing money is scary for anyone, but women are more fearful of losing money than men. Why? First, men typically earn more money than women do and therefore feel as if they have more to invest. Moreover, if men lost money in a bad investment, their reaction—that it can be replaced—differs from many women who may exaggerate the loss's significance in their overall financial situation.

Women are also less likely to take the more aggressive and riskier financial positions that men do. Risk-taking, in part, has to do with a man's familiarity with money. Men, in contrast to women, are generally exposed to the subject of money early on and by the time they reach adulthood, the topic is no longer unfamiliar or intimidating.[4]

The fact is, for both men and women, numerous factors contribute to our willingness or reluctance to take risks. These include family background, past experiences with money, and our basic temperament type. (We'll discuss many of these factors in part 2.) The other fact is that rarely do spouses share the exact perspective on risk versus caution. That's why money risks so often lead to marital rifts.

¢ If you can view the other's approach with respect and appreciation—valuing what the other person brings to the table—you can surge ahead financially.

Assessing Your Risk Tolerance

Do you relish risk or savor security? In chapter 18, where we discuss investments, we'll provide a risk-tolerance quiz to help guide your thinking and direction. For now, let's look at three scenarios where couples may differ.

1. Suppose a long-lost rich uncle gave you a gift of $100,000 with one stipulation: you must invest it, not spend it. Where would you invest the money? If you choose to put it in a savings account, a CD, or some other safe and slow-growth investment vehicle, you're probably on the cautious side. If you would rather to put it in stocks, precious metals, or options, then you're probably more of a risk-taker.

2. Let's say a trusted friend approaches you with an investment opportunity. He's getting several people to go in on an existing twenty-unit apartment building, and he invites you to join in. The buy-in cost: $25,000. The building needs repairs, and it has a history of vacancy problems. But it's located in an area that's turning around economically, so the upside potential is strong. What's your response? "Yes, it's a risk, but a good risk. The possible gains out-weigh the possible losses." Or, "No way. The building sounds like a black hole. It's in a dicey area, and the whole thing could be a boom or a bust. Forget it."

3. You've been on your job for ten years, and it provides a steady, reliable paycheck with decent benefits. The company is stable, and there's little chance you'll be laid off. But the truth is, you're getting bored and restless. A colleague approaches you with the idea of branch-ing out on your own—starting your own business together. This person is responsible and trustworthy, and the opportunity to be self-employed is quite appealing. Just imagine—no boss, no time clock, no endless meetings. True, but there are also no paychecks every two weeks, no paid vacation, no established retirement plan. What would you do? Go for it or stay put?

Obviously, each of these scenarios would require further investiga-tion and more research to make a wise decision, but what is your gut reaction? How would you approach each of these choices? Further, how would your own decisions either coincide with or contradict those of your partner?

Where Risk and Safety Collide

We have found that there are several key areas in which the differ-ences between risk-takers and security-seekers are clearly evident. These include the following:

Mortgage options. Most spouses want to lock in a thirty-year mort-gage at a fixed interest rate. It's predictable and steady over the long haul. Other people will go for a three-year adjustable-rate mortgage (ARM), which offers lower interest rates initially but substantially higher rates thereafter. They speculate that their financial situation will be improved by that point, so they'll be able to pay off the mortgage or make other favorable arrangements.

Cost of housing. Some people say, "Let's stretch ourselves and buy a bigger or nicer house than we can realistically afford at our current income level, assuming that we'll make more in the coming years. It'll pay off in the long run." Other folks are more cautious: "Let's buy into a house that we can comfortably afford *now*. If our financial situation improves, *then* we'll upgrade."

Saving for retirement. We recently worked with a couple—both in their early forties—in which the husband wanted to invest 2 percent of their combined salaries in retirement funds, while wife wanted to invest 20 percent. Quite a substantial difference. The woman was nervous because they had fallen far behind in saving for retirement; the man was banking on a significant jump in income (he was being groomed to take over as president of his company) or an inheritance at some point (he thought his parents would leave their entire estate to him, though he wasn't positive). Of course, neither of these scenarios is a sure thing, but he was willing to take the chance.

Investments. Many people like the security of CDs, which provide a fixed interest rate for a specific duration. Other people prefer more speculative investments. Some like the predictability of fixed annuities, while others will speculate on something like artwork, which could do well over time or do nothing.

Employment choices. Many people dream of being self-employed, which promises lots

WHAT'S YOUR PREFERENCE: RISK OR SECURITY?

To help you assess your risk tolerance, determine which of the following statements sound like something you would say:

1. "I can't stand being in a rut. I've got to try new things."
2. "I like to be able to plan and predict the future. I don't want to be hit with surprises later on."
3. "I don't like working for someone else. I'd much rather operate my own business."
4. "I love to check my bank account balance after payday. And I like to keep track of how much paid vacation time I have coming."
5. "Making money is kind of like a game. There's a thrill to it."
6. "I would never invest a lot money if there's a chance I'd lose it."
7. "Life's too short not to take a gamble every now and then. Why hold on to everything so tightly?"
8. "You know the fable about the tortoise and the hare? Well, I'm a tortoise and proud of it!"

As you've probably surmised, the even-numbered questions indicate comfort with risk, and odd-numbered questions point to a need for security.

of flexibility and the opportunity to boost your income beyond an annual salary provided by a traditional job. But this arrangement also comes with risks. It's up to you—not a boss or management team—to bring in the money. Working for someone else has its ups and downs as well: regular hours, a dress code, a boss you may or may not get along with. Some people could never work for someone else; others couldn't imagine going without a steady paycheck and benefits.

Saving for your kids' college tuition. This is similar to retirement savings. Some spouses start squirreling away money when their child is born; others assume that scholarships or financial aid will take care of it. Risk-takers sometimes say, "Not to worry. Junior is such a gifted athlete that he'll get a free ride through college." Security-seekers say, "Don't count on it. Let's be prudent and save a little over the years. Then we won't get hit with a huge bill all at once."

WORDS TO LIVE BY

Risk-takers and security-seekers govern their lives and make decisions by different sets of rules and guidelines. And they would surely select different mottos to live by. Which would you choose?

"Nothing ventured, nothing gained."

"If at first you don't succeed, try, try again."

"Fortune sides with him who dares."

"Slow and steady wins the race."

"Risk not, want not."

"A fool and his money are soon parted."

Let's Strike a Balance

You know, like we do, that rarely does anything in life reach the ideal, the perfect, the totally harmonious. That's certainly true when it comes money and marriage. But through our experience as financial professionals, we've come to see how a couple that includes a risk-taker and a security-seeker can complement each other—rather than combat each other. They find a middle ground that meets both of their needs and moves them toward prosperity.

Risk-takers may take too many chances or gamble unwisely. Security-seekers, on the other hand, may not risk enough. That person's cautiousness might lead to missed opportunities or failure to maximize potential for growth. When the aggressive and conservative partners learn to blend their styles, they can balance each other in a productive, prosperous way. In this spirit, we like to use the term "calculated risk" or "reasonable risk."

It was psychologist Maxwell Maltz who said, "Often the difference between a successful person and a failure is not one's better abilities or ideas, but the courage one has to bet on his ideas, to take a calculated risk—and to act." The more careful spouse brings the *calculated* part of that equation, while the more assertive person brings the willingness to *risk*. One person serves as the accelerator and the other as the brake. In tandem, they're a great team.

Couples who take informed, sensible financial risks are often the ones who get ahead. Those who take wild, shot-in-the-dark kinds of chances usually end up behind. A calculated, reasonable risk is one with the odds on your side. That's where differences within a marriage partnership become an asset.

If you can view the other's approach with respect and appreciation—valuing what the other person brings to the table—you can surge ahead financially. And naturally, this kind of cooperative, complementary attitude will bring about relationship gains as well. Couples who learn to blend their risk-taking and security-seeking impulses draw upon the strengths each partner has to offer.

CHAPTER FOUR

EXASPERATING EXPECTATIONS

T he famous writer Alexander Pope once said, "Blessed is he who expects nothing, for he shall never be disappointed." Besides being rather pessimistic, that sentiment seems unrealistic for nearly everyone who walks the earth. We each expect *something* from our work, our aspirations, and our relationships.

The truth is that every man and woman carries into marriage hundreds of expectations, assumptions, and beliefs about how things should be done. We all have preconceived ideas about how we'll spend holidays, where we'll vacation, how often we'll make love, who will be responsible for household chores, how we'll discipline the children, and how we'll decorate the house. When the expectations of both spouses coincide, there's no problem. But when they collide, conflicts are sure to arise.

A man may assume that he'll arrive home from work each night to a hot, four-course meal on the table, while his wife is content to make soup and grilled-cheese sandwiches a couple of evenings each week. A woman may assume that her parents will stay in the guest room for as long they want, while her husband believes the local Holiday Inn would be a more appropriate lodging place.

When we were first married, we encountered several differing assumptions we brought into the relationship. For instance, I (Scott) have always been a voracious consumer of milk, eggs, ice cream, and other dairy products and so assumed Bethany would share this passion. So I signed us up for a weekly home delivery of dairy supplies from a local company—the "deluxe" package, which probably could have fed a family of ten (with leftovers for the pets).

Bethany wasn't exactly thrilled by my brilliant plan, and I didn't understand why. She would say strange things like, "How are we

THE BEST
TIME TO TALK
IS BEFORE
YOU MARRY

¢

It's never too late for
couples to discuss
important issues and
get clear about each
other's expectations.
But sooner is better
than later in this case.
The more partners com-
municate and clarify
before marriage, the
more problems they will
avoid. In that spirit, we
put together twenty
questions dating or
engaged couples
should talk through in
detail. (As much as pos-
sible, give reasons for
your answers.)

1. Do you think joint
or separate checking
accounts are appropri-
ate in marriage?

2. How did your mom
and dad spend money?

3. How did your
mom and dad save
money?

4. Will we be a dual-
income family, or will
one of us stay home
with the children?

5. Do you think pay-
ing the bills should be
done separately or
together?

ever going to eat and drink all of those dairy products?"

But Bethany really is good about putting up with my "brilliant plans" and didn't say a word when month after month, the milk containers, cheese packages, and egg cartons piled up in the refrigerator—mostly untouched. I finally had to give in. We canceled our order, and our choles-terol levels have thanked us ever since. But I still think that if my wife had just joined me for a lumberjack breakfast now and then, things might have turned out a whole lot better!

All of this brings us to the fourth common conflict area related to finances. You and your partner carried into your relationship countless expectations about handling money. Some of these are relatively minor: who will do the shopping, pay the bills, or balance the check-book. Other expectations involve significant issues: how much you are willing to go into debt, to what extent you will financially sup-port your parents as they get older, what career and income sacrifices you will make in order to have children, and so on.

Just to complicate matters further, we are not consciously aware of many of our expectations. They are so ingrained in our subterranean thoughts that we aren't cognizant of why we act and respond in certain ways. As is true of all deep-down motivations and impulses, expecta-tions can cause damage if we don't seek to under-stand them. Unfortunately, often the only time we discover our assumptions is when someone has opposing ones. We heard one psychologist liken expectations to glass doors—you don't real-ize they're there until you crash into them.

To a large degree, you'll be either satisfied or dissatisfied in life depending on how many of your expectations are met or the degree to which you can accept and adjust to assumptions different from your own.

Dr. Judith Wallerstein, one the nation's foremost marriage experts, wrote, "Sometimes the man and woman are in accord from courtship on. More often they come to agree about fundamental issues during the early years of marriage. The core relationship emerges gradually as the partners weave the tapestry of their relationship. If the fit is right, the marriage itself helps shape the closeness in values and shared expectations. A marriage in which two people have incompatible expectations or unmodifiable demands is likely to fail."[1]

We have certainly found that to be true in our discussions with couples about their finances. When they cling steadfastly to their preconceived way of doing things, they're headed for trouble.

The Eight Most Provocative Presumptions

Through our years of financial counseling with husbands and wives, we've noticed many patterns and commonalities. Eight issues have surfaced repeatedly—issues in which differing expectations from partners created problems and perils for their relationship. See if any of these ring a bell for you.

Will Both Partners Work, and How Much Will Each Be Expected to Earn?

In our discussions with couples, we're constantly amazed at how many of them failed to talk through questions like this prior to marriage. It comes back to the issue of assumptions—they both *assumed* they'd play by a certain set of rules,

6. Are you a saver or a spender?

7. Do you work with a budget now?

8. Are you conservative or aggressive in your investing?

9. What are your income goals?

10. Should we consider entering into a prenuptial agreement?

11. Have you ever lost a large amount of money in investments?

12. Do you want to rent or own your home?

13. What mistakes have you made with money?

14. What is the most expensive item you have ever purchased?

15. What stresses you out when it comes to money?

16. Did your parents ever talk about money?

17. Do you track your saving and spending?

18. Do you utilize an employer retirement plan?

19. How important is planning for retirement to you?

20. Do you tithe and/or give to charitable organizations?

so it didn't occur to them to broach the subject. It is a shock, then, when one of them settles into a relaxed work schedule, while the other slaves away at a job for fifty or sixty hours a week. Or a spouse with a demanding, high-pressure position may feel cheated if his or her partner enjoys a cushy job, earning minimum wage.

A man named Steve told us recently, "When Tammy and I got married six years ago, I thought we would both work full time and earn as much we could. It was supposed to be a 50-50 deal. Surprise! Tammy is not career oriented, and she never intended to work more than part time. She works for a local florist twenty hours per week. If I'd known she didn't plan to work much, I still would have married her because I love her. But it would've been nice to know ahead of time—and it would have saved us some nasty fights."

Then there are Bryce and Shelly. He is a talented sculptor with undeniable skill—and, sadly, few sales to show for his craftsmanship. Shelly has largely supported him for nine years, though Bryce brings in a little money by working sporadically at an art-supply shop. Because Shelly believes in his artistic gifts and doesn't want to squash his dreams, she has felt comfortable with this arrangement—until recently. She's started to wonder if she'll always be footing the bill while he does the starving artist routine.

"I believe in pursuing dreams," she told us. "But I also believe in paying the rent."

Moreover, she feels her biological time clock clicking away, and she wants to start a family. What then? She assumed Bryce would give sculpting a shot for a couple of years and move on to a "real" career if things didn't pan out. Nope. For Bryce, this is a lifelong ambition that he intends to pursue indefinitely.

Who Will Pay the Bills and Handle "Administrative" Duties?

Most of us naturally follow the lead of our parents in this area. If Dad always sat down to write checks and fill out paperwork, we'll just assume it is part of the husband's job description. Same goes if it was Mom who handled these responsibilities. And if *both* parents were involved, that's what we'll expect, too.

Of course, it doesn't always work out that way. When our friends Chloe and Sam got married, they each assumed they would be in charge of the finances. That's what Chloe saw her mom do, and that's what Sam saw his dad do. To avoid a big fuss about it, Sam handed over the bill paying to his wife, secretly believing she'd blow it. She didn't. In fact, she handled everything so conscientiously that they were out of debt within a few years.

About that time, Sam got it into his head that this was a "man's job," and he assumed he would do even better than Chloe. He didn't. In fact, he handled everything so carelessly that they were back in debt within a few years. Did he learn his lesson that time? Let's just say that Chloe has been handling the money—with Sam's input—ever since. Much frustration—and debt—could have been avoided if they had talked through their expectations early on.

Who Controls the Purse Strings, and How Much Freedom Will We Have to Spend Money as We Choose?

This issue is a staple of screenwriters and comedians everywhere: the miserly man who hates to part with a penny and his shopaholic wife who constantly tries to weasel money out of him. In fact, those of us who grew up watching reruns of the hilarious "I Love Lucy" show remember this as a recurring story line. There was Ricky, reluctantly doling out Lucy's meager allowance. And there was Lucy, scheming to purloin a little more out of her husband's wallet. In the end, her conniving was always exposed, and Ricky would utter those famous words, "Lucy, you've got some 'splaining to do!" Though this situation brought big laughs in a sitcom, in real life it leads to big stress and squabbles.

Most couples today enter marriage assuming a degree of parity and shared control of the household funds. They anticipate equal opportunity when it comes to spending and managing money. Sometimes, though, this isn't the way things evolve in their relationship. One person—usually the man, but not always—may become the self-appointed keeper of the coffers and boss of the budget.

This arrangement might start out as a matter of expediency and efficiency: in hectic households, fewer details fall through the cracks if one person oversees the financial matters. Other times, it is a matter of power and control. Money and power go hand in hand, so the person who controls the money holds the power. This leaves the other person feeling subordinate and inferior.

We recall acquaintances of ours, Rachel and Howard, who were chronically short on money. They were both schoolteachers and didn't earn a high income. Howard handled all their money and scrupulously accounted for every penny. So Rachel had to plead her case like a court-room lawyer every time she wanted to buy a new pair of shoes, a coat, or a kitchen utensil. Not that she was extravagant—far from it. Though she never squandered money on unnecessary items, she felt as though she had to justify every nickel.

"It was a bad setup," Rachel told us. "I had to beg and plead with Howard for twenty bucks to buy the kids shoes on sale at Target. We bickered all the time because I didn't have any money to spend and he didn't want to give me any to spend. You can see how that would cause battles over the budget."

This situation doesn't happen only with couples feeling pinched financially. We know of a surgeon named Richard and his wife, Lisa, who is a dance instructor. Although Richard has always earned much more than she has, they each had ample spending money while they both worked. When they had children, they agreed that Lisa would be a stay-at-home mom until their kids were school age. This new arrangement tilted the balance of power in their relationship, since Lisa suddenly had to ask for money if she wanted to go out to lunch with friends, buy clothes, or see a movie. Richard freely paid for all the household expenses and happily provided for the children's needs, but he hassled Lisa every time she wanted spending money.

"You have plenty of clothes in your closet," he'd chide. "Why do you need sixty bucks for a new pair of jeans?" And, "I don't understand why you have to go out to lunch with your friends. Can't you go to each other's houses? That would be much cheaper."

Lisa said she started to feel like a kid asking her dad for pocket money, and this became a major source of contention for them. After many arguments, Lisa finally convinced him that caring for young children was as challenging and tiring as any full-time job (including being a physician). The clincher came when Lisa had to leave for a week to care for her elderly mother, and Richard was left to manage the household and care for the children. The meals, the laundry, the fussy kids, the sibling rivalry! When Lisa returned, Richard immediately offered to give her a generous amount of money each month that she could spend as she pleased.

Will the Man Be the Primary Breadwinner?

You might think that this would not be an issue in the twenty-first century, with women entering the workforce en masse over the past decades and occupying high-level positions in nearly every field. But for many couples, it becomes a sore spot when *he* expected to earn the larger income and *she* ends up outpacing him. For most men, ego and income are intertwined, at least to some degree. A man's self-esteem can be bruised when his wife brings home a bigger paycheck.

As the financial writer Kim Clark said, "Aha. Money. It's probably the only thing that complicates life between the sexes as much as sex. And when a woman makes more of it than her man, life really gets complicated. Even the most liberated man can feel threatened by a woman who earns more than he does. And even the most well-adjusted couples say they have to work extra hard to keep their relationships happy if the woman has the higher salary."[2]

> To a large degree, you'll be either satisfied or dissatisfied in life depending on how many of your expectations are met or the degree to which you can accept and adjust to assumptions different from your own.

There is another side to this issue. We've run across more than a few women who expected their husbands to be the principal provider, only to discover that he couldn't or wouldn't fulfill that role. This happens for a variety of reasons. Perhaps the man has suffered blows to his self-esteem because of failures on the job. It could be that his career started strong but stalled somewhere along the line, sending him into a slow decline. Other times it's a legitimate matter of emotional or physical setbacks, such as depression or disability. Maybe he's just plain ol' lazy or unmotivated. Whatever the cause, the woman ends up being the primary breadwinner, and not by choice. The expectations for one or both spouses are turned upside down, which naturally results in friction and fights.

Will We Give Big Gifts, Little Gifts, or No Gifts?

Gift giving seems so simple and straightforward, but it becomes a quandary when two partners disagree about how much is too much. You probably know someone who loves to proffer lavish gifts for birthdays, holidays, anniversaries, and other occasions. If you are the *recipient* of presents like that, you probably wouldn't complain. But if

MAKING CENTS

¢

What are money squabbles usually about? Most financial fights are about what to spend it on. Twenty percent of couples can't agree on financial goals. Fourteen percent of family feuds occur when the husband believes his wife spends too much, while 11 percent are caused by wives blaming their husbands for overspending. Another 11 percent of disputes arise over how much money a family can afford to save.

Does it cause problems when the woman earns more? Some 53 percent of women and 34 percent of men think that women bringing home more bacon would lead to dissension.[3]

that lavish gift giver happens to be your spouse—and you think less expensive gifts would suffice—you might complain loudly.

Maybe the situation is just the opposite. You feel that giving generous gifts demonstrates love and care, but your partner disagrees. He or she goes right to the bottom line: "You paid *how* much for that present?"

In the larger scheme of things, the gift-giving conflict may appear insignificant. But this issue has shown up so many times in our financial discussions with couples—and was mentioned repeatedly on the questionnaires we sent out—that we've become convinced it is, in fact, a divisive dilemma.

Will We Have Separate or Combined Accounts and Checkbooks?

Some couples enter marriage expecting to keep their finances separate. He'll have his accounts, she'll have hers, and never the twain shall meet. They figure that money management is neat and tidy with *individual* oversight, and besides, it gives each of them autonomy and freedom. It gives no room for partners to go poking around in each other's business.

We admit to having strong feelings on this issue, and we advocate combined and mutual finances for couples. Why? It comes back to the central theme of this book—money can unite partners or divide them. How you handle finances can enhance the quality of your relationship or undermine it. We've noticed that spouses who have joint accounts are forced to talk regularly about their spending and goals. By working together, they utilize the strengths of each individual and minimize the weaknesses. Teamwork, shared decision making, and mutual accountability increase. Money is such a central part of our lives and our future plans that it's helpful when two partners are directly involved in budgeting, investing, and spending decisions.

The main point here is that trouble looms when each partner has a different expectation. If one is adamant about keeping things separate and the other wants to merge all money matters, they're going to bump up against this conflict on a weekly or monthly basis.

Should We Pay Our Kids' College Tuition?

Not long ago, Stan and Nancy came to our office to map out a long-range financial strategy. Both of them were approaching age forty, and they had twin boys entering junior high school. After an hour of amiable discussion and decision making, Scott asked, "Since your kids are going into junior high school, have you given much thought to saving for college tuition?" That seemed like a straightforward and innocuous enough question, so we were surprised at the ensuing eruption of emotions.

It turned out that Stan and Nancy had never discussed in detail their boys' college education—but they both had clear and staunch expectations. Each wanted their boys to earn college degrees, but how they would achieve that was an entirely different matter. Nancy had always assumed she and Stan would pay for all or most of the college expenses. Her parents had funded a university education for Nancy and her three siblings, providing a free ride so they could focus on studies and enjoy campus life. This rite of passage was reinforced by Nancy's extended family and community, since all of the other parents she knew did the same thing.

"That's just part of parenting," Nancy said. "It's one of the last obligations a mom and dad have to prepare their kids to launch out on their own. You give your children a solid education—that's just basic parenting. Stan, I can't believe we're even having this discussion. Of course we're paying for college."

As Nancy spoke, Stan sat in stunned silence. He wore the pained look of someone whose wife had just whacked him on the noggin with a frying pan. And that's probably how he felt.

"Jason and Connor are going to college all right, but they're paying their own way," he insisted. "It will make them appreciate their education more—they'll work harder and buckle down if they know the money is coming out of their own pocket and not ours. Besides, it will prepare them for the real world, where they can't count on handouts

FORMING ASSUMPTIONS IS PART OF BEING HUMAN

The renowned writer C. S. Lewis once mused about the human condition and how prone we are to develop preconceptions. "Five senses, an incurably abstract intellect, a haphazardly selective memory, a set of preconceptions and assumptions so numerous I can never examine more than a minority of them—and never become conscious of them all. How much of total reality can such an apparatus let through?"[4]

and freebies. They're not going to learn to be industrious if we hand over money every month."

We came to learn that Stan's father had a pull-yourself-up-by-the-bootstraps philosophy of raising children, and he believed it was empowering for children to pay their own way as soon as possible. Stan had contributed to the family bank account since his first paper route at age twelve. It was no mystery where Stan got his ideas about paying for higher education.

Who was right in this college conundrum, Stan or Nancy? How you answer that depends on your own background, experiences, and expectations. Stan and Nancy both made strong arguments for their point of view, and they both had legitimate rationales. Besides, both of them had turned out to be stable, conscientious, hardworking individuals.

You can see that the expectations formed from their own experiences led this couple into a significant collision of ideologies. They did not solve the dilemma in our office that day, though they did continue their "discussion" in a decidedly animated fashion. Indeed, we anticipate many such lively conversations over the coming years.

To What Extent Should We Help Our Elderly Parents?

The vast majority of couples want to help their older parents if there is a genuine and legitimate need for assistance. We have noticed that sometimes conflicts arise among couples when one partner's parents require much more financial help than the other person's. A woman named Donna from Bellingham, Washington, included this message on the questionnaire we sent out.

My husband, Bill, and I both believe in the Bible's admonition to honor parents and care for the elderly. Even though we aren't wealthy by any means, we're happy to help pay for the needs of each of our mothers, who are in their eighties (our fathers passed away some years ago). But we've had several arguments about this matter. Bill's mom has far less money than mine because she and her husband were not good with their finances. They lived extravagantly and wasted lots of money. My parents scrimped and saved for decades, and they ended up with a decent retirement.

We have $500 a month set aside to send our moms, and $400 of it goes to Bill's mother. This isn't quite fair and balanced. I admit that it seems petty to complain about these things, since Bill and I love each other and we love our parents. But that's reality. Sending off those checks each month puts a strain on our budget and a strain on our relationship.

The pressure is ratcheted up even further when couples are in the "sandwich generation"—giving money to help their parents while incurring big expenses for their own kids. We hear comments like this all the time: "We get it coming and going! It takes a ton of money to raise kids these days—especially teenagers—and it's costing more and more to care for our older parents." How well couples navigate these bumpy roads depends largely on how closely aligned their expectations are. If they're united about their convictions and beliefs, they will sidestep much of the tension that other couples experience.

¢ **DOES INCOME INTERFERE WITH INTIMACY?**

Psychologist Olivia Mellan, who specializes in financial issues, commented on how some partners derive power from their money-making prowess—and how this sometimes causes problems. "When men make more money than their spouse, they believe their superior earnings entitle them to greater power in decision-making. By contrast, women who make more than their mates almost always desire democratic decision-making. As a woman and a therapist, I have a definite bias toward shared decision-making and shared power. It is the only arrangement that works.

"Men are trained to believe that money equals power and that power is the path to respect. However, power and control are not compatible with intimacy. Relationships succeed only when both partners are willing to display their vulnerabilities to each other. It's important for men to know that failing to share power cheats them of the intimacy and love they want."[5]

The Cure for Conflicting Expectations

We believe the best way to overcome opposing assumptions is to be perfectly clear about what they are, talk them through together, and compromise when necessary. We also realize that this sounds easy in principle—and is much harder in practice. Part 3 of this book is devoted entirely to helping you and your spouse develop healthy communication, problem-solving solutions, and goal-setting strategies. But for now, chew on these three ideas.

Get crystal clear about your own expectations. We all have blind spots and hidden motivations that drive us to think and act in certain ways. If you and your partner run into the same problem over and over, it's probably because you have conflicting expectations. And it may be that you've never thought them through individually or discussed them together. Set aside plenty of time to explore and understand your preconceived notions about spending, investing, financial security, long-range planning, and everything else related to money.

Be open to seeing your partner's point of view. Because our assumptions about money, love, and relationships are so deep-rooted, we hold tightly to them. It's hard to imagine that someone with an opposing opinion might just possibly have a valid point. As writer Jessamyn West said, "We want the facts to fit our preconceptions. When they don't, it is easier to ignore the facts than to change the preconceptions." Isn't that the truth! Take a giant step back, so you can view the big picture. With most conflicts about money, it isn't a matter of one person being absolutely right and the other being absolutely wrong. It's a matter of differing backgrounds, opinions, and beliefs.

Adjust your assumptions for the sake of the relationship. People often become so determined to win the argument, make a point, and demonstrate their correctness that they damage the relationship in the process. The quality of your relationship is far more important than proving you are right. As the saying goes, you may win the battle but lose the war. Sure, there may be times when you have to take a stand and hold firm boundaries. But most often, explosive conflicts can be defused by practicing give-and-take and making concessions for the sake of marital harmony.

CHAPTER FIVE

FLYING BLIND

The temperature in the cockpit of the Piper Arrow felt like 120 degrees. I (Scott) had been flying under a plastic hood for an hour and a half, and it had been a bumpy day. Fatigue and frustration were setting in. My flight instructor was obviously annoyed by my performance and decided that leaning on me a little harder would help me better prepare for our next cross-country IFR (Instrument Flight Reference) flight. As we circled around toward the runway, he barked orders and peppered me with questions about emergency procedures.

As I scanned the flight controls and recited answers, I felt like I was losing control of my cockpit—probably because I was. The heat, my instructor's harsh tone, and my preoccupation with other things made it tough to maintain focus.

As I turned into the final approach, I forced myself to concentrate and push everything else out of my mind. My instruments showed that I was on course and that my altitude was perfect. Five hundred feet above touchdown, my instructor suddenly ordered me to lift my hood, and then he jerked the controls from my hands. An unmistakable look of disgust formed on his face.

"Well, Mr. Palmer," he growled, "you finally straightened it out ... but forgetting to engage the landing gear would have ruined the day."

* * *

Scott's experience reminds us of some couples we've talked with who are "flying blind" financially. In fact, our research revealed that this is the fifth most common area of conflict for couples—they are simply unfocused and inattentive to their personal finances. They aren't on top of their bills, checking account, taxes, insurance, and other money matters.

Many husbands and wives don't balance their checkbook regularly, get behind in credit-card payments, couldn't tell you the amount in their savings account, sprint to the mailbox at 11:58 p.m. on April 15 with tax forms in hand, bounce checks, rummage through overstuffed boxes in search of missing receipts, procrastinate about returning insurance and medical forms, and avoid at all costs the overflowing box marked "bills" on the desk. Is it any wonder these couples feel stressed out and squabble over money? When finances are in disarray, trouble is on the way.

Nearly every couple in America has the occasional slipup: the bill that accidentally gets tossed out with the junk mail; the year-end bonus check that doesn't get deposited in time to cover checks already written; or the reimbursement form buried in the bottom of the stack. Those things happen in our hectic and harried society. But for "flying blind" couples, these are frequent occurrences. If we had eavesdropping equipment like the FBI, we could listen in on the conversations these couples have.

¢Not knowing how to manage the household finances in our era of rampant consumerism and pervasive debt can sabotage a marriage and thwart long-term goals.

BOB: Did you pay the phone bill?

JANE: Me? I thought you were going to pay it.

BOB: I never said that. I said I'd pay the Visa bill. And by the way, where *is* the Visa bill?

JANE: I think it's on the kitchen counter. No, wait—it's in the glove box of my car. No, *your* car. Oh yeah, I forget to mention that we got a call from Memorial Hospital saying we've been turned over to a collection agency. Something about an outstanding bill related to Tommy's surgery last April. I told them we paid it. We did—didn't we?

BOB: Last April ... gee, I don't know. I'll have to check. Speaking of April, that reminds me. We filed an extension for our taxes, and isn't that extension almost up? I wonder how many extensions we're allowed. Call your cousin tomorrow—she knows about those things.

If you are one of those supersaver types described in chapter 1—the kind who watches every penny and pays bills well before the due date—then you may be skeptical and even snooty about people like this. You may scoff at the idea of people playing so fast and loose with their finances. But it happens—and more often than you might think. Here's a snapshot.

- Nearly half (45 percent) of all Americans admit they occasionally pay their bills late. For 32 percent, tardiness is a routine occurrence.
- Almost everyone knows it's important to have a will, but more than 40 percent of people thirty-five and older don't have one. More amazing, 40 percent of those who haven't made a will don't expect they'll ever get around to it.
- When it comes to balancing the checkbook against bank statements, 43.3 percent of people admit they never do it. Of those, 31.9 percent believe it's a good idea but just don't find the time for it. The rest totally trust the bank to figure it out.[1]
- Nearly half of all Americans (46 percent) have less than $10,000 saved for their retirement. And 39 percent of Americans are anxious about their ability to achieve their desired retirement lifestyle.[2] It can either be the golden years or the golden arches.

We've had many couples come to us with their tails between their legs and say, "Help! We have no idea what's going on with our finances. You've got to help us get on top of things!" That's the good news. The bad news is that we've met even more couples in this situation who say, "We'll make an appointment so you can help us sort out this mess." And then we never hear from them. We can only imagine the deep, dark hole they're sinking into.

BRUSHING UP ON THE BASICS

A suggestion we give clients who want to understand finances is to read *USA Today's Money* section once a week. The articles are written in an easy-to-understand style and will introduce you to financial concepts and lingo without talking over your head.

Let us tell you two true stories that came from our interviews. Davis and Trisha of Long Beach, California, used to be the kind of couple that carefully checked their bank statements, kept up on payments, and closely watched their checking account balance. Note the operative words *used to be*. Somewhere along the line, things changed—and in a way you might not expect.

It isn't that they lost jobs, racked up huge debt, filed for bankruptcy, and threw in the towel on their finances. In fact, five years ago they started making big money when they both received promotions along with sizable pay increases. With their new positions came longer hours and higher stress, and they no longer felt motivated to sit down together every week to look at the budget and handle paperwork.

"We stopped using a budget altogether, and we kept tabs on our checking account by calling the bank's 800 number once a week to get the balance," Davis explained. "As long as there was money in the account, we kept spending. We set up automatic withdrawal through our bank to pay most bills, so we weren't even aware of many expenses. For the others that came through the mail, we just wrote a check as soon as they came in. We knew there was a lot of money coming and going, but we never knew exactly how much."

When we asked why they stopped keeping track of their finances, Trisha said, "For one thing, we were suddenly very busy with our high-pressure jobs. When we came home from work at seven-thirty or eight, we didn't want to deal with checkbooks, insurance forms, and all that. We wanted to collapse in front of the TV or soak in the hot tub. Second, we had a surplus of money. Our paychecks were big enough so that we just deposited them and assumed we had it all covered."

But on several occasions, Davis and Trisha assumed wrong, and that's when their negligence caused problems. Despite their income, they bounced checks when they both pulled money out of the ATM without telling each other and went wild with debit cards. They lost important papers. They paid more taxes than they needed to because of poor record keeping. Late payments—along with exorbitant fees—became commonplace.

And so did arguments about whose responsibility it was clean up the massive money mess. Ironically, they started fighting about money much more than when they had less of it.

Davis summed up their experience. "There we were, pulling in more money than we would've dreamed we could, and yet we argued about all kinds of problems related to that money. After one particularly heated fight, we stopped and said, 'Wait a second. We've got all this hostility between us because we've let our finances become a black hole. Let's take some time to get organized, so we can enjoy the income we're making—and enjoy each other.' We did just that, and our relationship has been back on track ever since."

The other story we want to tell you involves a couple whose disorganization nearly ended in disaster. Don and Laurel of Boulder, Colorado, were in many ways a typical husband-wife team trying hard to keep up with life's demands. He was a general contractor, and she was a social worker. Together, they owned four houses (besides the one they lived in), which they used as rentals. The parents of three young daughters, they bore the stress of family responsibilities while trying to get ahead financially. Frankly, they struggled to keep up with their bills, renters' demands, and the myriad of details that bear down on every American household.

Then they received the kind of news every couple dreads. Laurel was diagnosed with breast cancer. Within weeks, the entire family flew to Mayo Clinic in Rochester, Minnesota, since a good friend of Laurel's dad served as a top oncologist there. During the weeks Laurel was undergoing tests, Don received a phone call from their health insurance provider: their coverage was about to be dropped because they had failed to pay premiums for the previous six months. They had received notices and warnings, but Don had ignored them. He'd been too busy trying to keep up with the daily grind. Then when Laurel was diagnosed, everything else—meaning everything piled up on Don's desk—was pushed aside.

> Your family's finances can be as simple or as complex as you want to make them.

Some couples fly com-
pletely blind—they have
no clue about their
finances. Others have
"money myopia," a sort
of nearsightedness in
regards to their financial
situation. Still others
have 20/20 vision.
Check your own finan-
cial eyesight by answer-
ing true or false to the
following statements.

1. I have avoided
bouncing checks this year.

2. I can say within
$100 what my checking
account balance is at
this moment.

3. I know how much I
have—within $1,000—in
my retirement accounts.

4. I have an up-to-date
will (especially important
if you have children).

5. Last year, I filed my
taxes on time.

6. I know the interest
rate on my primary
credit card.

7. I have not spent
more than twenty min-
utes looking for a particular financial document
in the past six months.

8. I have not received
a phone call or written
notice from a collection
agency in the past year.

"That was the darkest point of my life," Laurel recalled. "There I was battling cancer, waiting to find out how bad it was, and facing the prospect of chemotherapy or a mastectomy. I had three young girls to think about. And then to hear that we might not be covered by health insurance—it was almost more than I could take. My illness could have wiped out our family's assets in a matter of weeks. I was devastated."

That's the same word Don used—devastated. The previous months had been a whirlwind of activity and upheaval. He had run from one rental property to another, attending to plumbing problems and water-heater failures. Plus he was in charge of taking the girls to their doctor appointments, soccer practices, and church activities.

Most of us—especially those of us with young kids—understand how life can become overwhelming and how easily things fall through the cracks. Unfortunately for Don and Laurel, this flying-blind incident came at the worst possible time.

"I felt like a total failure," Don told us. "I thought Laurel would never trust me again and that my kids would hate me. My own disorganization endangered our family's future, and even more so, Laurel's life."

Thankfully, it didn't. Laurel did go through several months of chemotherapy, and the treatment was successful. After five years, she still has a clean bill of health, and her long-term prognosis is positive. As for their insurance, they were able to reinstate coverage—but not without the help of a lawyer and many hours of consultation and negotiation. Their financial stress added to a far greater stress. Both Don and Laurel vowed to never let anything like that happen again, and since that frightening episode, they have been absolutely sure to keep on top of their money matters.

Why Couples End Up in a Muddled Money Mess

As we've counseled couples about their finances over the years, we have heard several comments surface repeatedly. These came from the flying-blind spouses who just couldn't seem to get a handle on their financial situation. See if any of these explanations (or excuses) sound familiar.

"We Don't Understand It, So We Don't Want to Deal with It."

Even though we are financial professionals and are well versed in all the terminology and procedures related to our field, we sympathize with couples who say this. Our society bombards us with mind-numbing amounts of information, confusing statistics, and perplexing lingo. The average person is hit with a daily barrage of mailings, Internet pop-ups, sales pitches, advertisements, and media reports that leave them more perplexed than informed.

Besides the information overload that muddles our minds, many people have never been taught the basics of money management. They are simply unclear about the nuts and bolts of budgeting, consumer credit, insurance, and retirement accounts. Most possess only a vague understanding about managing a paycheck, the type of insurance to carry, how to get out of debt rapidly, the pros and cons of

9. I have a life insurance policy.

10. I have checked my credit rating in the past two years.

11. I have not paid a late fee to a credit-card company during the past year.

12. I can say within $20 how much I spent on dining out last month.

13. During the past year, I did not withdraw money from the ATM machine if I didn't know what my balance was.

14. I can say what my phone bills (landline and cell) were last month within $20.

15. I have met with a financial professional to discuss retirement, budgeting, debt relief, and other financial issues.

Count up your "true" answers.

- 12 or more: You're seeing clearly.
- 10–11: Your financial vision is a bit fuzzy, and you should take steps to correct it.
- 9 or fewer: You're flying blind—seek help immediately!

paying off a mortgage, and so on. Not knowing how to manage the household finances in our era of rampant consumerism and pervasive debt can sabotage a marriage and thwart long-term goals.

As we said in the introduction, your family's finances can be as simple or as complex as you want to make them. We advocate a straightforward, uncomplicated approach. A colleague of ours is fond of saying that personal finance is "90 percent common sense and 10 percent rocket science." We would add that the vast majority of families today have no need to enter into that 10 percent zone where things get complicated.

Simplify Bill ¢ Paying

We found it helpful to change the payment dates for all of our bills to the same time during the month (ours is the twentieth). This allows us to pay bills all at one time, rather than having them scattered throughout the month. Arranging this is not difficult: simply call each of the accounts (there is usually a toll-free customer service number on the statement), and request the billing date be switched to whichever time is most convenient for you.

"Neither of Us Is a Numbers Person."

It's true that some men and women are not wired to be math minds. They may feel more comfortable with words, artistic endeavors, auto mechanics, or whatever. When you get *two* people together who are annoyed by arithmetic and baffled by budgets, finances can indeed spin out of control.

The good news is that many easy-to-use tools are available to assist even the most numbers-averse individuals. Many online calculators and CD-ROM programs can help you organize finances in a matter of minutes (we recommend several helpful tools in part 4). What's more, financial professionals are available to guide you, and most could help you devise a simple spending and saving plan in less than a half hour. The key is figure out a system that works for you and stick with it.

"Who's Got Time?"

We've noticed a common response when we ask people how they're doing: "Oh, I'm so busy!" *Busyness* has become the byword of our era, and a lack of time is often the rationale given for letting finances fall into disarray.

As we've counseled couples over the years, we've realized there is a widespread misconception about what it takes to handle finances. Many spouses assume that it takes hours each week, but that's not necessarily true. Overseeing your finances can take as much time—or as little time—as you want to devote to it. Some folks enjoy reading money magazines, watching stock reports on CNN, poring over the *Wall Street Journal*, and tinkering with their computer money-management programs. The average couple today, however, is too busy for all that. They prefer to spend their time doing other things.

We understand. Early in our marriage, we devoted a considerable amount of time each week to our household finances. We scrutinized the budget, read investment prospectuses, studied and cross-checked every bill, and spent hours talking about how to maximize our paychecks. Then we had kids. Suddenly, our discretionary time was consumed with changing diapers, cleaning up spills, and running to the store for necessities. Now that our boys, Cole and Cade, are older, our time is spent reading Dr. Seuss books, wrestling on the floor, and tossing the ball around (far more enjoyable than talking about budgets!). We were forced to simplify our personal-finance system and streamline all the paperwork and publications so we could invest our time in the most important things—our relationship with each other and our kids. Now we spend a maximum of two hours per month on our home finances, and usually less than that.

We don't mention this to hold ourselves up as shining examples; we simply want to convey that we understand what it's like to continually battle the time crunch. We also want to convince every flying-blind couple that only a small amount of time is required to stay on top of your finances.

"We're Buried in Paperwork, Forms, Check Registers, and All Kinds of Other Stuff."

In 1986, Roger Smith, chairman of General Motors, made a bold prediction. "By the end of the century, we will live in a paperless society."[4] Well, we're well into the new millenium—and paper looks like it's here to stay.

Consider the following: US companies sent 35 billion pieces of direct postal mail in 1980. In 1990, the number jumped to 64 billion. In 2000, the figure hit 90 billion.[5] Not all of those mailings had to do with money, but we're guessing that most of them did. No wonder people feel overwhelmed by paperwork, procedures, and red tape.

We've spoken with many people who shy away from their finances because of the daunting amount of paperwork and administrative details involved. But for better or worse, this is the world we live in, and we've got to deal with it. Thankfully, there are many things couples can do to minimize their paperwork and get clear about their finances (see sidebar).

"Our Finances Are Such a Mess That We Just Can't Face Them."

There's a word for this excuse: denial. Simply put, it means to purposely ignore a destructive situation or condition. We aren't psychologists, but we've worked with enough couples in financial dire straights to say with authority, "Money problems will not disappear on their own!" You've got to face the truth, even if it hurts.

Juliet Schor, Harvard professor and author of books such as *The Overspent American* and *Born to Buy*, said,

> Americans live with high levels of denial about their spending patterns. We spend more than we realize, hold more debt than we admit to, and ignore many of the moral conflicts surrounding our acquisitions.... Sixty-five percent [of people surveyed] agreed that "in looking back on my spending, I often wonder where the money goes." Eighty percent felt they should be saving more. Forty percent said they'd like a simpler life. But while 70 percent described "the average American" as "very materialistic," only 8 percent felt they were materialistic themselves.[6]

Yes, denial is alive and well in America. What denial does—whether we're talking about addictions, relationship problems, or money matters—is keep us blinded to the truth and perpetuate harmful patterns and habits.

Take debt, for example. Most people do not fully understand, or *want* to understand, the problem that debt is causing them. Suppose you have $8,000 worth of credit card debt. At a rate of 18 percent interest, it will take you more than twenty-five years and will cost you over $24,000 if you were to make only the minimum payments each month. Ouch! No one wonder people choose to ignore facts.

We believe the words of Jesus, who said, "Know the truth, and the truth will set you free" (John 8:32). Shielding ourselves—and our family members—from the truth only keeps us stuck and in bondage. Acknowledging where we are financially is the first step toward freedom and peace.

We'll close this chapter with the words from a woman named Beth, who lives with her husband and three kids in Wheaton, Illinois.

> Ken and I have been married thirteen years, and almost that entire time we lived from paycheck to paycheck. When a bill showed up in the mail, we paid it. When we needed groceries, we wrote a check for them. When we wanted to go on vacation, we charged it. We had absolutely no plan or strategy. Not surprisingly, we arrived at age thirty-nine with only a couple thousand dollars in retirement and many, many thousands of dollars in debt. We were in a desperate cycle of earn-spend-pay debts.

financial information you should keep and what you can throw out.

3. *Cancel every credit card, debit card, and other plastic card that isn't essential.* The fact is that every credit card comes with loads of mailings and emails that clutter your life. Who can keep track of it all? We suggest you keep the bare minimum of cards.

4. *Get your records in order.* Take a deep breath and plunge into the file cabinets and boxes in the garage. Many folks have boxes stuffed with old papers and files—lots of out-dated material that can be thrown away.

5. *Maintain a central "clearinghouse" for your most important documents.* Designate one safe, secure spot to keep your birth certificates, Social Security information, medical records, wills, 401(k) information, insurance policies, warranties for appliances, and anything else you may need to access. Again, see our Web site for a complete list of documents to retain.

Our "great awakening" came when we felt called to open our home to foster children. This had been a desire and dream for many years, and as we both approached age forty, we decided, "Now is the time!" But guess what? We soon discovered that we couldn't afford it. We would've had to make home modifications to meet the requirements for the Department of Social Services in our area. And we calculated the out-of-pocket expenses of caring for foster kids (food, clothes, gas, and so on). Even though the state gives foster parents a stipend, it would not have offset the costs. We just couldn't swing it financially, and our dream looked dead.

Thankfully, we decided not to give up that easily, and we've set a goal to get out of debt in five years and have home alterations done by then. At that point, we can fulfill our calling to be foster parents. We fooled ourselves for years, but no longer—we know the next five years we'll need to live like paupers and watch every penny. But it will be well worth it.

Beth's letter gets to the heart of the flying-blind fiasco. When couples are reckless with money and let their finances become jumbled, they jeopardize their dreams and goals. They also take on unnecessary stress and tension. If you and your partner are flying blind, we encourage you to open your eyes, face reality, and let the truth begin to set you free.

PART TWO

YOUR MONEY MAKEUP

Why You and Your Partner Approach Finances the Way You Do

CHAPTER SIX

IT'S ALL RELATIVE

C all it an early inheritance. This one doesn't come in the form of a check or a house or heirlooms. No precious metals, no antiques, no works of art. Nevertheless, your parents bequeathed you something extremely significant, something you have carried with you since you left home: a deeply ingrained and highly influential attitude toward money.

The way your parents managed or mismanaged finances during your childhood dramatically shaped the way you think about money as an adult. Perhaps you were fortunate enough to have a parent, grandparent, or other role model sit you down and teach you the basics of personal finance. Perhaps someone even talked to you about a "philosophy of finances"—the meaning of money, with all its moral and ethical implications.

But based on our research and interviews, we know that most people did not have those instructional conversations. That means the majority of us learned about money—its use and abuse—through observation, emulation, and osmosis.

The relationships that have probably influenced you most are those within your family of origin. For most people, this means a mom and dad (maybe just one of them) and siblings, who lived under the same roof or at least spent regular time together. For others, extended family members— grandparents, aunts, uncles, cousins—were also big influences. Some had parents who divorced, and they were raised by stepparents and shared a house with stepsiblings. So when we talk about family, we mean the circle of people closest to you while growing up.

Family financial background and childhood perceptions about money are topics that couples don't usually discuss before marriage (and often not *after* marriage either). That's because most adults have

¢
MAKING
CENTS

How was money handled in your family? In a third of families (31 percent), nobody talked about money, while in 45 percent they constantly worried about the way they spent it.[1]

never stopped to ask themselves, *What mind-set and feelings about money did my family convey? What perceptions and misconceptions did I pick up from Mom and Dad?* We also don't think much about our family attitude toward money because it's a rather abstract concept. Our memories tend to focus on much more concrete childhood experiences, such as the time Dad yelled at you for spilling cherry Kool-Aid on the new sofa or when your mean neighbor stuck gum in your hair.

Make no mistake, however. All of those intangible and vague attitudes toward money are powerful forces in our lives. That's why we believe couples can benefit from thinking about the past so that they can understand and take responsibility for the present.

Where Did *That* Belief Come From?

As we counsel couples, we find that conflicts often stem from money attitudes that were formed in childhood and carried into marriage. Dissimilar experiences, modeling, and training cause each spouse to have different expectations and motivations about handling finances.

Remember our discussion in chapter 4 about how differing assumptions cause marital conflicts? Where did those expectations come from? Largely from your childhood—watching Mom and Dad, aunts and uncles, grandparents, and others either enjoy their money or worry about it, share it or hoard it, invest it or squander it.

Recently we worked with a couple named Gary and Brittany who vividly illustrated this. As we explored their financial situation, it became obvious that they disagreed on the use of debt. Thumbing through their file of documents, Scott paused to ask how much credit-card debt they were carrying. When Gary nonchalantly responded that it was "around eight grand," Brittany became visibly agitated.

"I keep telling Gary I don't like that," she said. She clenched her fists into two tight balls. For a moment, it looked like she was going to slug him. "It's such a waste—all that interest. And what if we're late on payments? Think of the fees and the hit to our credit rating."

As we sat there and listened, Brittany ranted about how despicable debt was and how she used credit cards only in emergencies. She found it irksome that Gary used them so often, and she found it even more irksome that he was so cavalier about it.

Gary sat there with a smirk on his face as if he'd heard all this before. Finally, he said matter-of-factly that he didn't see any problem with credit cards and that he wished his wife wouldn't get so uptight about it. He also commented that debt was simply a tool to parlay his money—an investment vehicle. His father had gone into debt many times to purchase rental properties, and he amassed a small fortune by borrowing money. Gary concluded by saying, "Debt is only a problem when you can't pay it off."

We were starting to get the picture, so we asked Brittany about *her* parents' point of view. She said her mom and dad had a strict pay-as-you-go policy—cash and carry only. "If we couldn't pay up front, we didn't buy it," she explained. "You should have seen some of the junker cars we drove while saving up for a new one."

Talking about their parents provided much insight. Although debt appeared to be the reason for their conflict, in reality their different backgrounds were the contributing factors. Was one of them right and the other wrong? Not really. Gary and Brittany were merely applying to the present what they had learned in the past.

The way your parents managed or mismanaged finances during your childhood dramatically shaped the way you think about money as an adult.

Let us also tell you about a couple named Amanda and John, whom we know from our church. They asked us to get together one evening for coffee because they wanted our opinion about a decision they were debating.

"As you know, we've been house hunting, and we've found two we like," Amanda said as we all sat in a local coffee joint. "Well, that's not quite accurate. John likes one, and I like the other. And that's why we asked to see you—we want your advice."

We exchanged furtive glances that said, *Careful! We might get dragged into a family feud.* Scott defused the potentially awkward situation by saying, "Obviously, we wouldn't want to choose sides—for your sake and ours. But we'll be happy to help you think through the options."

They agreed and filled in some background for us. John—a computer programmer who was starting to earn good money—wanted to buy a five-bedroom, four-bath house with a three-car garage. The house came with a state-of-the-art theater system, oak cabinets, huge Jacuzzi tub, and many other amenities. When they mentioned where the house was located, we immediately recognized it as one of the most expensive parts of town.

"It is such an awesome house," John gushed. "You would love it. We enjoy entertaining people, and this place would be perfect for parties. Since we're planning on starting a family next year, I'm thinking it would be a great home for kids to grow up in."

Amanda sat slumped in her chair with her arms crossed. Her body language said it all. When she finally spoke, she used words such as *ostentatious* and *pretentious* to describe John's dream house. She took a sip of coffee and added, "I don't want people to think we're showing off or flaunting our money. Why do we need such a lavish house? I don't get it."

We asked about the house Amanda preferred. "It's in a nice quiet neighborhood near downtown," she replied. "Three bedrooms, two bathrooms, with about two thousand square feet, and not far from a park. It's more than adequate for what we need."

"And more than a little bland and humdrum," John put in. "Everything about it says, 'Standard, middle-class tract house.' Bor-*ing!*"

The face-off was clear. John wanted big, posh, and upscale. Amanda wanted comfortable, modest, and quaint.

We could have talked to them about the growth potential in the real estate market, the mortgage payments of each option, what interest rates were likely to do in the future, and other financial considerations. But they already knew the facts and figures. Something deeper and more powerful was at work.

"Here's something to think about," Bethany said. "What does a house represent to each of you? What does it signify and symbolize? After all, to nearly everyone in our culture, a house is much more than a place to hang pictures and store clothes."

Amanda and John thought for a while, and then he answered

first. It turned out that his dad had grown up in a dirt-poor family, and his entire childhood was spent in run-down, ramshackle houses "on the wrong side of the tracks." As an adult, he became driven to accumulate wealth, and he vowed that his children would never live in a shabby home and suffer the ridicule of peers like he had.

As a result, John grew up with a clear message: a large, elegant home in a fashionable area is a sign of personal and familial stability, security, strength. To him, it was not a sign of conceit or arrogance to own an opulent home; it was a sign of competence and confidence.

As for Amanda, she had grown up in a missionary family that served in India until she was fourteen. When the family moved back to the States for her high school years, they had little money and were barely able to scrape enough together for a down payment on a home.

"It was a cracker-box house in a low-income area," she recalled. "But my folks were proud of that house, because it was the first they ever owned. They used to make derogatory remarks about the 'rich people in their fancy houses'— how they were uppity and snobby. I can still hear my mom saying, 'If

FIGURING OUT YOUR FAMILY FINANCIAL HISTORY

To explore how your background shaped your money personality, think through the following questions:

• Did your parents argue about money—either loudly or the silent, fuming kind of fight? If so, what did they most often quarrel about (paying bills, debt, how to spend money, hours spent at work)?

• Who primarily oversaw the money and bills: mom, dad, both, neither? Looking back, how does this arrangement strike you? Was it fair or unfair? Did it work?

• How did your parents interact with you "monetarily"? Did you receive an allowance? What was expected from you in order to receive it? Did you ever feel manipulated by money given or taken away? Were your parents stingy or generous with you?

• How much or how little did your parents spend on birthdays, holidays, and vacations? In retrospect, does this seem tilted in one direction or the other? Why do you think they spent as much or as little as they did on these occasions?

• Were there recurring themes about money in your family? Did your dad badger your mother for spending too much on clothes? Did your mom pressure your dad to make more money? Did your parents frequently talk about getting a bigger, nicer house? Did they exude joy when they helped others? It is often these themes that tell us most about a family's financial attitudes.

they visited India for a week, they'd come back and put their houses up for sale. They'd feel so guilty and wasteful.'"

It didn't take a psychologist or marriage therapist to see what was going on here. John and Amanda each brought to their prospective home purchase messages laden with subtext and undertones. The type of house they lived in meant something different to each of them.

> Dissimilar experiences, modeling, and training cause each spouse to have different expectations and motivations about handling finances.

They didn't come to any conclusion that evening, but when we followed up a few weeks later, Amanda said, "It really helped to understand where we were each coming from. And we've agreed not to buy any house until we both feel comfortable with it. We'll wait until one of us changes our opinion or until we find a house we can compromise on." That's the kind of decision that will strengthen their marriage over the long haul.

The Messages Parents Send about Money

The classic film *Cat on a Hot Tin Roof*, with Paul Newman and Elizabeth Taylor, is based on Tennessee Williams' play about a wealthy patriarch named Big Daddy. While his children and in-laws squabble about the family inheritance, Big Daddy and his second son, Brick, try to come to terms with his failed fathering and his misplaced priorities.

In the basement of their family home, Big Daddy and Brick talk honestly among the clutter of discarded paintings, sculptures, and boxes of family heirlooms. Big Daddy looks around the room and says, "You know what I'm going to do before I die? I'm going to open up all these boxes." He tells Brick his wife bought most of the stuff during a European trip they took years earlier. He boasts that is he's worth $10 million in cash and blue-chip stocks. He also owns twenty-eight thousand acres of prime land.

"Well, that is pretty rich to me," Brick replies in a cynical tone.

Brick wonders why Big Daddy allowed Big Momma to buy all that stuff. Picking up an old suitcase, Big Daddy answers, "The human animal is a beast that eventually has to die. If he's got money, he buys and he buys and he buys. The reason why he buys everything he can is because of the crazy hope that one of the things he buys will be life everlasting."

Big Daddy then asks his son why he never came to him when he wanted something, why he didn't lean on the people who loved him. In an irritated tone, the father says, "What was there that you wanted that I didn't buy for you?"

Brick, raising his voice in anger, retorts, "You can't buy love! You bought yourself a million dollars' worth of junk! Look at it! Does it love you?"

Big Daddy, equally angry, shoots back, "Who do you think I bought it for? Me? It's yours! The place, the money—every rotten thing is yours!"

"I don't want things!" Brick answers. He shoves a sculpture and large vase to the floor. With a steel rod, Brick continues smashing things, including a life-size photograph of himself in a football uniform. He laments, "Worthless. Worthless. Worthless."

Finally, he stops demolishing things and breaks down crying.

Big Daddy pleads with Brick to stop weeping. A moment later, Brick regains his composure and says, "Can't you understand? I never wanted your place, your money, or to own anything. All I wanted was a father, not a boss. I wanted you to love me."[2]

That scene dramatically portrays how messages about money and work are passed down from parents to their kids. Sometimes, as with Brick, the child feels neglected and abandoned as his dad and mom obsessively chase wealth, perhaps telling themselves that they're "doing it all for the kids." Other times, kids listen to their parents brag about their big income— or complain about their small income. And some kids hear their folks grumble about having to work every day, while others hear their mom and dad praise the Lord for a job. As psychologist Olivia Mellan insightfully commented,

> When people love money so much that they cross over into greed and avarice, they will succumb to temptation.

LASTING ¢

LEGACY

When I (Bethany)
was growing up,
my mother *always*
bought generic
brands. She was
extravagant in
some ways—
expensive trips, for
instance—but any-
thing she pur-
chased had to be
generic. This made
such an impression
on me that I prom-
ised myself I
would never buy
generic products
when I got older. I
would be a brand-
name buyer!

Imagine my dis-
may when, a
month after I was
married, my new
husband came
home with a bag
full of generic
items. He quickly
learned that what
he'd done was
unacceptable. He
was surprised by
my reaction—and
I was surprised at
how strongly I felt
about his pur-
chases. Obviously,
it pushed an old
button.

We grow up in families where nobody talks about money. Most people will immediately protest: "Not true. My family talked about money all the time." When I ask, "How did you talk?" they reply, "My father worried about not having enough, and he yelled at my mother for spending too much."

The fact remains that people do not grow up with educational or philosophic conversations about what money is and isn't, what it can and can't do. We don't examine societal messages telling us that gratification lies in spending or that keeping up with the Joneses is important. Information-based money discussions are so taboo that we usually reach adulthood without a realistic sense of our family's finances.[3]

The point is that money messages are often unspoken but persuasive nonetheless. Perhaps you've never thought about the money messages your parents handed down to you. And it's likely your parents didn't even realize they were instilling beliefs in you, but they were. Let's look at several common messages parents transmit to their kids.

"Money brings power and prestige." For many people, it isn't the accumulation of money itself that motivates them—it's the societal and relational spoils that come with it. For better or worse, affluent people are treated differently than those of modest means.

"Money belongs to God, and we are only managers of it." Spiritually oriented people often believe that God owns everything and entrusts us with much or little. Our job, therefore, is to use wisely and generously whatever we have.

"Money equals achievement and accomplishment." Some people derive a sense of worth and

value because of the income they generate. Their identity is wrapped up in what they do and how much they make.

"Money is the root of all evil." Some people, usually those from strict religious traditions, believe that money is bad and will corrupt the unsuspecting. We like to point out that the Bible verse that gave rise to this notion is frequently misquoted and misconstrued. The apostle Paul said, "The *love* of money is a root of all kinds of evil" (1 Tim. 6:10). When people love money so much that they cross over into greed and avarice, they will succumb to temptation.

"Money can be used to manipulate and control." This is the carrot-and-stick method. Dangling a reward in front of someone, or threatening to withhold a reward, is often effective at getting people to comply with your wishes.

"Money should be used to enrich our lives." We know people who love nothing more than to spend their dollars on travel, dining out, classes, tours, and other experiences. They argue that there's little point in making money if you don't take advantage of the opportunities it affords.

"Money is something to fret about." Some men and women just need something to worry about, and money is a convenient target because it's such a necessary part of our everyday lives. It's interesting to note that there are money worrywarts among the desperately poor, the outrageously rich, and everyone in between.

"Money should be hoarded as a safeguard against calamity." You've heard about Depression-era people who lost all their savings and scrounged to put bread on the table—literally. Those agonizing experiences would surely reform a person's outlook on money. Even today, people who suffer dramatic loss—or have the fear drilled into them from parents—try to ward off hardship by stockpiling money.

Our list of common money messages is by no means exhaustive; you could add dozens more. It is simply intended to activate your memory and stimulate your thinking. We urge you to take some time to consider what money messages emanated from your family.

Realize that most families are not unilateral in their approach to money. That is, there are at least a couple—and often several—attitudes toward money competing for attention at the same time. This is especially true if you had two parents with differing attitudes.

To Repeat or Rebel, That Is the Question

Think back to our discussions with Gary and Brittany, and John and Amanda. They were all living out attitudes that had been modeled for them. They were following in their parents' footsteps. As *Wall Street Journal* columnist Jeff Opdyke said,

> Psychologists I've talked to say that our core beliefs about money are formed within the first twelve years of our lives. That means all the things we learn from Mom and Dad—and all the things that our kids, in turn, learn from us—serve as the financial foundation we rely on as adults. That's just peachy. Here we are, vowing never to be like our parents, and it turns out that we can't help but mimic them in many ways financially, often without even realizing it.
>
> For some of us, that's probably not so bad; for others of us, impersonating Mom and Dad just can't be good, because those beliefs ingrained in us dictate how we spend and save and, ultimately, the role money plays in our relationships with other people.[4]

We would add an addendum to that comment: all of us tend to either duplicate our parents' beliefs or distance ourselves from them, replicate them or reject them. We agree with the author and financial expert Emily Card, who said, "In some way, all financial behavior stems from what we experienced as children. It's either a reflection of what we learned or a rebellion against it."

This was apparent in the questionnaire we sent out. We asked people to comment on the way money was handled in their family growing up. The following responses are representative of many we received:

Debbie, Costa Mesa, California: "My parents were just like my husband and I are—always spending a little more than they had. I am one of seven kids, and things were constantly tight growing up, but I always got huge Christmas gifts. In the early years, I never questioned it—I was too young to think about how my parents could afford expensive gifts. But later I wondered how they did it. I have since found out that they went into debt every Christmas. Guess what? My husband and I do the same thing. My parents are now in their seventies and just got out of debt. Please, God, don't let it take us that long!"

Howie, Saint George, Utah: "My dad was such a tightwad when I was growing up that I vowed never to be like that. He wouldn't spend a dime on family outings or vacations. We hardly ever went anywhere. So here I am at age thirty-two, and my five-year-old son asks me the other day, 'Can you and me go to the skating rink this weekend?' The first words out of my mouth were, 'Sorry, we can't afford it.' Then I thought, *Where did that come from? Of course we can afford it!* I was being haunted by the ghost of my miserly past. I said, 'Son, I just came to my senses and realized we *can* afford it. Let's you and me go skating together. I can't wait!' I resolve to be openhanded rather than tightfisted."

Sarah, Bethesda, Maryland: "My father and stepmom were terrible with their money. Dad was a well-paid recording engineer who saw a lot of money go in and out of his hands (mostly out). My stepmom loved to buy junk and more clothes than she could possibly wear. You know that bumper sticker that says, 'I'm spending my children's inheritance'? Well, that was my parents. I don't want to think about the thousands of dollars they frittered away. Perhaps it's not surprising that my husband and I operate from a very strict budget."

What about you and your partner? Are you playing out the same patterns—be they healthy or unhealthy—from your family? Or are you creating new ones? Couples who are aware of their embedded money messages can understand their preferences and predilections. They are able to head off conflicts. Those spouses who have never examined their family financial history will continue to clash, perhaps without even knowing why. We encourage you to take a close look at your upbringing so you can move into the future with a positive, productive attitude.

CHAPTER SEVEN

SWAYED BY SOCIETY

I t was an eye-opening experience in more ways than one. There we were on June 29, 2001, at Penrose Community Hospital in Colorado Springs, following the birth of our first child, Cole. We were elated to be heading home after a grueling five days in the ICU. Born six weeks premature, Cole had to be held for observation because of low blood sugar. Now our bags were packed, gifts stowed, and baby boy bundled. We were ready to go home to begin our lives as a three-member family.

As we approached the maternity ward's hydraulic doors, one of the nurses said to us, "Oh, yeah, I almost forgot to give you this," and she handed us a diaper bag bulging with freebies and goodies. We said our last good-byes and thank-yous and drove away with our sleeping baby.

It was several hours later that I (Scott) brought the hospital-provided diaper bag into the house, along with armloads of other stuff. I thought, *That was sure nice of the hospital to give us this.* But as I looked through the items in the bag—samples of formula, diapers, bottles, CDs, coupons, and pamphlets—it dawned on me: these things weren't given as a helpful way to get us started with our new baby. All of these companies want us to buy their products. If we get started with a particular kind of diaper, we'll spend hundreds, maybe thousands, of dollars on that brand over the years. Same with formula and bottles and baby food. (This "aha moment" seems like a no-brainer now, but I was still on a new-baby adrenaline rush at the time!)

That was only the beginning. During the next few weeks, we received dozens and dozens of marketing mailers, promotional pieces, advertisements, and free samples. More than the usual amount of credit-card applications appeared, with not-so-subtle messages that babies are expensive and we'd better have a ready reserve of extra cash. Telemarketers called to congratulate us and invite us to take advantage of special offers for this product or that program. Glossy brochures for minivans, SUVs, and Volvo wagons magically materialized, promising "safety and comfort for your growing family."

It became obvious that there was massive machinery in place to market, promote, and pitch products, and by signing the Social Security form for a new baby, we flipped an invisible switch that set all those gears in motion. Unaware and unsolicited, we seemed to have been put on every baby-related mailing list in the country. What's worse, some of the marketing pitches were directed not at the proud parents, but at the child himself. Advertising pieces came addressed to Cole Palmer, and he was automatically signed up for an airline frequent flyer program and registered for restaurant birthday clubs.

¢In some cases, cultural influence is even *more* persuasive than family influence in determining how you spend, save, and utilize money.

After a couple of weeks of opening and discarding direct-mail pieces, Bethany commented in exasperation, "In this society, it sure doesn't take long for people to get indoctrinated into consumerism. Get 'em hooked early, and they'll become lifelong shoppers and buyers."

Without realizing it at the time, Bethany declared what is probably the mantra of corporations, chain stores, marketers, and advertisers everywhere: get 'em hooked early and they'll spend forever. If you have a child, you can probably relate to our feeling of inundation when our firstborn arrived. Even if you don't have children, you've surely had similar experiences somewhere along the line. You've been aware that you were being pitched, poked, and prodded by the purveyors of goods and services. It's unavoidable, as we're all exposed each day to hundreds of advertisements and messages that are incredibly clever, persuasive, and compelling. Not to mention *effective*.

The Power of Culture

In the previous chapter, we talked about the powerful influence your family of origin had in shaping your money personality. If family is the most significant influence, then the culture you live in surely runs a close second. In some cases, cultural influence is even *more* persuasive in determining how you spend, save, and utilize money. Author and social activist Lynne Twist expressed it well.

> We are born into a culture defined by money, and our initial relationship with money is the product of that culture, whether it is one based primarily in poverty [or] affluence and wealth. From our earliest experiences, we learn money's place and power in our families, our communities, and in our own lives. We see who earns it and who doesn't. We see what our parents are willing to do, and what they aren't willing to do, to acquire money or the things money buys. We see how money shapes personal perspective and public opinion.[1]

The issue is not *if* our attitude toward money is shaped by our culture, but *how* and *how much*. Many of the ideas and impressions transmitted by the society around us soak into our hearts and minds. They become a part of who we are. This doesn't mean that we automatically accept every message that passes in front our eyes or floats into our ears. Nor do we bite on every advertisement hook, line, and sinker. But there's no denying that we are greatly influenced by the world we live in. And the beliefs we adopt from our culture affect our individual lives, marriages, families, and friendships.

Let us be honest with each other. In most ways, we are all extremely fortunate to live at this time and in this place. Very few people would choose to live someplace other than America or in a generation other than this one. We have endless opportunities to better ourselves. The freedoms we enjoy make us the envy of the world. The transportation and technology at our fingertips can take us anywhere we want to go. Still, most of us would acknowledge that the society we live in suffers serious ills as well. Psychologists wonder how a country so prosperous could be riddled with so many emotional woes. Countless research studies have sought to answer the question, "In a society with such a high standard of living, why aren't people happier with their lives?"

We take the good with the bad. Try as we might to resist the distasteful aspects of the society surrounding us, it is nearly impossible to do so. As sociologist Ruth Benedict said, "Most people are plastic to the molding force of the society into which they are born. The great mass of individuals quite readily take on the form that is presented to them."[2]

CONSUMER ¢
COUNTRY

Harvard economist Juliet
Schor sheds light on our
shopaholic society. "The
United States is the most
consumer-oriented society
in the world. People work
longer hours than in any
other industrialized country. Savings rates are
lower. Consumer credit has
exploded, and roughly a
million and a half house-
holds declare bankruptcy
every year. There are more
than 46,000 shopping
centers in the country, a
nearly two-thirds increase
since 1986. Despite fewer
people per household, the
size of houses continues to
expand rapidly, with new
construction featuring walk-
in closets and three- and
four-car garages to store
record quantities of stuff.
According to my estimates,
the average adult acquires
forty-eight new pieces of
apparel a year."3

A culture imposes its values, standards,
and expectations on people in many ways.
The primary way our society shapes attitudes about money is through entertainment outlets and mass media. Daily we are
bombarded with messages from radio, television, movies, newspapers, magazines,
billboards, and the Internet. But some
forms of persuasion are more subtle. Our
attitudes are also swayed as we observe the
kind of cars neighbors drive, the clothes
coworkers wear, and the home furnishings
friends have. Cultural influence, then, happens not only on a widespread, national
level, but also at a community and neighborhood level. We may be aware of the
emotional tug of a Super Bowl ad, but we
may not be aware of the messages that
shape us just as powerfully as we drive
around town or chat with neighbors.

The key point is that the messages we
absorb do, in fact, shape our attitudes toward
many things—money perhaps most of all.
Cultural cues can change what we want,
what we think we need, and what we assume
should happen in our relationships. Many
messages we absorb from the media and our
communities are not selling anything at all,
but they are nevertheless conveying important ideals and expectations about the way
we ought to handle money.

Most folks can't be bothered with all of this. They think societal soul-
searching is pointless and pessimistic. Harvard economist Juliet Schor,
one of the nation's most astute researchers on socioeconomic issues,
said, "Many adults respond to the critique of media and consumerism by
shrugging it off, on the grounds that this culture is inescapable. Some are
fatalistic; others contend that the critics exaggerate or are missing the
true causes [of] distress. Many reason that they themselves grew up on

television with no untoward effects. But this stance is increasingly untenable. Day by day, marketers are growing bolder. Year by year, the scientific evidence about harmful effects is mounting."[4]

Both directly and indirectly, you have accumulated impressions from many different sources and translated them into assumptions—assumptions you bring to your marriage. Understanding your assumptions and how they were formed is critical as you and your partner seek unity on personal finances. Acknowledging and discussing your expectations can bring closeness to your relationship and help both of you become more discerning money managers.

Can This Be Good?

As we discovered when our first son was born, the call to consume begins early. This is particularly insidious, since children lack the cognitive development to filter out manipulative messages. Real life and the false life presented by the media blend together in such a way that young kids don't know the difference. Consider these findings.

> The issue is not *if* our attitude toward money is shaped by our culture, but *how* and *how much.*

- The average child views as many as forty thousand television commercials every year.[5]
- Children as young as age three recognize brand logos, with brand loyalty influence starting at age two.[6]
- Young children are not able to distinguish between commercials and television programs. They do not recognize that advertisements are trying to sell them something.[7]

Why are advertisers so aggressively appealing to children these days? Because they have money to spend or they influence what their parents buy. With children either spending or influencing 55 billion dollars' worth of purchases, marketing techniques have become more sophisticated and assertive.[8] In the past, the most effective way to sell children's products was appealing to moms and dads. Now the opposite is true. Children are the target for intense advertising pressure. Advertisers know that children influence the purchase of not just kids' products anymore, but everything in the household from cereal to cars.

Thus these "adult" products are being paired with kid-friendly logos, images, and movie character tie-ins.

Again, we appreciate the perspective of author Lynne Twist:

> In our distinctly aggressive American consumer culture, even our youngest children are drawn into that fierce relationship with money. Much as we did, only more so today, they grow up in a media milieu and popular culture that encourages an insatiable appetite for spending and acquiring, without regard to personal or environmental consequences. Distortions in our relationship with money emerge from a lifetime of these seemingly innocuous everyday experiences in the money culture. Personal money issues ... are clearly rooted in the soil of our relationship with money and the money culture into which we are born and which we come to accept as natural.[9]

What's come to be accepted as normal is the desire for more stuff, a bigger house, a sportier car, a more exotic vacation. A couple of years ago, the British Broadcasting Corporation aired a documentary called "Shopology," in which psychologists looked into the psychology of shopping and consumerism in places like Britain, the United States, and Japan. They conducted interviews and studied realms of research. The key findings are as follows:

> Even though we know money does not bring happiness, we are often persuaded to at least give it a shot.

- Consumption now helps to define and answer who we are as individuals.
- Social definition revolves around consumption.
- People don't so much buy products as they do a "lifestyle."
- Brands help turn perceptions into reality, thus encouraging purchases based on fashion and peer/social pressures to fit in.
- Consumerism can increase stress for various reasons. Rising consumer debt puts pressure on families.[10]

The world in which we live determines, at least in part, the way we think, behave, and respond. All of the ideas that swirl around us each day affect not only our checkbook and bank account, but also our relationships.

Decoding Cultural Messages

Our point in all of this is not to preach a finger-waving sermon about the evils of our greedy and materialistic society. We assume that most people reading this book acknowledge that twenty-first-century America is badly out of whack in regards to consumerism and the pursuit of wealth. Our encouragement to you is to be discerning and discriminating about the messages they continually press on you. Stop and consider the ways in which our culture shapes your money personality. Here are just a few of the prevailing beliefs our society propagates.

Money Really Does Bring Happiness

Rationally and intellectually, most people would insist that money can't buy love and can't buy happiness. Unfortunately, our consumer culture does not always promote rational thinking. So many folks buy in order to get a little jolt of good feeling. Even though we know money does not bring happiness, we are often persuaded to at least give it a shot.

We appreciate the perspective of respected educator and pastor Haddon Robinson, who said,

> If there is one message that comes to us in ten thousand seductive voices, it's the message of our country and our century that life really does consist of things. You can see it on a hundred billboards as you drive down the highway. It is the message from the sponsor on television. It is sung to you in jingles on the radio. It is blared at you in four-color ads in the newspapers.
>
> We're like the donkey that has the carrot extended before it on a stick. The donkey sees the carrot and wants it, so the donkey moves toward it, but the carrot moves, too. The carrot is always there, promising to fill the appetite. But what it promises, it does not deliver.[11]

MAKING CENTS

Percentage of American teenage girls who say shopping is their favorite activity: 93.

People in the world who live on less than $2 a day: 3 billion.[12]

If we are looking for happiness in the things we buy and the money we make, we'll continue to be disappointed. Earning money and buying things are not wrong—so long as you know *why* you're doing it and understand the limitations finances offer in terms of personal fulfillment and contentment.

¢It's interesting—and disconcerting—to think that at this very moment, hundreds of smart and savvy people are meeting in boardrooms and conference rooms to brainstorm more efficient ways to separate us from our money.

You Can Have It All Now

Sociologists and historians often assign labels to generations in attempt to summarize an era's prevailing characteristics. The World War II era has been called the "Greatest Generation," owing to its courage and selflessness during perilous wartime. Far less flattering, the '70s era has been dubbed the "Me Generation," signifying the widespread self-centeredness that epitomized that period.

What about our current era? It very well might be dubbed the "Buy-Now-Pay-Later Generation." At every turn, we are encouraged to satisfy our appetites now and count the costs later. Want a new outfit? Charge it on your credit card. Want a new car? Dealer financing is available.

To be sure, the society in which we live makes enticements and inducements of every kind extremely difficult to fend off. Why? Because we have access to virtually anything we want at any moment.

In captivating and compelling ways, the media, advertisers, and others shout, "Don't deprive yourself! Get what you want. You deserve it. In fact, if you have to work hard and endure adversity, something must be wrong. Everything should come easily and effortlessly."

Enough Is Never Enough

It's interesting—and disconcerting—to think that at this very moment, hundreds of smart and savvy people are meeting in boardrooms and conference rooms to brainstorm more efficient ways to separate us from our money. Teams of researchers are poring over data to determine our spending habits. Retail psychologists are advising corporations on which ad campaigns will move us enough to reach into our wallets and pull out a credit card.

All of this is done to advance one idea: you need more. Whatever you have, it isn't enough. You lack something.

In their book *Your Money or Your Life*, Joe Dominguez and Vicki Robin wrote,

> If you live for having it all, what you have is never enough. In an environment of *more is better*, "enough" is like the horizon, always receding. You lose the ability to identify that point of sufficiency at which you can choose to stop.... Even if I do get the "more" I was convinced would make my life "better," however, I am still operating out of the belief that more is better—so the more I now have *still* isn't enough. We get deeper in debt and often deeper in despair. The "more" that was supposed to make life better can *never* be enough.[13]

We see it over and over again in our financial counseling service. Couples get themselves into big trouble—and bring big trouble into their relationship—by running on this treadmill of more, more, more. We believe that the happiest couples are those who can say, "We have enough. We are content with what we have." This doesn't mean they stop looking ahead and seeking ways to better themselves. But they've learned that if they can't be happy *right now*, they probably never will be—no matter how much stuff and how much money they acquire.

Bigger Is Better

It doesn't matter how big your house is, you need a bigger one. The same goes for your car, your boat, and your home theater system. The message we hear constantly is that you have just *got to* supersize, upgrade, and expand. So what if your three-bedroom house is adequate for your family—a five-bedroom place would be so much better!

¢ WE'VE GOT A LOT OF STUFF

In an *Atlanta Journal Constitution* article, columnist Jim Auchmutey quoted comedian George Carlin as saying, "The essence of life is trying to find a place to put all your stuff."

Auchmutey wrote that there are 32,000 self-storage businesses nationwide (or the equivalent of 1.3 billion feet of rentable space), 620 in Atlanta alone (twice as many as a decade ago), and 100 million storage containers are sold by Rubbermaid every year.

This "stuff" explosion peculiar to Americans has led to a new profession: the professional organizer. Some POs charge as much as $75 an hour to help people get organized in this culture of clutter.[14]

The companion message to "bigger is better" is "more is merrier." If you move to a bigger house, you've got to fill it with more stuff. Recently, I (Bethany) went to a baby shower and sat next to an executive who, I assume, earns a healthy income. I had met her before, so this lady had no hesitation about leaning toward me and saying, "Bethany, I heard a sermon in church that was *so* convicting. It was titled 'How much stuff do you need?' I was excited to hear it, since my husband and I downsized our house from six thousand square feet to thirty-five hundred after our kids left. We had cleaned out all of our closets and gotten rid of tons of things. So I was feeling pretty smug about our 'stuff' situation. So smug, in fact, that I decided go browse at Williams-Sonoma in the mall. A half hour later, I walked out with several bulging bags full of stuff. More stuff! I guess I needed to hear that sermon after all."

We imagine most people can relate to this woman's struggle. The temptation is ever present to acquire more and more things.

You Don't Have to Kowtow to Culture

In the classic 1946 film *It's a Wonderful Life*, Jimmy Stewart plays George Bailey, a generous and compassionate proprietor of a local building and loan institution. George offers loans to individuals denied by the bank, which is headed by the greedy Mr. Potter. George helps countless young families move out of Potter-owned rentals and buy their own homes. Threatened by George and his loan company, Mr. Potter invites George to join his operation.

In a pivotal scene, George sits in Mr. Potter's ornately carved chair, a symbol of Potter's success. A blazing fire roars in the fireplace, and the old miser sits in a wheelchair positioned in front of a massive desk. After offering George an expensive cigar, Potter paints a picture of the struggles this twenty-eight-year-old man, George Bailey, must have: a young wife, family needs, a precarious business, and a meager salary of $40 a week.

"What's your point, Mr. Potter?" George asks.

"My point is I want to hire you," Potter blurts out. "I want you to manage my affairs and run my properties. George, I'll start you at twenty thousand a year." (A handsome salary at that time.)

Shocked, George drops his lit cigar in his lap, and his eyes widen. "Twenty thousand a year?" he asks in disbelief.

"You wouldn't mind living in the nicest house in town, buying your wife a lot of fine clothes, a couple of business trips to New York a year—maybe once in a while Europe. You wouldn't mind that, would you, George?"

Looking over his shoulder, George asks, "You're not talking to someone else, are you? This is me, George Bailey."

"I know who you are. George Bailey, whose ship has just come in, providing he has the brains to climb aboard."

George is enticed by the promise of financial security, though it would mean relinquishing his family business and overseeing a ruthless and unethical operation. Potter agrees to let George sleep on the decision and holds out his hand. As George grips the hand, he pulls back, coming to his senses.

"I don't need twenty-four hours," he says. "I know right now the answer is no. You sit around here, and you spin your little web, and you think the world revolves around you and your money. Well, it doesn't, Mr. Potter. In the whole vast configuration of things, I'd say you were nothing but a scurvy little spider."

We love that movie, and that scene in particular, because it depicts someone who stays true to his values despite enormous cultural pressure. The allure of money, power, and prestige was powerful, but George held fast to his convictions. Thankfully, there are some real-life people like George Bailey, people who remain true to their values and beliefs, people who refuse to succumb to pressure exerted by the society around them.

In this chapter, we've made the point that we each are influenced to some degree by the culture we live in. But that doesn't mean we have to blindly accept the messages foisted upon us. We can choose to walk a different path and follow a different calling. We can decide to say, "Enough is enough. We'll live according to our convictions and not by the messages we're force-fed by the media." Let's determine to be discerning and discriminating about the consumer culture we live in.

CHAPTER EIGHT

IT'S THE WAY YOU'RE WIRED

W e'll call them Skip and Nadine. When they came to our office for financial counseling, it didn't take long to see why they were squabbling about money and work decisions.

Skip bounded into the office, full of energy and enthusiasm. He shook our hands as if he were trying to pump water into a bucket. Boisterous and bouncy, he could hardly sit still. He peppered us with questions, chitchatted with our office staff, and generally made himself right at home. When we asked where Nadine was, he shrugged and said she was parking the car.

"She'll be along," he said and then zipped onto another topic. "Say, have you guys ever been to Cancun? I was there last month with my buddy. We were scuba diving—"

Just as Skip was plunging into his scuba story, Nadine slunk into the room, with shoulders slumped and wearing a gray sweater. She silently took a seat—the farthest one from us—and nodded in greeting.

If Skip was a frisky puppy bursting with energy, Nadine was a Siamese cat, stealthy and suspicious.

Have you ever interacted with a couple and thought, *How in the world did these two get together?* Well, this was one of those couples.

We soon learned the reason for their visit to us. Though Skip was one of the top salespeople at the Toyota dealership where he worked, he was restless and eager to start his own business. He wanted to become a Realtor, which would require classes, exams, and lots of time to build a clientele. Nadine, who worked as a medical transcriptionist in their basement office, wasn't hip to the idea.

So they came to us for a close look at their financial picture and a reality check about the feasibility of Skip's plan. We got the feeling right off that they didn't so much want our counsel and guidance as corroboration for their different agendas. Skip wanted us to say, "Sure, you can pull this off. Go for it! You'll be an awesome Realtor—a millionaire by forty!" Nadine wanted us to say, "Gee, the figures just aren't adding up. Seems *very* risky. Why jeopardize the great gig you have right now—good commissions, year-end bonus—for a leap into the unknown? Not a good idea."

As we talked with them for the next hour, their markedly different personality types kept revealing themselves.

"You're so into security and stability," Skip said to Nadine. "I see a doorway, and I'm ready to step through. C'mon! Let's take the step together."

> ¢ Financial issues seem to magnify the temperament differences—and especially if partners don't understand their own personality type and that of their spouse.

Nadine sat with a blank expression on her face. Finally, she said, "So what if I want security? What's the matter with that? And what's with your constant need for change? I don't understand why you can't just relax and stay put for a while."

Those three words—"I don't understand"—summed up our meeting together. Skip and Nadine didn't understand each other, and they didn't seem to recognize how their different personality types brought them into conflict over issues both big and small. From a financial standpoint, they were fine. Skip could have launched out on his own, since he'd saved enough to provide an eight-month cushion. But that wasn't the real issue. The issue was two spouses with very different temperaments struggling to come to agreement on a major decision.

A Tempest over Temperaments

Although Skip and Nadine were an extreme case, we've seen over and over how dissimilar temperament types create problems. Many times, a lack of understanding about personality types generates conflict in marriage. It's as if the spouses never stop to acknowledge that they are simply wired differently.

We suppose that nearly every married person on earth has thought at some point, *Why can't my spouse be more like me? When will my spouse see that my point of view is right?* No wonder marriage is so complex and confusing. Not only do a husband and wife bring under the same roof significant *gender* differences, but usually personality differences as well.

Judith Viorst, in her book *Grown-up Marriage*, wrote about the collision of different personalities.

> Those of us who expected that we would always be a team confronting the world together soon learn the many ways we can be divided. One of these ways is by temperament, as some of us have discovered to our sorrow by picking a marriage partner with a temperament quite different from our own. Although well aware of this difference, we may choose to ignore its potential for divisiveness, hoping that our mate's temperament will complement ours and offer our life some balance, and cheerfully noting that opposites attract.

Viorst went on to mention several scenarios where differing personality types become obvious.

> He takes forever and ever to make a decision. She comes to a decision right away. He's a saver. She's a tosser. He holds everything in. She lets everything out. He is self-effacing. She is bold. He's generous, open-handed, a big-time spender. She's afraid that if they don't watch every single penny, they'll end up in the poorhouse when they're old. Maybe the notion that opposites attract is more viable in theory than in practice.[1]

Does any of this ring true for you? Even if you and your partner are not polar opposites, chances are that at least a few personality differences within your relationship cause friction. What's more, financial issues seem to magnify the temperament differences—and especially if partners don't understand their own personality type and that of their spouse. A key to successfully managing marriage and money, then, is to understand that your spouse has a certain temperament that offers both strengths and weaknesses.

Temperament Types 101

Research about personality types expanded greatly over the past few decades, but the topic is hardly new. Historians tell us that the basic temperament types were identified as far back as 450 BC, when a physician named Hippocrates observed four dispositions he called melancholic, sanguine, phlegmatic, and choleric.

Those designations have largely stood intact for all these centuries, with several attempts at improvement and clarification along the way. In the 1500s, Paracelsus gave the four temperament types new names: changeable, industrious, inspired, and curious. A few centuries later, in the 1940s, German psychiatrist Erich Fromm came up with four new labels: exploitative, hoarding, receptive, and marketing.

Still the adaptations continue. A few years ago, popular relationship experts Gary Smalley and John Trent assigned animal names to the personality types: otters, lions, golden retrievers, and beavers.[2] As if all this help isn't enough, many sophisticated and involved personality tests have been developed, including the Minnesota Multiphasic Personality Inventory (MMPI) and the Myers-Briggs Type Indicator, which identifies four subgroups under each primary temperament type, for a total of sixteen possibilities.[3]

> A key to successfully managing marriage and money, then, is to understand that your spouse has a certain temperament that offers both strengths and weaknesses.

For the sake of our discussion—and with our preference for keeping things simple and straightforward—we'll stick with the tried-and-true personality types developed by good old Hippocrates. What follows is a brief sketch of each temperament type followed by how these people typically handle money. (Our thanks to financial writer Matt Bell, who, in his column "The Steward's Wallet," addressed many of these issues.)[4]

Melancholic

Key characteristics: Perfectionistic, analytical, conscientious, artistic, aesthetic, indecisive, introspective, creative, loyal, precise, and anxious.

Money methodology: These people love to balance the checkbook down to the penny. Usually introverted, they are self-disciplined and detail oriented. Owing to their analytical nature, melancholies carefully think though purchases, researching all the options. But when they finally make a choice, it's usually a good one. These folks typically have the best financial instincts—and they are the type most likely to develop and follow a budget.

On the downside, melancholies are sometimes apprehensive and tentative, so they may be overly conservative in their investments. Artistic and drawn to beautiful things, these people might overspend on aesthetic items: gourmet food, fine clothing, entertainment, books, music, and artwork.

Sanguine

Key characteristics: Outgoing, conversational, persuasive, impulsive, relational, unorganized, fun-loving, restless, colorful, and enthusiastic.

Money methodology: These are the people who are fun to be with, even if they can be a bit flaky and undependable. They don't mind spending money to have a good time and enrich relationships. They are often generous, happy to give their money to help people in need. These are the kind of people you want at a dinner party—they're funny, energetic, and they'll spring for a pricey bottle of wine.

On the downside, they can be impulsive, spending without regard to the consequences. They enjoy approval and attention, so they might be the ones driving the new sports car and wearing trendy clothes. These folks like to be cutting-edge trendsetters, and they'll spend money to achieve that position. Also, they are usually free spirited and spontaneous, so following a budget is a problem. Not ones to be bothered by details, their paperwork is usually in disarray.

Phlegmatic

Key characteristics: Easygoing, harmonious, dependable, efficient, unmotivated, orderly, cautious, reserved, diplomatic.

Money methodology: These people are steady, reliable, pleasant,

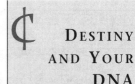

DESTINY AND YOUR DNA

We agree with financial consultant Ray Linder—it's impossible to separate who we are from what we do. "Temperament determines our development as individuals, for as we grow, who we are becomes more of what we are. Our behaviors cluster into patterns and actions that attempt to satisfy our inner core needs according to personally held values. Temperament influences everything we do, from what we aspire to, to what we strive zealously to accomplish. And it clearly influences how we manage money."[5]

The way you're wired—your basic temperament type—has a direct effect on your spending and saving habits.

and not easily ruffled. They keep their jobs for a long time, because they are responsible and rarely do anything rash. They are also careful with their money—often the best savers are found among this group. These men and women are usually thrifty, frugal, and penny-wise.

On the downside, they aren't the kind to take charge and be aggressive, so they tend to be passive when it comes to work and finances. Their desire for peace and distaste for confrontation may mean they get talked into investments or purchases. Owing to their laidback personality, they may not be motivated to follow a budget and may not actively pursue opportunities. They prefer just to go with the flow.

Choleric

Key characteristics: Single-minded, hard-charging, resolute, eager, fastidious, goal-oriented, insensitive, opinionated, pragmatic, decisive, and argumentative.

Money methodology: These are often the take-charge leaders, who like to get things done. Frequently control freaks, they can be demanding, challenging, and tough—but no one can deny that they are the movers and shakers. They might bulldoze over people, but, boy, can they go places and do things.

On the downside, these folks are so eager to move ahead that they may not explore options as carefully as they should. They tend to make decisions quickly, which can lead them into ill-advised investments. Sure of themselves, they usually don't feel the need to seek out counsel from others. Although they see the wisdom of a budget, they may be too restless to sit down and discuss it.

Applying Those Personality Types to Real Life

Now that you know the general profiles of the four personality types, let's get specific. You probably saw yourself in one of those temperament types, but how do they play out in real life? As we've studied temperaments and thought about the many clients we've worked with over the years, we've discovered that these general types fall into one of six specific types. These relate back to the primary conflict areas we discussed in part 1. See if you can identify yourself and your partner on the personality chart located on page 112.

You might be thinking, *Yes, I saw myself—in couple of those categories.* That makes sense. We have found that most people have a *primary* and a *secondary* money personality. Although one is the dominant trait, the subordinate trait vies for attention on occasion. Here's a peek into our money personalities.

Bethany: I am primarily a "Sue the Spender" and secondarily a "Rhonda the Risk-Taker." What can I say—I love to shop and spend money. Also, if I see an opportunity in business or investing, my first inclination is to go for it. The reason it was important to identify my money personality is because I don't want to be a "Debbie the Debtor" and pile up debt or get into a lousy business venture.

Scott: I am primarily a "Steve the Security-Seeker" and secondarily a "Stu the Spender." (No wonder I am so complicated). I feel secure when I know the bills are paid and the kids' college and our retirement accounts are fully funded. But don't let that fool you! When those obligations are met, bring on the big-ticket items—such as a giant, state-of-the-art home-entertainment system (see our story in chapter 1 for a prime example). I'm compelled to save, but I can spend with the best of them, too!

Now let's talk about you. Let's explore further where you might land on our six-person grid. Keep in mind that you may not fit neatly and cleanly in one category. Like us, you probably

> Most people have ¢ a *primary* and a *secondary* money personality.

have a primary type and a secondary type. And just to complicate matters, these two types are often contradictory.

Sally or Sam the Saver

Financial professionals love to work with the Sallys and Sams of the world (we know!). They have a budget and stick to it. They always know their checking account balance and where additional money can be saved. They often don't care if their investments are aggressive or conservative as long as they are increasing. Sally and Sam are the type who will retire early and have plenty of money in the kids' college accounts.

Sally and Sam, however, may not stop to "smell the roses." They'll forgo a weekend getaway or a night on the town and sock the money away instead. These people will often get labeled as cheap and are known as "coupon cutters." Often Sally and Sam will spend hours trying to find the best deal and do thorough research before buying a product. Sometimes the time spent on research and looking for the deal could be better used in other areas of their lives.

We have a Sally in our lives who would never dream of buying a name-brand item. She will spend hours at the grocery store comparing prices and feels great in the end because she knows "cheapest is best."

Stu or Sue the Spender

Stu and Sue probably know how much is in the checking account—because they want to know how much they can spend. They don't necessarily worry about a sale as much as the product they're buying. They find great pleasure in spending time at the outlet malls, appliance stores, and home-remodeling shops. Browsing on eBay and other Internet shopping sites is the perfect way to pass an afternoon. Stu and Sue always have the cool new gadget, and they're on the lookout for the *new* new gadget.

Although Stu and Sue aren't necessarily spiraling into debt, they probably aren't saving or planning ahead either. After the bills are paid, they see what is left over and start dreaming of a shopping spree. Stu and Sue often look at the tax return at the end of the year and say, "Where did all my money go?"

We are well acquainted with a Stu who loves new gadgets and toys. Frankly, we enjoy going to his house to see his latest, greatest purchase. His sheer delight in his recent acquisition is contagious, and we have to fight the urge to go and buy one for ourselves.

Debbie or Dan the Debtor

While most people immediately toss the dozens of credit-card applications that arrive in the mail each month, Debbie and Dan see them as an opportunity. They can transfer balances for lower rates, increase credit limits, and have a picture of their dog on the front of the new one. Debbie and Dan are not necessarily people who like to spend a great deal of money, but they would much rather have a credit card than a wad of cash.

As we said in an earlier chapter, not all debt and credit cards are bad. We use our credit cards to obtain frequent flyer miles—but we're careful to pay them off at the end of the month. But the Debbies and Dans of the world don't pay theirs off, and after ten years of utilizing credit cards, they find themselves in quite a predicament.

We know a Debbie who is experiencing great anxiety because of this situation. After agreeing to a debt-payoff plan, she now has a strategy and a schedule to get this monkey off her back. We do not have visions of grandeur about her debt situation, but at least she is making a concerted effort.

Rob or Rhonda the Risk-Taker

Rob licks his lips as he reads the information his broker gave him about an initial public offering (IPO). If this investment goes the way he hopes, he could parlay $10,000 into $100,000 in a matter of months. This would help pay for kids' college and get that new kitchen for his wife. After reviewing the prospectus, he's convinced it is a surefire winner.

Rob, and his counterpart Rhonda, live by the adage "Nothing ventured, nothing gained." Numerous stories and great examples in history prove this adage true. Many entrepreneurs have stood at the brink of bankruptcy before their company, investments, or inventions brought them riches and glory. People such as Thomas Edison, Henry Ford, and Bill Gates spring to mind.

Of course, for every Edison, Ford, and Gates there are thousands of people whose ships *didn't* come in. But Rob and Rhonda never consider that possibility. Such pessimistic thinking would sink the ship!

We know a Rob who left the comfort and security of his corporate job. He was a rising star at one of the largest accounting firms in the country, but he had always dreamed of launching out on his own. So he took the leap. He started his own accounting practice, which grew and grew over the years. Eventually, this Rob sold his practice for a high price, allowing him to put his three kids through college and retire early. Now he volunteers at church, skis three days a week, and spends lots of time with his grandkids. There's a guy whose risk paid off in a big way.

Steve or Stephanie the Security-Seeker

Stephanie's stomach tightens as she hears on the radio that the stock market has closed down for the day—*way* down. She breathes a sigh of relief, knowing that she invested conservatively. She feels a little smug and congratulates herself for playing it safe. However, she is concerned that her husband, Phil, is talking about how aggressive his 401(k) plan is. Later that day, she will go online to compare the balances of their respective investments.

Stephanie (or Steve, as the case may be) believes that once you make the money, risking it would be foolish. She often looks for ways to minimize risk and even pays things off early so that interest rates will not get the better of her.

We work with a Stephanie, and after a few aggressive investments that didn't go her way, she retreated to completely conservative investments. If the principal is not guaranteed, she won't touch it with a ten-foot pole. Understanding her money personality, we find the highest fixed rates and leave it at that. She would get too stressed otherwise.

Fred or Fran the Flyer

Fred comes in the door after a long day at work. As he takes off his coat and pushes the play button on his message machine, he hears the words that send his blood pressure soaring: "You are now sixty days late on your car payment. If we do not receive payment on your outstanding balance within seven days, you will be turned over to a collection agency." Fred sighs and says to himself, *Where is that payment booklet? It's gotta be around here somewhere.*

It's not that Fred (or Fran) does not have the money; it's just that he is unorganized, short on time, distracted, overcommitted, and tired of paperwork. After all, he has just accepted a new position at work, making him project manager over two divisions. Hey, who's got time for all the details in life ... like car payments?

The Fred in our life is struggling with this very situation. The problem is not money, but time and organization. The free time he *does* have, he'd rather use to play racquetball or golf. After hearing his concerns and issues, we gave him a helpful suggestion: hire someone to help you get the mess in order. Fred did his research and hired a company to pay his bills and track his spending.

* * *

The way you're wired—your basic temperament type—has a direct effect on your spending and saving habits. And that temperament has helped to shape you into a Stu or Sue, Rob or Rhonda, or anyone else among the cast of characters described above. Simply understanding your temperament and your partner's can relieve much tension and eliminate conflict. You may still disagree on some issues, but you will at least know why you each respond the way you do. And that is a big step toward achieving unity and harmony.

Name	Sally or Sam the Saver	Stu or Sue the Spender	Debbie or Dan the Debtor	Rob or Rhonda the Risk-Taker	Steve or Stephanie the Security-Seeker	Fred or Fran the Flyer
Description	save, save, save; never buys anything unless the money is in the bank; often saves for a purchase	shop till you drop; pay the bills, spend the rest; acquires lots of "stuff" to the detriment of savings account	debt — no sweat; comfortable using credit cards; sees debt as leverage, a vehicle to be used	you only live once; new business ventures, no problem; sees the opportunity and not potential dangers	analyze and research, then buy; will research investments and large purchases before diving in; wants to know the pros and cons of most decisions and purchases	I'll figure it out later; because of time constraints and general pressure of life, puts off paying bills and making decisions; often pays bills as they come in or late
Feeling Pattern	feels good when they get a good deal; feels bad when pressured into a purchase	feels good when purchases are made; feels bad when there is no money in savings	feels good when the debt is low; feels bad when the debt is getting out of control	feels good when money is directed toward a possible high return; feels bad when they lose on the deal	feels good when financial obligations are met; feels bad when worrying about money because of risk level	feels good when get "on top" of bills; feels bad when doing nothing and control is lost
Action Pattern	solicits advice; often takes time when purchasing large item	quick decision maker; makes a purchase without seeking advice	doesn't base purchase decision on available dollars	often swayed by others' advice; makes decisions and moves to next subject	slow decision maker; likes to "sleep on it"; bases decision on facts; often pessimistic	often doesn't take action; when they do take action it is usually based on catch-up
Strengths	prudent planner with long-range thinking	enjoys life; doesn't over-analyze	not afraid to leverage	finds good opportunities	tends to analyze and do research	doesn't take on stress with finances
Weaknesses	miserly	often gets in debt; doesn't have savings account	often feels guilt	often becomes disheartened after failed ventures	tends to get caught up in the details	overdue bills and late charge

CHAPTER NINE

THE POWER OF PARADIGM

Money is always on its way somewhere," said author Rosalie Maggio. "What we do with it while it's in our keeping says much about us—as will the direction it takes after we speed it on its way."[1]

The way we use the money that passes through our hands does, indeed, reveal much about us—particularly our beliefs, values, and convictions. We have seen this principle played out with every one of the clients we've worked with. Wait a second—did we say *every* one?

Yes. Each person's attitudes about finances flow directly from the deepest places within the heart and soul. The decisions we make about money—how much to save, how to spend, where to invest—are guided by the set of standards and ideals that make up the core of who we are.

For the last several chapters, we've been talking about the key factors that shape your money personality. This is another extremely significant factor. Your spiritual beliefs, values, worldview, and eternal perspective greatly influence the way you think about and use money. We wholeheartedly agree with the financial writer Michael Phillips, who said, "Money is a mirror. An examination of your money and the way you use money is a way of understanding yourself in the same way that a mirror provides a way of seeing yourself."[2]

Since money serves as a mirror that reflects our deep-down beliefs, we would all do well to take a long, hard look into it. This is another step in understanding ourselves and our partners, so we can achieve a higher level of compatibility and cooperation within our relationships.

What's Your Point of View?

What we've come to realize is that everyone operates from a particular paradigm. Are you familiar with that word? If you go online and "Ask Jeeves" what *paradigm* means, you will learn that it is a "set of assumptions and perspectives; a framework, held in common, used to interpret reality; a set of rules and regulations that establish boundaries, and that tell us what to do to be successful within those boundaries."

We all have a certain grid or context from which we view life, and this reference point influences virtually every decision we make. Stephen Covey, in his best-selling book *The Seven Habits of Highly Effective People,* said that paradigms are like road maps that lead us in a particular direction.

> Each of us has many, many maps in our head [and] we inter-
> pret everything we experience through these mental maps. We sel-
> dom question their accuracy; we're usually even unaware that we
> have them. We simply assume that the way we see things is the
> way they really are or the way they should be. And our attitudes
> and behaviors grow out of these assumptions. The way we see
> things is the source of the way we think and the way we act....
> Paradigms are powerful because they create the lens through
> which we see the world.[3]

How much consideration have you given to the "road map" you follow in life? Have you thought about the "lens" through which you view
your place in the world? Are you clear about the big questions of life: What
is your purpose here? Why were you created? What are your beliefs about eternity and God's plan for humankind? How you answer these questions directly relates to your decisions about work, time management, sharing your resources, use of money, and a whole host of other issues.

The way we use the money that passes through our hands does, indeed, reveal much about us—particularly our beliefs, values, and convictions.

We've noticed that some peo-
ple haven't given much thought to the connection between finances and spiritual beliefs. These people consider the two issues separate and shrug off the notion that they might overlap. Other men and women recognize *some* points of intersection between money and faith. Perhaps they feel compelled to put money in the offering plate at church or give to charities

at Christmastime. Still others view those two issues as tightly woven together. Their views on money management, giving, and stewardship emerge from their deeply held values, and they can't see how it could be any other way.

Let us tell you about two conversations we had during the past month that illustrate this point. When Jeremy came to us for financial advice, we asked lots of questions to ascertain how he'd like to invest, what goals he was pursuing, and so on. We gently broached the subject of giving money to charities or a church. Was that important to him?

"Money is a mirror."

"Well, I'll be honest with you," he said. "I've never been what you'd call religious. That's just not the way I was raised. I'm open-minded to the possibility of a supreme being, the afterlife, and all of that. But I just don't know. It's not something I give much thought to." He chuckled and added, "Besides, I've got enough on my mind with my job, the MBA I'm finishing, and my house renovation. Who's got time to ponder the mysteries of the universe?"

After a few more questions from us, Jeremy made clear that religious or spiritual beliefs of any kind had no bearing on his financial matters. And no, he did not want to give any of his money away unless there was an overriding tax benefit.

Our point in mentioning Jeremy is not to criticize him, but to highlight the fact that his perspective or paradigm certainly *did* influence his actions and attitudes toward money. Because he viewed life in terms of here and now—with no regard for God and eternity—he chose to use his money accordingly. He may have insisted that an absence of spiritual beliefs meant all his decisions were based solely on reason and rationality. We would disagree.

Then there are Jamaal and Olivia, who were both in their mid-forties and starting to think about their retirement years. They came to us for help with financial planning as well, but their perspective was far different from Jeremy's.

"Our top two priorities," Olivia announced almost immediately, "are to give our kids a good upbringing and a solid education, and to help support the church we attend here in town. We also have three missionaries we've committed to support, and we don't want to let them down."

SOMEDAY, IT'S ALL GOING BACK IN THE BOX

We like the perspective offered by John Ortberg, teaching pastor at Menlo Park Presbyterian Church in Menlo Park, California. He once told a story about playing Monopoly as a child with his grandmother. He suffered defeat after defeat, until one summer, when he made up his mind to learn the game well enough to beat her. Sure enough, the day came that he won, and he was so thrilled that he considered having the board bronzed as a testimony to his newfound skill in capitalism. But then his grandmother reminded him, "It all goes back in the box."

Ortberg says that was a great lesson and metaphor for life. All our money, houses, and things are ours to use for a while, and then they go away. He concluded with this thought: "None of it was ever really yours. It was here long before you were, and it will be here long after you're gone."[4] The apostle Paul put it succinctly: "For we brought nothing into the world, and we can take nothing out of it" (1 Tim. 6:7).

"Knowing your priorities certainty helps us in coming up with plan for you," Scott said. "Anything else we should know?"

"Yes," Jamaal said. "We'd like to see if we could retire in our early sixties. It's been a dream of ours to serve a couple of months together each year in rural Mississippi. We have family history there, and we feel a strong need to give back to the low-income people in that area. You might say it's a calling we have. That's something we want to do when we retire, and we're willing to make sacrifices now to make it happen."

We were more than happy to help Jamaal and Olivia devise a plan to reach their goals. We have to be honest, though. They had tough choices to make, since neither of them earns a high income. He is a human resources specialist with a small nonprofit organization, and she is an elementary schoolteacher. But because they were so clear about—and committed to—their priorities, they were willing do what it took to bring them to fruition.

As we concluded our meeting with them, Olivia said, "The spending plan you put us on is going to take some creative belt-tightening on our part. But we'll do it because we know it's what God would have us do."

Understand our reason for sharing these two stories. We aren't saying that people without spiritual beliefs are *always* tight-fisted and self-centered. Nor are we saying that people of faith are always generous and eager to share. Frankly, we've worked with some people who proclaim no belief in God whatsoever, and yet they give of their resources willingly and liberally. And, sadly, the opposite is sometimes true: people who profess to live according to Christian principles may be miserly and stingy.

Our point is simply this: whatever your core beliefs and values, those are sure to direct your decisions about money. Just as your family upbringing had significant influence on your financial personality, your spiritual beliefs shape who you are and how you use all of your resources—talents, time, and money.

Where We Stand

Since we deal with money and financial decisions on a daily basis, we have spent considerable time thinking through our own paradigm. We were both raised in Christian homes and heard teachings about money from the time we were little. Although we have numerous thoughts and convictions about finances, they can be distilled into three core principles.

God Owns It All

Whose money is it? This is the most fundamental question of all. Who owns our dollars, the house we live in, the car we drive, and the clothes we wear? Many people would answer, "I own those things! I worked hard to earn a paycheck. It's my name on the mortgage papers and the automobile title. Those things belong to me." That makes sense on a practical level, but how about on a spiritual level? We believe that, ultimately, God owns everything because he created everything.

We point to three key Bible passages that lay the foundation for our spiritual paradigm.

> You may say to yourself, "My power and the strength of my hands have produced this wealth for me." But remember the LORD your God, for it is he who gives you the ability to produce wealth. (Deut. 8:17–18)

> "Do not store up for yourselves treasures on earth, where moth and rust destroy, and where thieves break in and steal. But store up for yourselves treasures in heaven, where moth and rust do not destroy, and where thieves do not break in and steal. For where your treasure is, there your heart will be also." (Matt. 6:19–21)

> For by him all things were created: things in heaven and on
> earth, visible and invisible ... all things were created by him and
> for him. (Col. 1:16)

We believe that God entrusts money, possessions, and talents to us. It's our job to use those gifts to the best of our ability. We've worked with some people who believe that God is entitled to 10 percent of their income (which is often referred to as a "tithe") and that the other 90 percent belongs to them. We support the idea of tithing—giving away 10 percent to help others—but we take that concept a giant step further. God owns not only the 10 percent; he owns the entire 100 percent. Every dollar and every cent ultimately comes from the Creator. If you accept this concept, it becomes clear that every financial decision is a spiritual decision.

> We all have a certain grid or context from which we view life, and this reference point influences virtually every decision we make.

Spending money is not wrong, whether that means paying for kids' college, purchasing furniture, or taking a nice vacation. But it comes back to your basic attitude. Do we filter those spending decisions through our grid of spiritual awareness and divine direction?

We Have Responsibilities, Not Rights

Many people in our society are fierce defenders of personal rights and civil liberties. When it comes to freedom of speech, freedom of religion, and other freedoms our country affords us, we *should* stand up and defend those rights. But the whole issue of rights has been taken to an extreme over the past few decades, and now people claim the "right" to do just about anything. It's not unusual to hear someone proclaim, "It's my money, and I have the right to spend it any way I please!"

We have a different perspective in that we believe money carries with it *responsibilities*, not rights. This goes back to the previous point about the ultimate ownership of money and possessions. If all that we have is on loan from God, then we have the responsibility to use those resources according to his purposes. In fact, the Bible mentions money issues more than twenty-five hundred times—more than almost any other topic. Why? Because using our money wisely, morally, and gener-ously is a huge responsibility.

It's the Attitude, Not the Amount, That Matters

We are fortunate to work with many men and women in full-time ministry. We've noticed with some people of faith have the misconception that poverty equals spirituality. They seem to think if they make a lot of money that their values would misplaced, that they'd be greedy and self-centered. To us, the real issue is a person's attitude or heart toward money. We agree with a statement posted on the Web site of the Pallotti Center, a Catholic organization that offers insights about money and faith.

> How does the Bible judge money? For example, does the New Testament consider money good or bad? If one were to answer, bad, on what biblical text would that judgment be based? Scripture does not teach us that money is the root of all evil. Rather, "it is the love of money [not money itself] which is evil" (1 Timothy 6:10). It is when we allow financial security to lessen our perception of God as our true source of security that money becomes a block to our spirituality.[5]

Some people interpret the Bible as telling us that we need to sell all of our possessions and follow God. We believe that you can have a great relationship with God whether or not you sell all your possessions.

For many years, we attended Lake Avenue Church in Pasadena, California. The pastor, Dr. Gordon Kirk, continually challenged people to examine the attitudes behind their actions and the motivations underlying their methods. Regarding the use money, Dr. Kirk wrote,

Every dollar and every cent ultimately comes from the Creator. If you accept this concept, it becomes clear that every financial decision is a spiritual decision.

> In Matthew 19:21 and Luke 12:33, Christ requests His fol-lowers to "sell their possessions and give to the poor." The full account in Matthew reveals that Christ is specifically speaking to the rich young ruler and in Luke He is distinctly speaking to

His disciples and the applicable principle is that "it is hard for a rich man to enter the kingdom of heaven" (Matt. 19:23).... The matter of one's priority and ownership to either God or mammon is fundamental to financial stewardship. While it is not necessary or even suggested in the Scriptures to sell all of one's goods to obtain eternal life, Christ clearly reveals the detachment and unpossessive control one must have with regard to material temporal matters.[6]

Those words—*detachment* and *unpossessive control*—are at the root of this entire discussion. We can possess money, we can try to make more money, and we can enjoy our money. But when it becomes a priority in our lives and a primary pursuit, then money begins to harm us in a variety of ways. The detachment Dr. Kirk speaks about means maintaining a healthy, balanced regard for the place money has in our lives. Money does not give us worth; it does not determine our identity. Our value comes from being children of God, regardless of how much or how little we have in the bank.

DO YOU TALK ABOUT MONEY?

The adage warning people to avoid discussing religion and politics with friends and family has fallen on deaf ears in modern-day America. A new survey from the Barna Research Group has discovered that in a typical week more than 100 million adults discuss political issues with others while about 90 million adults delve into religious or spiritual matters.[7]

Couples Conflict When Spiritual Beliefs Differ

As with every other money issue raised in this book, this one presents problems for couples when their opinions and beliefs differ. These differences may be slight or they may be significant, but they're sure to create some conflicts along the way. Here are a few examples from the couples we queried.

Sasha and Tom, Gresham, Oregon: "I (Sasha) was raised in a strict Baptist home, and our family tithed 10 percent to church no matter what. Tom, on the other hand, grew up in a family where giving to the church and charities wasn't even discussed. It just never came up. Now I want to give 10 percent of our money to the church we've started going to, and Tom is reluctant. It's not that he's against the idea completely—he just thinks we should give whatever and whenever we feel led to do so. This issue has become a bone of contention for us, since we share our finances and obviously see things differently."

Russell and Kris, Sarasota, Florida: "I (Russell) grew up in a family that participated in food and clothing drives for local charities—not just at holiday time, but throughout the year. It was big part of our lives. My parents would spend time and money organizing donation drives and fund-raising events, and this was a financial priority for our family. Kris wasn't raised in a family that did volunteer work of any kind. She thinks too much money and time is going into these charity endeavors. I say she's holding me back from a true calling and passion; she says I should be spending more *time* with her and more *money* on our house. This isn't something we should argue about, but we do!"

Naomi and Len, Austin, Texas: "I (Naomi) feel strongly about environmental issues since I believe God created this beautiful world and we should preserve it. Len respects my opinions but doesn't participate in any of my efforts. For instance, I think a bare minimum is to recycle newspapers, plastic bottles, and tin cans. Len gets tired of all the 'junk' piling up in the garage. (We have to haul it to the recycling center since our city doesn't have home pickup service.) He doesn't like the mess and wants to throw it out with the weekly garbage. Since we have similar beliefs on most issues, I never thought we'd have a conflict over how to protect God's creation."

> Money does not give us worth; it does not determine our identity.

Dave and Amber, Tulsa, Oklahoma: "Our struggle pertains to what constitutes 'giving.' I (Dave) am a family law attorney, and I do a fair amount of *pro bono* work for low-income families. I keep a log of hours and assign a dollar amount to what I would normally bill for the time. I then deduct that amount from what Amber and I have agreed to give to our church and other ministries. To me, that's fair and honorable. But Amber says I'm cutting corners. She thinks I'm looking for a convenient rationale to give less of our money. I tell her that's ridiculous, and she tells me, 'Then why don't you give more money to church?' She says I'm being cheap, and I say she's being irrational. Every time we sit down with our budget and come to that column labeled 'giving,' we get into it all over again."

We've heard hundreds of stories like these. Sensitive issues arise when two partners hold different beliefs about the interplay between money, values, and faith. These couples will mend rifts and assuage tension by making an extra effort to communicate, negotiate, and compromise. (We'll discuss those subjects in part 3.) Rarely is it a matter of one partner being absolutely right and the other being absolutely wrong. The challenge, therefore, is to express beliefs clearly and thoroughly with each other, and to find a middle ground both partners feel good about.

Guided by Values

At age eighty-four, Tom White has almost achieved his life's goal—to give away his entire fortune. White is a Boston businessman who has given away $75 million. When people ask him why he's done it, he responds by saying, "Give me three reasons I shouldn't." He proceeds to give three reasons he should: "I can't take it with me, my kids are okay, and my wife's taken care of." Then he gets to the heart of the matter: "I'm motivated a lot by what Jesus wants me to do, and I think he wants me to help make the world a better place."

White has been on the boards of Harvard Divinity School, Boston College, the JFK Library, and the New England Patriots. But his proudest relationship is with the poorest country in the Western Hemisphere, Haiti. He's involved in health and justice projects there.

When his alma mater, Harvard University, calls to request a donation, White says, "You've got fifteen billion dollars over there, and I've got people over here starving to death. You tell me what I should do." He adds with a chuckle, "I still give a thousand dollars a year [to Harvard] so my classmates will talk to me."

Tom White's one regret? "I'm sorry I don't have more money to give away."[8]

We share that story because it encapsulates so much of what we've expressed in this chapter. Money can be used as a great blessing and benefit for ourselves, our families, and others. Or it can be a huge stumbling block, the source of hardship and heartache. It all boils down to a simple principle: it's what is in your heart, not in your bank account, that matters most.

THE PAST INFORMS THE PRESENT

A few years ago, prolific author Stephen King delivered a speech at the Vassar College commencement. He titled his talk "Scaring You to Action," and he told how two years earlier he had been lying in a ditch beside a country road. He'd been seriously injured after being hit by a van as he was out walking.

"I had a MasterCard in my wallet, but when you're lying in the ditch with broken glass in your hair, no one accepts MasterCard," he told the audience.

On that day and in the following months, King got a painful but important lesson in many of life's simple truths. "We came in naked and broke. We may be dressed when we go out, but we're just as broke." He cautioned his listeners against chasing after wealth, fancy cars, and other false symbols of success. "None of that is real. All that lasts is what you pass on. The rest is smoke and mirrors."

Of all the power most Americans have, King said, "... the greatest is undoubtedly the power of compassion, the ability to give. We have enormous resources in this country, but they are only yours on loan, only yours to give for a short while.... I want you to consider making your lives one long gift to others, and why not? All you have is on loan anyway."

King invited the audience to imagine a typical American backyard, with Mom, Dad, and the kids enjoying a delicious barbecue next to their swimming pool. "And standing around that fence, looking in, are emaciated men and women, starving children. They are silent. They only watch."

Stephen King, master of horror stories, was left changed by his near-death experience. A man of great fame and wealth, his priorities were radically readjusted when he realized it could all vanish in an instant.[1]

In the past four chapters, we've discussed the influences that shape our money personality—our outlook and attitude toward finances. Now we come to the fifth factor: past experiences that have served to modify our views about money. Thankfully, most of us have not endured a tragedy like the one that nearly killed Stephen King. But every one of us has had experiences, momentous or minor, that altered his or her perspective of money.

Sometimes these were difficult events—divorce, bankruptcy, illness, job loss, theft, natural disaster, extended periods of unemployment, or a bad decision that cost a bundle. Other times, these incidents were positive. Perhaps you landed a plum job, started a business that took off, received a hefty inheritance, invented a gizmo that sold like hotcakes, or invested in property that quadrupled in value. Those delightful happenings shift our attitude toward money just as disastrous ones do.

> Arduous experiences can be instructive if we look squarely at the situation and take responsibility for our own contribution to the problem.

We want to challenge you to identify the experiences you've had that have contributed to your current money personality. You will gain insight as you discuss with your partner the turning-point events each of you has had. This is another step toward better understanding yourself and your spouse, and in the process, you will achieve greater compatibility and cooperation in your relationship.

Sometimes We Learn from Mistakes

The writer James Russell Lowell said, "One thorn of experience is worth a whole wilderness of warning." It's true that painful events usually transform our actions and attitudes. In chapter 2, we told you about how we plummeted into a pit of debt and our subsequent effort to crawl out. That was hard for us, mostly because we should have known better. We're financial professionals, after all, and we tell people to avoid debt!

But that experience was valuable, too, and we're glad it came early in our marriage so we could benefit from it. After we sent off the last credit-card payment, we vowed to each other that we would never, ever go into debt again (unless we had no other choice because of a health crisis or other emergency). Since that time, we have lived debt free. Frankly, we probably would not have been motivated to stay out of debt had it not been for those tough years of belt-tightening and self-recrimination.

No one enjoys going through hardship or suffering the consequences of bad decisions. We can, however, choose to learn from mistakes and be wiser the next time. We were fascinated to find a research study in which people were asked what taught them the most about personal money management. Their responses follow:

- mistakes: 64 percent
- school: 31 percent
- unsure: 5 percent[2]

The key, of course, is the ability to glean wisdom and discernment from our setbacks and slipups. Arduous experiences can be instructive if we look squarely at the situation and take responsibility for our own contribution to the problem.

As we were thinking through this issue, we asked several friends and clients if they would tell about past setbacks and what they learned as a result. We received some insightful responses.

Seth, age 37: "For six years, I was self-employed as a graphic designer in Seattle. I landed a few big clients, and I eventually hired a couple of friends. We were pulling in good money, producing excellent work, and having a ton of fun. Too much fun, I see now. What I mean is that I didn't really treat it as a business. The office structure became very loose, details fell through the cracks, and I didn't pay attention to the bottom line. We made a lot of money, but spent even more. After that sixth year, the business went bust and we closed up shop. If I ever start a business again, I will treat it as a *business*. I'll be much more careful and conscientious."

LETTING GO, MOVING ON

Part of the process of moving beyond past experiences is learning the fine art of forgiveness. You may need to forgive yourself for mistakes you've made, hurts brought on by someone else, or broken commitments on the part of your partner.

Mary Beth, age 31: "My biggest blunder is fairly typical, I imagine. When I got a promotion and raise at work, I figured I deserved a new car. I decided in advance how much I could spend, but when I went to the dealership ... well, my eyes got bigger than my budget. I drove away in a brand-new, top-of-the-line Jeep. I loved it. What I didn't love were the monthly payments, which were much more than I could realistically afford. But then I was stuck. I couldn't sell the Jeep because it had depreciated as soon as I drove off the lot. It took me five years to pay off that car (and I don't even want to think of the real cost after figuring in the interest!). Lesson learned: never let yourself be persuaded to spend more than you've determined beforehand. Stick to your guns!"

Brandon, age 30: "A few years ago, my grandfather gave each of his six grandkids an early inheritance of twelve thousand dollars. I was a newlywed at the time, and my wife and I thought we'd hit the jackpot. Because we didn't own much, we went on a shopping spree—furniture, kitchen appliances, stereo equipment. We could have—and should have—put that money toward our debts, since we owed on credit cards and each had substantial student loans. In fact, much of the stuff we bought is already gone, but our debts are still here!"

¢ Learn from past experiences, but don't become jaded by them, and don't let them keep you from taking positive steps forward.

Susan, age 41: "This is difficult to talk about because I have strong feelings of failure. My biggest mistake was not so much about money as it was about marriage (though I've since learned the two are interconnected). I agreed to marry Tom even though I knew deep down that we weren't right for each other. Sure enough, we got divorced two years ago. It's been a heart-wrenching experience from an emotional standpoint—and a real hardship from a financial standpoint."

Can you relate to any of these stories? If you can't see yourself in the particulars of what these people shared, you can almost certainly think of some mistake you've made or a misfortune that has befallen you. Dwelling on what might have been, obsessing about the woulda-coulda-shouldas, isn't going to help anything; but choosing to learn from your mistakes can give you insight that helps you to avoid mistakes in the future.

Sometimes We Learn from Success

Thankfully, not every experience that shapes our money personality is a bad one. It may be that a good decision confirmed that you were headed in the right direction. Perhaps an unexpected windfall encouraged you to become more generous and giving. Sometimes even the pinnacle of success brings new insights that set us on a new, healthier course.

That was the case with Peter Lynch, one the nation's top financial experts. During the thirteen years he was the manager of the Fidelity Magellan Fund, Magellan was the top-ranked general equity fund. *Time* magazine called Lynch the country's "number-one money manager." But Lynch's financial genius came with a price. He wrote the following in his autobiography:

> As much as I enjoyed managing a portfolio the size of the GNP of Ecuador, I missed being home to watch the children grow up. They change fast. They almost had to introduce themselves to me every weekend. I was spending more time with Fannie Mae, Freddie Mac, and Sallie Mae than I spent with them. When you start to confuse Freddie Mac, Sallie Mae, and Fannie Mae with members of your family, and you remember 2,000

THE ONLY CERTAINTY IS UNCERTAINTY

We agree with financial commentator Terry Savage, who said it's our ability to adapt to change and setbacks that makes the difference between success and failure.

"Sometimes we are confronted by issues and events we never see coming because we don't know they're even a possibility. Of course, we try to stay on guard against the unexpected. We seek advice from experts to try to make the future less uncertain. We buy insurance against financial disaster and property damage. We set aside savings or investments to tide us over through rough times.

"But what happens when, after all your planning, the tide changes? You think you're in control of life because you've made decisions based on the commonly accepted wisdom. The lessons that hurt the most, cost the most, and teach the most come from suddenly being awakened to the reality that your strongly held beliefs have been turned upside down.... Change is a certainty. Accepting change means setting aside beliefs, recent experiences, and even the common wisdom. How well you adapt to change determines success in life, as well as in personal finances."[3]

stock symbols but forget your children's birthdays, there's a good chance you've become too wrapped up in your work.

In 1989, I was celebrating my forty-sixth birthday with my wife, Carolyn, and my daughters, Mary, Annie, and Beth. In the middle of the party, I had a revelation. I remembered that my father had died when he was forty-six years old. You start to feel mortal when you realize you're going to exist for a little while, whereas you're going to be dead for a long time. You start wishing you'd seen more school plays and ski meets and afternoon soccer games. You remind yourself that nobody on his deathbed ever said, "I wish I'd spent more time at the office."[4]

For Lynch, reflecting on his success led him to see the trade-offs he'd made—and led him to live a more balanced life. Though highly successful, he had given up a lot. What experiences have you had that taught you positive lessons? Here are a few responses from the friends and clients we queried.

Matt and Cindy, ages 38 and 37: "We were always extremely cautious with our money. Any extra savings we parked in a CD. So it was only with great reluctance that we agreed to join friends in an investment of several rental properties. Though it was out of character for us, boy, are we glad we risked! It's been a terrific investment for everyone involved. We learned not to always play it safe and take some well-thought-out risks."

Neta, age 43: "The best thing that ever happened to me was going on a two-year missions trip to Guinea, Africa. It totally changed by perspective of money and work. Before, I was really tight was money and, frankly, very stingy. But my eyes were opened by spending those years in a dirt-poor village among people who had nothing and yet were joyful. I asked myself many times, *Why I am holding on so tightly to my money and things?* I came back from Africa a changed person, and now I love to share what I have with others."

Andrew, age 35: "I had always wanted to be my own boss. After years of working for someone else, I decided it was time to

> Exploring your history will help you understand why you handle finances the way you do.

venture out on my own. I had saved money for the previous five years and came up with a well-thought-out sales and marketing plan. After three or four years of struggle, that small business is now growing along with my income. It was a big risk—and sometimes I wondered if I'd done the right thing—but now I'm reaping the rewards and fulfilling a dream."

Learn from the Past—Don't Live in It

One last thought before we leave this topic. We've worked with plenty of people who remain stuck in the past because of hard experiences. Perhaps they had an investment turn sour, and they vowed to be cautious forevermore. Maybe they loaned money to a friend and got burned when the person failed to repay. Now they say, "That's the last time I try to help someone!" And we've all heard stories about grandparents who stuck money in a shoebox under the bed after they lost it all during the Great Depression. Their previous hardships prevented them from investing in vehicles that would have given them a much higher yield than a cardboard box. As we've said throughout this chapter, you surely want to learn from past experiences, but don't become jaded by them, and don't let them keep you from taking positive steps forward.

We've also met several individuals who project past experiences onto their current partner. One of our clients, whom we'll call Fred, was previously married to a woman who was reckless and rash with money. She spent and charged like mad and burdened her husband with massive debt.

Now, years later, Fred is remarried and is encountering conflicts with his wife, Katie. Why? He put her on a strict allowance and looks over her shoulder on every purchase. Katie feels imprisoned by his controlling, persnickety behavior. She has shown no signs of being irresponsible with money, but the shadow cast by Fred's first wife is falling on his current relationship. Unless Fred can leave the past behind and start living in the present, his marriage is going to be jeopardized.

Fred and others like him would do well to remember the words of Judith Rossner: "The past isn't useful until its place in the present is found." Learn as much from past experiences as you can—then leave them behind. All of those important events have shaped and molded your money personality into what it is today. Exploring your history will help you understand why you handle finances the way you do.

PART THREE

CHECKS AND BALANCES

Building Financial Compatibility and Cooperation

Chapter Eleven

Take Time to Talk

Money must be one of the most delicate and dicey issues any couple will face. You can understand why. *Any* kind of communication within a relationship can be tricky, with two people bringing different personalities, needs, feelings, and styles of relating. Add to that mix the hot-button issue of money—laden with messages about power, security, and family history—and you've got a real challenge on your hands.

Talking about money is simple and easy if you and your spouse are feeling loving toward each other, if you're well rested, if your bills are paid up, if your budget is under control, if your taxes were filed on time, and if you're anticipating a big fat Christmas bonus. In other words, communication happens smoothly when everything is going great. But life is rarely ideal. So communication isn't nearly as simple and easy when you're under stress, when someone forgets to pay the phone bill, when the car breaks down, or when the collection agency is hounding you. Since life in the twenty-first century is full of pressures and hassles, we spouses need to find ways to communicate even when the conditions are less than ideal. That includes when the conditions involve financials stresses and strains.

Every marriage counselor in America will tell you that good communication dramatically enhances relationships. Every financial counselor will tell you that good communication also enhances a couple's economic situation. Husbands and wives who talk through money issues are in a position to make great decisions, strategically work together, and utilize the strengths each has to offer. Financial writer Jeff Opdyke put it succinctly. "Talk is cheap. It's the silence that's expensive.... Communicating about your money will better your financial life and help you and your partner build not just a stronger bank balance, but a more robust relationship."[1]

The Power of a Powwow

John and Elaine Johnson entered our office holding hands, with organized files and a very positive vibe about them. Our meeting was light, positive, and creative. Their finances were in order, and their relationship was thriving.

Husbands and wives who talk through money issues are in a position to make great decisions, strategically work together, and utilize the strengths each has to offer.

Ten months earlier, if you would have told us the meeting was going to be so upbeat and optimistic, we would have laughed out loud. The Johnsons were a couple that took the term "flying blind" to a whole new level. Their finances were a complete mess. Even worse, they virtually never talked about money.

After they left our office after that initial meeting, Bethany said, "If they don't take our advice seriously and start to communicate clearly, I'm afraid we're going to hear that they've divorced."

So what helped transform this couple? The "Johnson powwow."

You're probably asking, "What's a 'Johnson powwow,' and how did it transform their relationship so quickly?" We want to explain a communication strategy that can dramatically improve your relationship—and give a huge boost to your finances.

What Is a Powwow and Why Is It Important?

We started using the powwow when we were engaged and planning for our wedding. Bethany just loved talking wedding, wedding, wedding. What flowers were we going to have? What music selections? What napkin fold were we going to use at the reception? She just couldn't get enough of it. Scott, on the other hand, *could* get enough of it—and did. Although excited about the wedding, he got tired of talking about it every minute.

Our solution: a once-a-week meeting set aside for wedding planning only. It was contained to a definite time allotment, and the total focus was on wedding plans. This worked great because Bethany knew she had a specific time and place to talk about plans and to make decisions. Scott knew he was there to focus on the big event, be open to ideas, and show his enthusiasm. At the same time, we both knew this was the *only* time during the week that wedding talk would take place. In doing so, we eliminated conflict caused by Bethany thinking Scott was disinterested and Scott thinking Bethany was obsessing about it. End result: a smooth and wonderful wedding and a great time for all.

After we were married and found ourselves in our awful debt situation (described in chapter 2), we knew the "Palmer powwow" must be resurrected again. We met every week to stay focused on our goal to become debt free and to keep each other accountable. The end result that time: no debt and much better communication about finances.

¢ MAKING CENTS

Do you know how much your spouse earns? Three out of ten husbands and wives are in the dark about the amount of income their partner makes.

Is it okay for married folks to keep separate accounts? Two-thirds of people surveyed think it's fine for a husband and wife to have separate accounts, but one in four thinks it indicates lack of trust.

How many spouses keep a "secret stash"? More than 60 percent of people hoard a private pile of cash. Almost three-quarters of women admitted to having hidden money from their spouse, compared to 53 percent of men.[2]

We encourage you to use this technique in your relationship. We've seen it work many, many times with fantastic results. Let us explain how to take your relationship to the next level and apply the powwow principles.

Getting Your Powwow Powered Up

We have our powwow on or around the fifteenth of every month. Don't get us wrong—*weekly* meetings were required for quite a while. But after years of marriage and a concerted effort to get our finances in order, a monthly meeting suffices at this point. For thirty minutes, we talk about "money stuff." That's it. No discussion about kids or vacations or leaky faucets. We review our budget, talk through decisions, and identify anything new that has popped on our money radar screen.

You might choose to call your powwow something else—a money meeting, a budget-brainstorm session, or whatever—but the idea is to have a consistent, regularly scheduled get-together to go over finances.

Look over your budget, review goals, discuss purchases, share feelings, and so on. The key is to make this a nonnegotiable part of your schedule so it doesn't get forgotten or put off. And the goal is to have an undemanding and stress-free chat about money.

The powwow should feature at least four elements.

1. A positive reflection on what went well for the month (or week)
2. A basic check-in to stay current on financial matters and how each of you is feeling
3. Identification of any action items necessary for the coming month
4. Delegation of assignments with specific criteria ("I will call our insurance agent no later than Friday, and you drop those bills in the mail by Thursday.")

Besides stimulating helpful conversations, another benefit is that you don't have to talk about money issues *all the time*. We've noticed that communication sometimes gets stifled when one partner brings up financial matters throughout the week; the other person starts to feel pestered. A powwow limits money talk to a specific time and gives partners the assurance that they will, indeed, have a chance to voice opinions and address issues. (If one or both partners have let things fall through the cracks to the degree that it's causing relationship problems, you may want to meet two or three times a week until trust is rebuilt and a reliable system is in place. We'll discuss this in detail in chapter 13.)

The Dos: Six Principles for a Productive Powwow

These meetings should be positive, upbeat, useful, and fruitful. Here's how to make sure that happens.

1. Listen Intently

We put this one first because this should be the highest priority within marital communication. Sometimes we think of communication as *how things are said*, but the true key is listening. We all need to learn to be expert listeners. As the book of Proverbs says, "He who answers before listening—that is his folly and his shame" (18:13).

Most of us do not think of listening as a skill. We assume it just happens naturally since our ears are in a permanently "open" position. However, you can probably think of a recent incident where you did not listen intently to some communication and the result was misunderstanding or confusion. Think for a moment about how most of us listen. If someone is speaking, we usually begin to formulate a response before the person is finished. Sometimes we even interrupt with our responses as soon as we get the gist of what's being said.

Respected family counselor Norm Wright didn't mince words when he wrote, "Listening intently with one's mouth shut is a basic communication skill needed in marriages."[3] Great listening involves steady eye contact, maintaining a posture that shows you're engaged and interested, not interrupting, pushing distractions out of your mind, and focusing your complete attention on what's being said.

2. Use Positive Reinforcement

Dr. John Gottman is one the nation's leading experts on how relationships function and malfunction. He and his colleagues at the University of Washington conducted a groundbreaking study that was able to predict with 94 percent accuracy those couples who would later divorce. The one determining factor that led to their accuracy was the ratio of positive statements to negative statements that spouses made to each other. Dr. Gottman found that the optimal ratio was five positive statements to one negative. In healthy relationships, he reported, partners gave each other "five compliments for each noncommittal answer or complaint; five expressions of affection for every outburst or anger or blame; five good things for every bad. The lesson? People need warm, positive reinforcement from their partners in order to stay the course."[4]

The upshot is that one of the best ways to foster communication is to be positive. When having your powwows, look for ways to provide praise and reinforcement to the other. When discussing money matters, be sure to use—with authenticity—lots of statements like, "That's an excellent point," "I appreciate that perspective," and "I'm so glad we're in this together!"

> Communication sometimes gets stifled when one partner brings up financial matters throughout the week; the other person starts to feel pestered.

SECRETS ¢ SABOTAGE A RELATIONSHIP

We agree with writer Mary Loftus, who said, "Keeping secrets about money is not only tempting in our cultural carnival of consumption, it's also on the rise. The ability to spend and borrow money impulsively has never been greater, with ubiquitous ATMs, Internet banking and online shopping, to say nothing of refinancing deals and new credit card offers arriving almost daily in the mail....

"Given the avoidance, accessibility and ambivalence that now swirl around money, it's creating an explosive new dynamic in relationships. However small the money deceptions are, however well they are rationalized, they can nevertheless create fissures in a relationship that feel like flagrant betrayal to the other partner."[5]

3. Strive for Equal Time

In many relationships, one partner dominates the conversation to the exclusion of the other.

Some people consider themselves skilled communicators because they can talk nonstop. But the ability to speak is only one part of the equation— and not the most important part. Communication, as we said, requires talking *and* listening. Therefore, productive powwows occur with an even and equal exchange between two people.

Think of good communication during a powwow like two people on a teeter-totter. As they find a consistent rhythm and use teamwork, their goals are achieved. Similarly, great communication occurs as each person alternately talks and listens, talks and listens.

4. State Your Feelings and Beliefs

Communication often breaks down because we assume the other person knows what we mean. We may think, *I know what I'm saying, so my partner must, too.* Not so. This is why women sometimes complain that men are not "in tune" and are maddeningly imperceptive (or insensitive or thickheaded). And this is why men say, "I'm not a mind reader, you know. If you want me to do something, you've got to tell me."

Partners understand each other not by "picking up vibes" or "reading between the lines," but by dialoguing in a clear and direct manner. If you want to be understood by your spouse, it will happen because you clarify your thoughts and feelings. We encourage you to err on the side overcommunicating. Especially if you're trying to convey something important, state it a couple of times and in different ways.

One technique to make sure your powwow communication is getting through is to repeat back what the other person has said. "I hear you saying that you feel nervous and insecure when I don't keep the checkbook balanced." And then ask, "Is that accurate?" It may take a couple of times to get it exactly right. Your spouse may respond, "That's not quite it. It's not that I feel nervous and insecure; it's that I don't feel valued when you don't follow through on your commitments." Then you repeat that back and keep going through the process until you *both* agree that you understand clearly. This technique can seem clunky and contrived, but it really does work.

5. See Your Partner's Point of View

Psychologist Olivia Mellan observed, "Money issues are different from other problems in relationships. They're harder to resolve because of our extensive cultural conditioning. The most important thing in couples communication is empathy, or putting yourself in your partner's place. It is almost always more important to be heard and understood than to have a partner agree with what you say."[6]

Empathy is a matter of seeing and experiencing the world the way the other person does. You put yourself in the shoes of your partner. You make every effort to understand from his or her viewpoint everything that is said. In previous chapters, we explored in detail why we are the way we are in regard to money (family background, spiritual beliefs, and so on). This information can better help us understand ourselves and our partner. Instead of saying, "How can you believe *that?*" you can say, "Since I know how your parents operated, what you're telling me makes a lot of sense."

Trying to empathize and understand takes a lot of effort. There is nothing easy about trying to understand the complex, inner world of another human being. But it is a necessary part of great powwow communication.

6. Accept Disagreement

When we're talking about an intense money issue and emotions get stoked up, it's tempting to think about our partner's perspective as right or wrong, good or bad. But assigning those black-and-white labels does nothing to encourage a healthy flow of information and feelings. Instead of putting opinions in "acceptable" or "unacceptable" categories, consider everything shared a legitimate and valid point of view. Just because you're different doesn't mean either of you is wrong.

You may totally disagree with your partner's opinion. That's fine.

But that doesn't mean you are correct and on target, while your spouse is incorrect and off target. It may be that you have differing points of view—and each of them is valid and well founded.

Emotions may flare at times during your powwows. In the following chapter, we will discuss a solution and key communication system—which we call "meeting at the fence"—to work through highly volatile or emotional topics.

The Don'ts: Five Ways to Undermine the Powwow

Just as steps can be taken to promote a productive powwow, certain actions can be avoided so you don't impede the process.

1. Don't Criticize

While you're offering lots of praise and affirmation, remember to also hold your tongue when tempted to criticize and condemn. Nothing shuts down a powwow faster than a put-down. Watch how quickly your partner will stop sharing thoughts and feelings when you say, "Oh, that's ridiculous!" If you disapprove of everything your partner says, you're likely to find yourself sitting in silence.

It is a natural and understandable human response to protect ourselves if we feel demeaned and disparaged. We erect a barrier to fend off further attack. It's a learned defensive mechanism designed to reduce the possibility of criticism and judgment. Therefore, keep in mind this simple rule: when tempted to criticize, don't! When a negative comment comes to mind, don't let it come out of your mouth.

> With deceptive communication, couples do indeed talk about spending and saving but in a sneaky way that undermines both their financial and relational health.

2. Don't Clam Up

When you're discussing money matters, it's easy for one person to stay silent. Don't let that happen! For healthy communication and a successful powwow, each partner must be willing to talk openly and honestly. This may be difficult at times, especially for those who are most introverted and reticent by nature. But remember that your goal is a straightforward and candid discussion—and that requires *two* people being willing to talk.

3. Don't Lecture

We frequently work with couples in which one of them is the "money person." This often happens when someone works in the area of finance professionally or simply enjoys handling money matters. The other spouse relinquishes control and doesn't get involved. In this case, the couple's style of relating is tilted in one direction. The money manager ends up talking *to*, instead of *with*, the other partner. The powwow is a monologue rather than a dialogue. The downsides here are obvious. The "silent partner" is not given the chance to express opinions, beliefs, and feelings. Power issues may be at play, as the person controlling the purse strings holds all the decision-making authority. What's more, the uninvolved partner will not be prepared to handle finances should the need arise.

4. Don't Deceive

Sadly, a lot of couples talk about money, but not in a way that's completely open and truthful. They are disingenuous and dishonest with each other. A recent survey revealed that 42 percent of men and 36 percent of women keep secrets from their spouses, and the most widespread secret involves money. The survey found that almost half of all husbands and wives hid the cost of something from their spouse.[7] With deceptive communication, couples do indeed talk about spending and saving but in a sneaky way that undermines both their financial and relational health.

We believe that anything less than the whole truth is destructive to relationships. Unfortunately, money is one of those issues that some couples have a hard time telling the whole truth about.

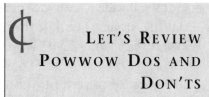

LET'S REVIEW POWWOW DOS AND DON'TS

Do
1. Listen intently
2. Use positive reinforcement
3. Strive for equal time
4. State your feelings and beliefs
5. See your partner's point of view
6. Accept disagreement

Don't
1. Criticize
2. Clam up
3. Lecture
4. Deceive
5. Get distracted

BE AWARE OF YOUR BODY LANGUAGE

The old cliché says that "actions speak louder than words." And this includes your nonverbal communication. Be sure you are not sending negative and critical messages to your partner through your posture, gestures, and facial expression. Rolling your eyes, sighing dramatically, folding your arms, and slouching in your chair are all signs that you're disinterested or disapproving.

5. Don't Get Distracted

Distraction is surely the most common of all communication conundrums. Most of the husbands and wives we know make a sincere and heartfelt effort to communicate clearly and openly with each other. They explain themselves, they express their feelings, and they try to enlighten each other. And yet there's a disconnect somewhere. They're not in sync. They become baffled, bewildered, befuddled.

As our friend Derek told us recently, "Lora and I sat down the other night to make a very simple decision—what to do with our tax refund. We were either going to put it in an IRA or pay down our Visa balance. Somehow we started talking about her parents and my parents and where we'll retire and some irrelevant article in *Forbes* magazine. And then she got upset about something—I don't know what—and then I got upset because she was upset. And we never did make a decision about the money. Frankly, that's typical! I listen to her talk, and I think, *Where is she coming from? What is she saying? I just don't get it.*"

To be fair, we imagine Lora would say the same thing about Derek. That's because communication between men and women is incredibly complex and complicated. The *content* of any conversation—what to do with a tax refund or what kind of vacuum to buy—is insignificant compared with *process* of validating each other, seeking to understand hidden messages, and being receptive to emotional cues. No wonder the simplest topic can turn into a muddled mess.

***

It's critical that you and your spouse keep the dialogue flowing with clear and straightforward messages to each other. You can get on the same "money page" with honest, heartfelt communication. You may need outside help in a time of crisis, but it all starts with honesty and commitment to talk things through. A powwow is a great way to start.

CHAPTER TWELVE

WE CAN WORK IT OUT

Just up the road from us is the University of Denver, where some of the most innovative research is being done regarding marriage, families, and relationships. One of the top researchers there is Dr. Scott Stanley. Read what this relationship expert has to say. "Money is the intersecting point where couples make most of their decisions. Money arguments have added potency because they allow for power and control dynamics to be triggered. It's an area of conflict where one partner can make unilateral decisions that affect both partners, sometimes for the rest of their lives."[1]

So true. We hope you know by now that we are optimists when it comes to marriage and money. We believe that marriage should be a great source of joy and that money—whether you've got a little or a lot—can enrich your lives and the lives of people you care about. We are also realists. After working with a wide variety of clients over many years, we know that money is a sore spot for most couples at some point. Psychologists often talk about the "big three" sources of conflict for spouses: money, sex, and in-laws. It's interesting—and probably no accident—that money is usually mentioned first in this testy triad.

Even if you and your partner become expert communicators, as we discussed in the previous chapter, you're bound to run into squabbles over money. Learning to talk through issues and having a pow-wow can prevent some quarrels—but not all of them. That's because hardly a day goes by that both you and your spouse don't use money in some way. For better or worse, money is woven into the fabric of our everyday lives. With so many individual and collective decisions about our dollars, it's not surprising that bad feelings occasionally bubble to the surface like molten lava. We agree with the financial writer Mary Loftus, who said,

If you are in a serious relationship, no matter how long you've been together or how much money you have, your next fight is likely to be about money. Money is inextricably connected to our hopes and our dreams, our sense of security and self-worth, almost all of our core emotions and familial expectations.

Disagreements about money are also more intense, and more negative, than those about other topics. Due to an invisible web of intention that underlies financial transactions, we endlessly attribute unspoken motives and consequences to the financial choices people make. When tweaked, the delicate threads of these decisions, woven throughout our homes and around our daily activities, can instantly become high-tension wires.[2]

What was your last money spat about? Perhaps it involved a spending decision, an impulsive buy, an unbudgeted purchase. The more significant issue is not what the disagreement was *about*, but how the issue got resolved—or didn't get resolved. Fights over finances will happen. It's how we handle those fights that matters most.

Dealing with Disagreements

We don't like conflict, and we're guessing that you don't either. Squabbling makes our pulses quicken, blood pressure soar, and stomachs churn. Worse, arguments often bring out the worst in us, and we may resort to childish and immature behavior.

All of this is why most people avoid conflict and consider it bad. Indeed, most married people think that arguments are damaging, that there must be something wrong with their relationship if they fight. If they had their way, conflict would not exist in marriage.

We want you to hear loud and clear from two of the nation's top relationship experts, Dr. John Gottman and Dr. Neil Clark Warren. Both have practiced psychology for decades and have written and researched extensively.

Dr. Gottman: "If there is one lesson I have learned from my years of research, it is that a lasting marriage results from a couple's ability to resolve the conflicts that are inevitable in any relationship. Many couples tend to equate a low level of conflict with happiness and believe the claim that 'we never fight' is a sign of marital health. But I believe we grow in our relationships by reconciling our differences. That's how we become more loving people and truly experience the fruits of marriage."[3]

Dr. Warren: "I believe marital conflict can be a valuable natural resource for spouses who learn to manage it wisely. It can provide a steady flow of healthy energy and vitality to a marriage.... If you and your partner master the skills to make conflict constructive, you will create freedom for the development of the uniqueness in each of you. You will have a generous supply of energy to propel your union toward greatness."[4]

Did you catch that? Arguments can be a source of growth and understanding for couples. Rather than being a bad thing, conflict can be a *great* thing. Because marriage is a union of two imperfect individuals with unique viewpoints, backgrounds, and values, conflict will occur from time to time.

You and your spouse will differ sometimes, and your differences will stir up emotions. That's only normal. But the key is what happens next. The happily married couple learns how to deal with conflict in creative, constructive ways.

How do you handle conflict? The ways you have learned to communicate and confront differences will influence how you approach and resolve conflict. The family you grew up in had a definite impact on your problem-solving style. Over the course of your life, you and your partner have each developed your own way of handling differences, difficult issues, and conflicts.

Consider these six basic conflict styles and determine which is your own personal resolution style.

Avoiders. These people physically or emotionally withdraw to avoid conflict. They will clam up, go to another part of the house, and insist nothing is wrong. They would rather retreat into their shell than deal with disputes. Avoiders say, "Me, upset? No, nothing's bothering me. I've got to go now."

Competitors. These men and women look at conflict as a contest to win. They are intent on achieving victory, which means making the other person lose. In their quest for triumph, they can be ruthless. Competitors say, "If we're going to fight, I'm going to win!"

Blamers. These persons do not take responsibility and don't see how they could be at fault for any portion of the argument. They'll point fingers—but never at themselves. They try to remain above the

MAKING ¢ CENTS

What do you argue about more—sex or money? Money is the number one cause of disagreements in marriages, sparking nearly twice as many arguments as sex. Twenty-nine percent of couples say they "frequently disagree" about whether to spend or save. Seventeen percent have ended a relationship because of money.

Do you trust your partner with your money? Forty percent of folks say it's madness to trust anyone else with your money— even your husband, wife, or steady partner. Fourteen percent don't even let their spouses know their PIN numbers.[5]

fray by disavowing responsibility. Blamers say, "If you want to make a big deal of it, that's your business. But don't try to put the blame on me."

Yielders. Men and women who face conflict as yielders would rather concede and give in than risk confrontation. They won't stand up for themselves. They may even be taken advantage of and walked on as a way to sidestep tension. Yielders say, "Okay, you're right. Have it your way. Let's just get over it."

Minimizers. These people diminish and downplay any issue. If someone gets upset, these folks will insist the other person is being irrational, melodramatic, and overly sensitive. Minimizers say, "I don't see what the big deal is. Why make a mountain out of a molehill?"

Resolvers. These people understand that conflict is a part of life and seek to deal with it as it comes up. They may not be perfect, but they seek solutions. Resolvers say, "Let's settle this matter so we can move on. Let's air our differences and agree to hold no grudges."

Obviously, conflicts can be handled and mishandled in many ways. Some couples sidestep arguments to keep the peace. Others feel overwhelmed by heated emotions. The whole process makes them uncomfortable, since they have never learned how to argue productively. So it's easiest just to skip it. The truth is, conflict management requires patience and persistence.

Let's be honest—some conflict is destructive. There's nothing good about arguments that cause harm and hurt. But there is a big difference between well-managed conflict and the kind that results in physical or emotional damage. Hold on to the primary premise: conflict can be extremely helpful or hurtful depending on how it's handled day in and day out.

Principles for Productive Conflict

If you agree that some disputes are inevitable, then it's important to establish ground rules for healthy conflict. Let's look at eight principles of constructive conflict.

Focus on How *You're Arguing as Well as* Why

Although it's important to address the specific issue that causes tension, it's even more important to make sure the *tone* of the argument does not become cruel and nasty. Psychology professor Dr. David Niven explains.

> Think of the disagreements you've had with your partner in the past six months. They blend together, don't they?... Now try to remember how you *felt* during those disagreements. It's much, much easier to remember that, isn't it? You might have felt belittled, or you might have felt disrespected. The point is that we remember the atmosphere, the feelings of a disagreement, long after we forget the specifics of the disagreement. Regardless of the disagreement at hand, remember to always put the feelings of your partner ahead of the specific complaint, because the feelings will linger long after the complaint is solved and forgotten.[6]

Determine Exactly What You're Arguing About

We ran across a quote from a nineteenth-century writer named Sara Coleridge, who said, "Much waste of words and thought would be avoided if disputants would always begin with a clear statement of the question, and not proceed to argue till they had agreed upon what it was that they were arguing about." Many disagreements could be settled quickly if both partners knew *exactly* what the disagreement was about. So often when emotions escalate, communication becomes muddled. It's helpful to stop and say, "What precisely is the issue here? What are we really fighting about?"

Brainstorm Solutions

Suggesting possible solutions is probably one of the most important aspects of resolving conflict. Considering options helps to develop alternatives instead of staying stuck in a particular direction. In brainstorming, both partners express ideas they have about solving the problem.

Settle Disagreements as Quickly as Possible

Conflict can almost always be managed more successfully in the early phases rather than when it builds up steam. It was the apostle Paul who said, "Do not let the sun go down while you are still angry" (Eph. 4:26). Whether you interpret that statement literally or not, the principle is clear: don't allow disputes to linger; take care of them as soon as possible.

Seek a Victory for Both of You

Conflicts activate our competitive instincts, and winning the argument can become critical. This doesn't just happen with the "competitor" style of conflict described above. In the heat of battle, it's tempting to pursue what's best for *me* rather than what's best for *us*. It feels great if I win the argument—but it hasn't helped to strengthen the relationship.

Refuse to Make Cutting Remarks or Call Names

If the goal of conflict resolution is to settle the matter in a fair and equitable manner, put-downs and name-calling serve no purpose. It will only drive you and your partner further apart to say, "You're being ridiculous!" Or, "That's the stupidest thing I've ever heard!" Any comment intended to demean or degrade the other person should be strictly off limits.

Remain Open-minded

Sometimes individuals become so convinced of their own rightness that they resist considering other options. The best solution may be one you haven't thought of yet. You should both seek an attitude that says, "Let's consider all the possibilities."

Keep Your Eye on the Primary Goals: Unity and Understanding

When couples encounter conflict, they can choose to let it divide them or unify them. They can either decide to fight mean and nasty, or fairly and open-mindedly. Each choice will reap consequences to their advantage or disadvantage.

Let's Meet at the Fence

The reason for a powwow, as described in the previous chapter, is to provide a consistent system in which to talk about money. However, during those talks or at other times, conflicts may arise. When those disagreements come up, they should be handled in an efficient, constructive way.

Recently, our government sent top officials to the Vatican in what they described as a "mission of fence-mending" over differences in the way international conflicts were being handled. "Mending fences" is a term used to describe coming together, resolving conflict, and moving forward in a positive way. That is why we named this conflict-resolution system "meeting at the fence."

Sometimes emotions flare, and there doesn't seem to be a way to calm down and talk rationally about a money issue. We know people who have knock-down, drag-out fights about money. Does anything get accomplished? No. And each side feels miserable afterward. What's worse, conflicts that become heated and go unresolved are toxic to relationships. Too many vicious fights, and a marriage is headed for trouble in a hurry.

Meeting at the fence is a conflict-resolution strategy that addresses money squabbles in a thorough, timely, and fair manner. Let's get specific. Here are the seven ground rules for meeting at the fence.

1. Agree to disagree at the moment. You don't have to achieve consensus *right then and there*. When emotions are running high, it may be counterproductive to force an agreement. You can say, "We see things differently, and let's leave it at that for now. Later, we can talk things out and seek common ground." This helps to de-escalate emotions and defuse an explosive situation. You're not avoiding the issue; you're

SIDESTEPPING SQUABBLES

Although some disagreements about money are inevitable, if you can circumvent conflict in a healthy way (meaning not just sweeping it under the rug), all the better! Consider these ideas.

Give each partner an "allowance." Many spats occur because of differences in how money should be spent. This can be avoided by allotting some "mad money" to each person. Agree on a personal monthly allowance, and don't question what your spouse does with his or her money.

Review goals regularly. Conflicts arise when we lose sight of the big picture and focus on immediate desires and wishes. Suppose a husband and wife agreed at the beginning of the year to put $5,000 in a savings account for the kids' college education. Around May, the husband decides he would rather use the money for home improvements, and a battle ensues. By reviewing the goal weekly or even monthly, this couple could have avoided being distracted from their primary aim.

agreeing to address it when you have the time and space to do it in a constructive way.

2. Meet within twenty-four hours. Rather than let conflicts brew and boil, it's best to address them in a timely manner. A twenty-four-hour deadline is a good rule of thumb, but sooner is better.

3. Give each person the opportunity to clearly state his or her concerns without interruption. Take turns and do not interrupt. Both people should feel as if they presented their side of the issue and aired out feelings. Don't short-circuit this process. Let both people have their say!

4. Allow each person to ask three questions for clarification. To make sure you're communicating clearly and precisely, ask a few questions that will elicit more information and insight. We limit the number to three in order to keep the process moving forward and eliminate the possibility of an endless stream of queries (which can avoid getting to the real issue).

5. Let each person state three possible solutions. Once the contentious issue is clear to both of you, it's time to turn up your creativity, expand your thinking, and suggest ways to resolve the matter. Propose concrete solutions that truly resolve the matter.

6. Agree on the solution. Use the solutions discussed as a foundation to get the creative juices flowing. This is where negotiation, compromise, and teamwork all come into play. Use one solution or part of several to come to a fence-mending answer that is win-win for both people.

7. Celebrate together when the issue is resolved. Conflict is not easy—there's lots of anxiety and pressure involved—so for resolution to happen, both people must be committed to the process. Therefore, when you do reach an agreement, congratulate each other and celebrate your success.

* * *

Conflict about money may be inevitable, but that doesn't mean it has to drag on and drag you down! By regularly reviewing the principles of constructive conflict, you and your partner can learn to resolve differences quickly and efficiently. And when you run into a particularly pressing issue, you can "mend fences" by using our meeting-at-the-fence technique. Make a commitment to work through problems in a way that leaves both of you feeling respected, appreciated, and valued.

CHAPTER THIRTEEN

THE CASE FOR CREATIVE COMPROMISE

Since we work together as financial professionals, we are usually in agreement when it comes to our personal money issues. But not always!

One area of disagreement we ran into during the last couple of years was whether to put extra money toward our house payment or save that money toward large expenses. Bethany had earlier agreed with Scott to refinance the house with a fifteen-year mortgage. Because Scott sees the house as an investment rather than debt, paying it off quicker is exciting to him.

Bethany, however, second-guessed the decision. She would much rather set aside additional funds for future expenses, such as a car purchase or home-improvement projects. This was not a major source of conflict, but a nagging disagreement we felt unsettled about. We discussed it at one of our monthly powwows and came up with a compromise we both felt good about.

Scott promised not to bring up the subject anymore and to make one extra house payment per year, which drops the payoff to twelve instead of fifteen years. That gave Bethany the flexibility to decide (with Scott's help, of course) where the additional cash will go.

This is just one example of the dozens of compromises we've made over the years. In fact, as we thought about our marriage and talked with many other couples and relationship experts, the point has been reinforced over and over: compromise is a key ingredient for the success of any marriage—and for the healthy handling of money.

If you're struggling with differences in perspective about saving and spending, those discrepancies can drive a wedge between you and your partner. But, like we did, you can successfully resolve any disagreements you're currently facing.

Regardless of how solid your relationship is, you're bound to encounter differences. As we've said previously, money is a lightning rod for disputes that can erupt into full-fledged conflict. These differences need to be resolved through a sensible, reasonable process. That process involves compromise and negotiation. This means communicating openly with the purpose of reaching a mutually satisfying decision. During negotiation, couples explore their dissimilarities, discuss their priorities, and develop a commonly held set of operating principles.

When you negotiate, you learn more and more about your mate. You must confront issues and be willing to state your thoughts and feelings in order to resolve the matter. One purpose of negotiation is to quell anger in such a way that open and honest discussion of the facts is encouraged. But there's more. Compromise also deepens your love, trust, and respect for each other. Successfully working through disagreements shows that you are united and committed to your relationship.

> Compromise is a key ingredient for the success of any marriage—and for the healthy handling of money.

Within successful relationships, compromise happens every day—perhaps dozens of times each day—and often without the partners being consciously aware of it. Some of the trade-offs are small; some are huge. Negotiation may take a few seconds if a man and woman are debating which kind of pasta sauce to buy at the grocery store—the expensive gourmet kind she likes or the cheap generic brand he wants. Or negotiation may take months or years as a couple grapples with where to live or how best to care for elderly parents.

Major or minor, every point of disagreement requires compromise of some kind. Perhaps one partner compromises, while the other doesn't. Better yet, both partners give a little and find a happy medium. In either case, the partners engage in the dance of cooperation and conciliation.

There's a word for relationships in which neither partner is willing to compromise: *miserable.* And miserable is not what you and your lover want to be. Like us, you want to navigate your way through all of life's potential snags and snares so you can enjoy a thoroughly happy and harmonious marriage.

View Yourselves as Allies, Not Adversaries

As kids, most of us went to events—camps, church picnics, school celebrations—where we played all kinds of games on a big grassy field. Everyone gathered to toss water balloons, hop like bunnies in gunnysacks, and run relay races. Two other popular competitions were the three-legged race and the tug-of-war.

These two activities provide an apt metaphor for marriage. As we've worked with thousands of couples on financial issues, it's become blatantly apparent that the ones who struggle most have an adversarial attitude toward each other. They are in a tug-of-war over ideas, beliefs, and goals. They each cling to opposite ends of the rope and pull with all their might, trying valiantly to yank the other person over to their side. And what happens when one of them feels the momentum shifting and the rising fear that they're losing ground? They dig in even deeper, hold on tighter, and redouble their effort.

If you've been in an actual tug-of-war, you know the two possible outcomes: a stalemate, where both teams eventually give up; or a victory for one side and, of course, defeat for the other. All of that makes for high-spirited fun at a party or picnic, but it makes for high-spirited *fights* in relationships.

Ah, but there is another alternative. Forget the tug-of-war, and sign up for the three-legged race instead. You've probably participated in one of those competitions before, too. You found a partner, stood side by side, and tied a rope around two of your legs. Then you grabbed hold of each other and waited for someone to yell, "Ready, set, go!" Off you went, fumbling and stumbling, perhaps falling to the ground before picking yourselves up and trying again. Eventually, you found your rhythm, figured out how to run in sync, and crossed the finish line.

There's a word for relationships in which neither partner is willing to compromise: *miserable.*

Whether you came in first place or not, you and your partner gave each

> ¢Creative compromise requires *two* partners fully engaged in the process.

other a hug and a high five and said, "Hey, we did pretty well together!"

Sounds a lot like marriage. At least that's how marriage *should* be—rather than the fierce competition of a tug-of-war.

Absolutely essential to any effort at compromise is an attitude of *teammates striving together*. Allies help each move toward a common goal, cheering and encouraging all along the way. Adversaries hold each other back, chiding and discouraging all along the way.

When you give your relationship priority over the two individuals who make it up, conflicts become a challenge that, when handled successfully, will enhance and improve your union. No longer a wedge that drives you and your spouse apart, problems approached with a team perspective can be like a rope that binds you together. Rather than two people asking, "How can I win this disagreement?" you can each say, "How can we benefit from this disagreement?"

You and your spouse are a team, and you will have to cooperate and communicate with each other as you strive for victory. You need to talk things through as you determine your priorities and decide how you will achieve them. You'll need to keep each other informed as you assume your roles and execute your unique assignments.

Look for Win-Win Solutions

Sometimes when we mention the word *compromise* to couples, the expressions on their faces convey skepticism and suspicion. We've talked through these issues enough with people to know what's usually going on in their minds: *You want us to compromise? Sure, that means we'll settle for some mediocre, middling solution. Then neither of us will be completely happy and satisfied.*

That is exactly opposite of what we mean by compromise. Now, suppose a man wants to eat at his favorite Italian restaurant and his wife is craving French cuisine. They argue about it for a half hour and end up at a nearby greasy spoon. That's a lousy compromise! Or suppose one partner wants to vacation in Hawaii, while the other would like a trip to Disney World. They settle for a week of RV camping, which they both find boring and frustrating. That, too, is a regrettable compromise.

What we're suggesting is that you turn up your creative energy and find a third alternative with which you're both delighted.

Earlier in this book, we cited leadership expert Stephen Covey, and another one of his insightful principles is apropos here. He encourages people to focus on win-win solutions. Whenever you encounter a situation that requires compromise, that doesn't mean one person has to win, while the other has to lose. Nor does it mean that you both sacrifice to the degree that neither of you is pleased with the outcome. Here's the goal, as described by Covey.

> Win-Win is a frame of mind and heart that constantly seeks mutual benefit in all human interactions. Win-Win means that agreements or solutions are mutually beneficial, mutually satisfying. With a Win-Win solution, all parties feel good about the decision and feel committed to the action plan. Win-Win sees life as a cooperative, not a competitive, arena. Most people tend to think in terms of dichotomies: strong or weak, hardball or softball, win or lose. But that kind of thinking is fundamentally flawed. It's based on power and position rather than on principle. Win-Win is based on the paradigm that there is plenty for everybody, that one person's success is not achieved at the expense or exclusion of the success of others.[1]

That is precisely the point we're making. In all of the disagreements we've tried to help couples overcome, rarely have there been only two options available. In other words, it isn't a matter of moving in one direction or the other. Usually another path that both partners would be happy to travel can be found.

GO, TEAM!

Dr. Allan Cordova has conducted extensive research at the University of Denver on teamwork with couples. He said, "Research suggests that teamwork—how coordinated, committed, and 'in sync' couples feel and act—is a cornerstone of marital adjustment. The stakes of thinking and acting like a team may be the highest under stressful circumstances, such as when trying to talk about a 'hot' topic. I've found that couples who score higher on measures of teamwork are couples who also score highly on general marital satisfaction, commitment, confidence in the ability to constructively solve relationship problems, and communication quality."[2]

Let Go of Either-Or Thinking

Compromise is thwarted when couples think they have to choose *either* his way *or* her way. A big step toward win-win solutions is identifying a third alternative that neither partner thought of originally. With open-minded discussion and creative exploration, a scenario that meets the needs of both individuals can usually be found.

Last year, we worked with a couple named Ian and Joy. He absolutely hated carrying any kind of debt, and he especially deplored credit cards with their interest rates, finance fees, and other costs. Early in their marriage, Ian had laid down the law: "No credit-card debt. Period." This was a law Joy didn't believe in and, consequently, had a hard time abiding by. To her, debt was no big deal. She had grown up with parents who were happy to borrow money as long as they paid it off before it became too burdensome.

This debt dilemma caused many heated confrontations for Ian and Joy. Often he said, "You're undermining our financial well-being and sabotaging our goals! We're never going to get ahead if you keep this up. Besides, you're disrespecting me by not complying with my wishes." She would respond, "When we got married, your money and my money became *our* money—but that doesn't mean I should have no freedom over spending decisions. We're just different in this area. I should be able to buy things, so long as I don't go overboard. Just let me be me—and *me* wants to spend a little money when I want to."

After a few years of this back-and-forth bickering, Joy came up with a compromise idea that underscores the point we're making. She told Ian, "You hate debt, and I don't mind it. So let's agree that I can have a limit of $1,000 of credit-card debt at any one time. It will never exceed that amount. And if it does, I will immediately cease and desist all debt henceforth and forevermore."

Ian thought about it. "A $1,000 cap on your debt? All right, I can live with that. But this is serious. You're agreeing that if you go over that amount—even one month by one dollar—you pay off the card and never borrow again. Right?"

Joy agreed, and they even put the agreement

MAKING CENTS

Amount of money spent in Britain by women buying things to say sorry to their partners: £2 billion (3.6 billion US dollars).

Amount of money spent in Britain by men buying things to say sorry to their partners: £10 billion (18 billion US dollars).[3]

in writing with both of their signatures at the bottom of the page. When last we checked, Joy had not exceeded her debt limit, and Ian, though still not thrilled about carrying a balance, hasn't hassled her about it since.

Let us tell you another real-life incident to help crystallize this point. We read about a situation involving Michael McManus, who directs Marriage Savers, an organization that provides resources for engaged and married couples. A few summers ago, Michael and his family were living in Connecticut, but he wanted to move back to Washington, D.C. His wife loved their house in Connecticut, and she didn't want to uproot their youngest son, who was about to start high school. They were at an impasse about a life-changing decision.

Eventually, they settled on a workable arrangement. The house would go on the market at a high price. If it sold by August, they'd move. If it didn't, they'd stay put for a few years. The house did sell, and the profit enabled the couple to buy another home in Washington and bank some cash for college. Michael and his wife both ended up feeling like winners.

Reflecting on the experience, he said, "Instead of browbeating the other person, it's important for a compromise to surface that you can both live with."[4]

¢ **COMPROMISE CASE STUDY: GIFT GIVING**

The following story comes from John and Larissa of Henderson, Nevada.

Problem: "From the very beginning of our marriage, we fought about what kinds of gifts to give other people—specifically, how much to spend on those gifts. I (Larissa) love to give big, extravagant presents for weddings, birthdays, and other special occasions. To me, it's a demonstration of my love. John has a different view. He thinks a little cash tucked into a card is fine (emphasis on the word *little*). We've had major battles over this issue!"

Solution: "For a while, we just split the difference. If I wanted to give a $50 gift and John thought $10 was more appropriate, we would meet halfway at $30. But I still felt we were being cheap, and John thought we were being excessive. We both felt uneasy. Then we landed on an arrangement we're both happy with. We increased the amount of spending money I'm allowed each month, and I am totally responsible for gift giving throughout the year. This provides me the freedom and flexibility to budget for all the gifts and buy whatever I want. I can go big on a wedding gift and smaller on a graduation present if I choose. I can spend as I see fit, and John doesn't have to worry about busting the budget."

¢

COMPROMISE CASE STUDY: MONTHLY ALLOTMENT OF SPENDING MONEY

Lamar and Trina of Shreveport, Louisiana, told us their tale of compromise.

Problem: "Since we both entered marriage with hefty school loans, we spent the first five years together climbing out of debt. After that, we agreed to go on a strict budget and to stick with it. But Trina found that *saying* she'd stick to a budget and actually doing it are two different things. We each had $75 in cash to spend as we liked throughout the month. Trina, however, couldn't stay within her $75 allowance and would continually say she needed more. On several occasions, she simply used her ATM card to get cash out of the machine (without consulting me beforehand). We were getting nickel-and-dimed into oblivion because of Trina's propensity to spend."

Solution: "Frankly, it took several attempts before we found something that worked. Lectures from me and self-discipline by Trina

As these two situations show, a different alternative than partners first conceive can nearly always be found. Couples who let go of my-way-or-the-highway thinking usually find a creative solution that suits everyone well.

The Content of Compromise

We aren't suggesting for a moment that compromise is easy. Far from it! When you mix together definite opinions with strong feelings, you're going to have some complicated clashes. But the hard work of negotiation pays off in the long run. Here are six guidelines to keep in mind as you and your partner work toward creative compromise.

Both partners must commit to be open-minded, flexible, and willing to change. Give-and-take must be a two-way street, or compromise is doomed from the start. If one person is entrenched in his or her position, progress will be impossible. Creative compromise requires *two* partners fully engaged in the process.

Become crystal clear about what you want and why. When partners have only a vague sense of why they're holding on to a certain position—or what they want to happen in a situation—discussions go round and round without resolution. Become as clear as possible about the outcome you desire and the motivations behind it. If you want to buy a house in the suburbs and your spouse wants to live downtown, you each should know *exactly* why you feel this way. Objectively articulating your reasons will help your partner understand.

Keep negotiations grounded in reality. As we've helped couples break through financial impasses, it has been clear that sometimes one person has unrealistic expectations. The individual's *starting point* for compromise is inflated and idealistic. Suppose a couple is ready to buy a new car, and the man says, "I think we should get a loaded BMW." In fact, their budget would allow for a nice, midrange Honda or Toyota—without leather interior and an upgraded CD player. So when the wife says, "I was thinking about a VW, not a BMW," they'll find a wide gulf between them as they begin discussions. That gulf—which is wider than it needs to be or should be—makes compromise much more difficult to achieve.

Set aside ample time for a discussion of options. Compromises are hard to work out if dialogue takes place "on the fly." Since we have two young boys, we know it's impossible to hear each other and feel heard with screaming kids running in and out of the room or while cartoons are blaring in the background. It's best to call for a "meeting at the fence" (as we discussed in chapter 12), when you can push all other matters aside and totally concentrate on the issue at hand.

Remain solution oriented. When hashing out an issue, it's easy to defend your position and make sure you don't lose the debate. That's when negotiations stall and become unproductive. Both partners should stay focused on the end result—a great solution they'll both enjoy.

Submit to one another in love. Sometimes negotiation and compromise boil down to a matter of submission. We certainly don't use that term with the connotation of one person taking advantage of the other or one partner

were futile. We had a 'meeting at the fence' to address the issue, and we came up with a four-point plan. First, we increased Trina's monthly allowance. It may seem strange to give a spender *more* money, but this actually provided her a cushion and room to maneuver. Second, we confiscated all credit cards and ATM cards. No cards, no expenses unaccounted for. Third, we agreed to dole out her cash on a week-to-week basis. Before, she got all her cash all the beginning of the month, and it was gone within the first week. This way, she could anticipate 'payday' each Monday to start fresh. Fourth, any expenses beyond her monthly allowance had to be cleared by me. Honestly, neither of us was thrilled about my being assigned the role of 'judge and jury' (too many potential arguments), but we had to do something. It's been two years since we made this agreement, and it's worked marvelously."

being a doormat to be stepped on. An imbalance of power and respect, where one individual always gets his or her way while the other person continually capitulates, is unhealthy.

We're talking about a willing and generous deference to your partner—free of coercion, arm-twisting, or power plays. Compromise may mean saying, "Honey, this wouldn't be my first choice, but I know how important this is to you. So I choose to let you have your way because I love you and honor you." This isn't a matter of disregarding win-win solutions—it may be a matter of "you win this time, and I can win next time." Another way we refer to this is to "choose your battles." Does the issue involve an absolute *must have*, or is it something you can let go?

Of course, the bigger picture goes far beyond how to invest, where to vacation, or what kind of house to buy. The quality of your relationship matters more than any financial decision. In nearly every dispute related to money, you have an opportunity to strengthen your relationship or weaken it. We appreciate the insight offered by the New Testament writer James. "Wisdom that comes from heaven is first of all pure and full of quiet gentleness. Then it is peace-loving and courteous. It allows discussion and is willing to yield to others; it is full of mercy and good deeds. It is wholehearted and straightforward and sincere. And those who are peacemakers will plant seeds of peace and reap a harvest of goodness" (James 3:17–18 TLB).

Those words ought to guide every aspect of our relationships. And when it comes to compromise, sometimes the willingness to "yield to others" and be "full of mercy" is the best solution of all.

CHAPTER FOURTEEN

ACCENTUATE ACCOUNTABILITY

It was supposed to be a routine review of a couple's personal finances and investment strategy. But it didn't turn out that way.

As we sat with Grant and Melinda in a big conference room with file folders and papers spread out in front of us, we could sense the tension between them. They sat several feet away from each other, didn't make eye contact, and uttered only short, clipped responses. It didn't take a body language expert to sense the hostility in the room.

We talked with Grant and Melinda about a few general matters, and then we asked about their goals for the coming year. That's when the dam burst.

"I'm happy to talk about our goals," Grant practically sneered, "but Melinda doesn't believe in goals. We make decisions, but she doesn't keep her end of the bargain. We agree on a budget, but she doesn't stick to it. We set goals, but she doesn't do anything to accomplish them." He stopped and sighed deeply. Then he said in a sheepish voice, "I'm sorry. That was uncalled for. I'm just so frustrated."

We remained silent, giving them the space to say what needed to be said.

Grant composed himself and spoke in a gentler voice. "We have more credit-card debt than we had a year ago. We have a roof to replace—about eight thousand bucks—without the cash to pay for it. And we're no closer to paying back my parents the twenty grand they loaned us for our down payment than we were four years ago. Somehow we're sliding backward rather than moving forward."

Finally, Melinda spoke up. "I admit it. It's my fault. Grant's right—I spend too much money. I just can't seem to get a handle on things. We talk about plans that sound great at the time. But I don't know. I just ..."

She didn't need to finish her sentence, because we were all pretty well knew what she was going to say anyway.

As we talked further with Grant and Melinda, we learned that they are the quintessential saver-versus-spender couple we described in chapter 1. He is self-disciplined; she is undisciplined. He's careful; she's careless. He watches every dollar; she wants to spend every dollar.

Yet there was something deeper going on. Melinda agreed to their goals, plans, and spending limitations, but she never followed through. She didn't seem to take seriously any of their heart-to-heart discussions, and she didn't respond to any of Grant's motivational techniques. She would promise not to use her MasterCard, and then she'd use it. She would agree to track down receipts for their tax return and then never get around to it. The issue was more than a financial one; it was a matter of trust, dependability, and good judgment.

We have heard so many similar stories—from clients, friends, and respondents to our questionnaire—that we felt the need to address the issue in this book. It happens frequently that one or both partners sabotage their financial well-being and hinder their progress. The husband or wife acts in ways that are reckless, rash, or irresponsible. Often they are dishonest with each other. In the process, they damage their relationship. Here is a sampling of what we're talking about.

Kelly, age 31: "When Jon and I got married three years ago, I knew he'd had credit problems. He had alluded to his poor credit rating and kind of laughed it off. Just recently, I found out that he filed for bankruptcy and has about the worst credit rating a person can have. Now I'm stuck with it, too. I feel deceived because he was not completely honest with me before we got married."

Reese, age 26: "This sounds so silly and insignificant that I hesitate to write it ... but it bugs me! Julie and I keep a jar full of change in the kitchen, and this is our entertainment fund. At the end of each day, we throw our coins in the jar, and every couple of weeks we use that money to go out for pizza or see a movie. Well, over the past six months, the amount of change has been getting smaller and smaller. I suspected that Julie was dipping into our entertainment fund to buy stuff for herself. When I asked her, she admitted it and shrugged it off as no big deal. Like I said, it seems ridiculous and petty to make an issue out of it. But it's the principle of the matter. I feel cheated, like she's stealing from me."

Gwen, age 42: "For most of our married life, I handled the budget, bill paying, and paperwork. I'm more detail oriented than my husband, Lloyd. Last year, I decided to go back to work full time as an RN, since our two kids are in school. Lloyd thought that would be a good time to switch roles and have him take over our money management. I reluctantly agreed. Turns out I was reluctant for good reason. Under his supervision (or lack of it), our finances became a complete mess. I'm upset that he made such a shambles of my airtight system, but I'm even more upset that he kept assuring me everything was peachy keen. For the past year, he said, 'I'm on top of it. No problem.' Actually, we've got a *big* problem."

Do you detect a thread running through these stories? One partner let the other down or failed to follow through. One partner dropped the ball, blew it, made a mess of things. Countless times we've heard spouses complain that they can't make any financial progress because their partner makes poor decisions, behaves dishonestly, or shows no commitment to their plans. Such carelessness and thoughtlessness are not only tough on financial goals, but they are also hard on the relationship.

Relationships in which one person pulls most of the weight—or

¢ OUR ADVENTURE IN ACCOUNTABILITY

It was a warm spring morning, the sun was shining, and the mountains were coming to life. I (Scott) sprang out of bed with one thing on my mind: *This is the weekend I'm going to conquer a Fourteener!* (That's what folks in Colorado call a mountain over 14,000 feet). Naturally, I needed some new equipment. I headed off to REI with visions of a new pack, boots, and other cool gear.

I never should have left the house without Bethany.

After an hour-long shopping spree, I drove home with $300 worth of equipment. Since Bethany and I have a standing agreement to check in with each other before purchasing anything over $100, I knew I'd blown it. Now I had to be accountable for my impulsive acquisitions.

After showing Bethany my new equipment, I confessed that I broke our $100 rule and awaited my "punishment." Bethany, who is gracious about these things, looked over my purchases and proposed a solution—one that involved accountability. How about if I kept $200 worth of gear and returned the rest? Fair enough. Minutes later, I was in the car and headed back to REI. An argument was diverted and no voices were raised, because we made a quick decision and exercised mutual accountability.

worse, when one person feels deceived by the other—are bound to sputter and stagger. That's not what you want. You want a relationship built on mutual trust, respect, honesty, and reliability. You want to know you can count on each other, so you can make financial progress and enjoy your marriage.

Why Some Partners Are Unreliable

When our partner lets us down in some way, we're often left scratching our heads. We wonder how the person could have said one thing and done another. As we've counseled couples regarding their personal finances and talked with many frustrated spouses, we've come to believe there are four typical reasons a partner will be erratic and unreliable with money decisions.

Ambivalence about Priorities

Leadership and business experts talk about the importance of "buy-in" from employees to keep them motivated and moving toward objectives. They have to believe wholeheartedly in the course of action they're pursuing or their vacillation will show up in their performance. What's true for the workplace is also true at home. We've noticed that some couples are not on the same page financially—and have the feeling of being let down—because they are not in complete agreement about their priorities and goals. Or maybe they do agree, but one person is much more committed than the other.

Not long ago, a woman named Jean told us, "I don't get it. Mark and I sat down on New Year's Day and identified one goal for the year: pay off our Visa bill. We both agreed, and Mark even wrote out the goal in big, bold letters on a piece of paper, which is now hanging on our refrigerator. But Mark keeps buying power tools and woodworking supplies, and just last week he bought a new set of golf clubs. Our Visa bill is expanding, not shrinking! I assumed he was with me in this, but I guess not."

Mark may have agreed to their resolution, but it's obvious he wasn't seriously committed to it—at least not to the degree Jean was. In the next chapter, we'll talk in detail about the value of dreaming together and setting mutual goals. When two people join forces in pursuit of a shared ambition, the result is powerful! For now, it's important to realize that when one person is not sharing the burden of working toward set financial goals, it may be that he or she is simply not wholeheartedly devoted to the goal.

Outright Deception

It's a fact of life that money brings out the best in some people and the worst in others. We've known folks whose healthy perspective toward money enabled them to be generous, charitable, and big hearted. And unfortunately, we've also known people whose distorted view of money leads them to lie, cheat, and deceive. Sometimes these lies are blatant, as with the woman who tells her husband, "I haven't bought a single piece of clothing for six months." Yet tucked in the back of her closet is a brand-new Nordstrom outfit. Sometimes the lies are less obvious, as with the man who "rounds down" the cost of his new car to make it more palatable to his wife. Honesty is a mandatory prerequisite to a healthy relationship; sadly, some partners haven't embraced this truth—and the relationship suffers.

> When two people join forces in pursuit of a shared ambition, the result is powerful!

Benign Neglect

Unlike those who knowingly and willfully deceive their partner, other people have no malicious intent—they just forget things, procrastinate, or avoid undesirable tasks. They don't mean any harm, but their behavior is frustrating nonetheless. These are the men and women who are "flying blind" (see chapter 5), and this is especially tough when a "blind" person is married to someone whose financial vision is 20/20.

A Serious Money Problem

A growing number of people in our consumer-driven society develop chronic spending problems, such as compulsive shopping. It's tempting to laugh this off ("She's never met a sale she didn't like!") or minimize the significance ("At least she's not an alcoholic or gambling addict"), but compulsive shopping can be a serious issue that affects *both* partners. These people hide purchases, buy things with cash so their spouse won't notice, and open secret charge accounts. It's easy to justify spending, since shopping is a social activity and our culture zealously encourages buying. At some point, though, the spouse who doesn't shop is going to wake up and say, "Where's all our money going? It just seems to disappear."

The Importance of Mutual Accountability

Many people in our society bristle at the thought of being accountable to someone else in any way, shape, or form. These folks cling to the attitude that says, "My business is my business—and my business is none of your business." They don't want to be told what to do, and they don't want to be held responsible for their actions.

This kind of thinking is toxic for marriages. When two people agree to marry, they also agree to give up some of their freedoms. This doesn't mean they sacrifice their individuality and uniqueness. It does mean, however, that their two lives overlap and intertwine. Let's face it—spouses are interconnected in a thousand different ways, and their actions dramatically affect each other.

The best couples we know—by that we mean the most happily married and financially prosperous—are mutually accountable to each other. It's not that they try to control each other, nitpick about every dollar spent, and harangue one another about mistakes. They communicate openly, refuse to hide things, and commit to making mutual decisions. In short, they accept the fact that their individual actions affect both of them.

Linda Waite, in her book *The Case for Marriage*, stressed how tight the connection is between marriage and money.

¢

REQUIRED: PERSONAL RESPONSIBILITY

In order for accountability to work within a relationship, both partners must be willing to take responsibility for their actions and attitudes. Shifting blame for past mistakes and giving excuses make progress impossible.

Of course, personal responsibility is in short supply these days. People blame their parents, their DNA, their teachers—anyone but themselves—for failures and flaws. If you want to change your course, you have to *own* your decisions. You cannot blame anyone for your situation. Your partner will be more willing to offer forgiveness and commit to the future together if you 'fess up rather than say, "It wasn't my fault!"

Married couples monitor each other's spending, but in a way that emphasizes their joint economic future rather than each person's right to spend his or her own money. Because they see themselves as an economic unit, married couples also benefit from specialization—the partner who is better at budgeting and handling money, for example, can act for the two of them....

Married people consider their money and their property to be shared. This financial union is one of the cornerstones (along with sexual union) of what Americans means by marriage. In fact, marriage can almost be defined as a twin union of bed and bank account.[1]

Dr. Waite raises a point that we emphasize with every couple we work with: mutual accountability in marriage is a way to build unity and create a bright future together. It is not a straitjacket, prison, or ball-and-chain. We often say that accountability is not punitive but positive. It is a way to utilize each person's strengths, avoid blind spots, and get a second opinion about important decisions. Psychologist Archibald Hart hit the nail on the head when he said, "Accountability to another is the only way to safeguard against poor judgment, unconscious motivations, and self-deception."[2]

We like to think of accountability in the way biblical writers intended. The writer of Proverbs wrote that "as iron sharpens iron, so one man sharpens another" (27:17). And in Ecclesiastes, Solomon wrote, "Two can accomplish more than twice as much as one, for the results can be much better. If one falls, the other pulls him up; but if a man falls when he is alone, he's in trouble" (4:9–10 TLB). That's the idea. A man and woman agree to be honest, open, and vulnerable with each other for the sake of their collective success.

The Ingredients of Accountability

In the previous chapter, we encouraged you and your spouse to view each other as allies, not adversaries. Teamwork is the key not only to marital happiness, but also to financial success. Let's amplify that theme for the purpose of our discussion about accountability. We like to use the acronym TEAM to break down the components of accountability into four easy-to-remember parts.

Tell the truth. For mutual accountability to succeed and serve a purpose, you both need to tell the truth, the whole truth, and nothing but the truth. A marriage has so much to gain if both partners can rest assured that every message they send each other is honest and true.

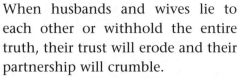

HOW CHANGE HAPPENS

Leadership expert John Maxwell offers these thoughts on transformation. "When it comes to change, there are three seasons of timing: People change when they hurt enough that they have to, when they learn enough that they want to, and when they receive enough that they are able to."[3]

When husbands and wives lie to each other or withhold the entire truth, their trust will erode and their partnership will crumble.

Encourage each other. Every person on earth responds better to the carrot than to the stick. It's hard to imagine anyone being nagged, badgered, and belittled into changing. So if you want to see your partner improve in a particular area, offer lots of encouragement and affirmation. As the apostle Paul said, "Speak encouraging words to one another. Build up hope so you'll all be together in this" (1 Thess. 5:11 MSG). Hope is what keeps people moving forward, and encouragement is what gives people hope.

Agree on action steps. Both you and your partner must consent to a plan of action to keep your financial situation and your relationship moving forward. Identify specific assignments and roles for each person, utilizing the strengths offered by both.

Meet consistently. Accountability won't happen if there is no regular communication. If one partner has a history of letting things fall through the cracks, it would be helpful to meet at least once a week. It may take only five minutes to discuss spending decisions, budget updates, and tasks that need to be accomplished. Consistent check-in times will assure both spouses that they're fulfilling their assignments.

* * *

We can imagine that some people reading this chapter find the idea of accountability intimidating, if not infuriating. Keep in mind that this is a positive tool to help ensure financial growth and marital harmony. Committing to work together and to take responsibility will foster a strong partnership.

CHAPTER FIFTEEN

DARE TO DREAM

C all this the parable of the two Winnebagos.

In the movie *About Schmidt*, Jack Nicholson stars as Warren Schmidt, a man leading a life of quiet desperation. As he retires from a vice president's job at Woodmen of the World Insurance Company, he looks back on a meaningless life and ahead to a meaningless retirement.

The only plans Warren and his wife have are to travel the highways and byways in their new Winnebago. But everything about Warren's countenance—his slumped shoulders and hangdog expression—betrays his lack of enthusiasm about cruising the country in a massive motor home. When his wife serves him a surprise breakfast at the tiny kitchen table in the RV, Warren can hardly conceal his displeasure with the turn his life has taken.

One day, while watching television, Warren sees an opportunity to give money and write letters to an underprivileged child in Tanzania. Warren responds to the appeal, and throughout the movie he faithfully sends the $22 a month and writes poignant letters to a child named Ndugu.

Not long after Warren's retirement, his wife dies unexpectedly, intensifying Warren's lack of purpose and direction. He decides to carry on with the travel plans, and the aimless wandering in the huge vehicle becomes a metaphor for his life. He rambles through desolate countryside with gray clouds overhead. He stops at cheesy tourist spots that are insipid and impersonal. Even his attempt to stop his only daughter from marrying an underachieving waterbed salesman is in vain.

After one long road trip, Warren comes home to his soundless, empty house. He reluctantly walks in with an armload of tedious junk mail. Warren ambles up the stairs and looks disappointedly at the disheveled state of his bedroom. Throughout the scene, the audience hears Warren's voice-over narration of a letter he composed to Ndugu in which he pours out his feelings of futility.

> I know we are all pretty small in the scheme of things, and I guess the best you can hope for is to make some kind of difference. What difference have I made? What in the world is better because of me? I am weak, and I am a failure. There's just no getting around it. Real soon I will die. Maybe twenty years, maybe tomorrow, it doesn't matter. Once I am dead and everyone who knew me dies, it is as though I never existed. What difference has my life made to anyone? None that I can think of. Hope things are fine with you.

> Yours truly, Warren Schmidt

The movie ends on a high note (such as it is) when Warren receives a letter and crayoned picture from Ndugu. Warren lifts his tired hands to his face and cries, realizing he has had at least a small measure of influence on someone's life.[1]

If that story sounds dreary, stay tuned for the second part of our parable. This is a tale that also features a Winnebago—but this one is true and decidedly more uplifting. Fifteen years ago, I (Bethany) sat down with a pastor named Sam. He had a dream of putting himself in a financial position to buy a nice Winnebago and drive around the country with his wife, Sally. If that ambition is reminiscent of Warren Schmidt and his wife, all similarities end there.

If used wisely, money can help you achieve your ambitions and aspirations.

Although Sam and Sally looked forward to seeing the United States, they had a much bigger aim in mind. They wanted to invest their retirement years in worthwhile ministry. Specifically, their goal was to help struggling churches throughout the country and encourage stressed-out pastors. With financial freedom and mobility, they could go wherever they felt God calling them.

Sam and Sally had the foresight to look ahead and plan for a fruitful retirement, and I helped them devise a savings schedule to help accomplish their goal. It worked. Sam and Sally stuck with their savings plan, and today they are living their dream. They travel all over the country, meeting wonderful people and serving in truly meaningful ways.

"We're having the time of our lives," Sam told us recently. "Every day is rich and rewarding as we are given great opportunities to serve people and make a difference. Plus, our marriage is as strong as ever, because we're working side by side. This may be the best part of our entire lives."

Next time you pass a Winnebago on the highway and notice the driver and passenger wearing wide, contented smiles, you might have seen Sam and Sally en route to their next adventure.

The Power of Dreams

Our work as financial professionals is fulfilling in many ways, but perhaps the most fulfilling is this: we get to hear about couples' dreams and help them devise plans to accomplish them. Isn't this the primary reason all of us work and earn money—to be able to pursue our hopes and dreams? We often tell couples that money in itself has no power; it's just a tool, a commodity. But it does have the

¢ FOUR DISTINCTIVES OF DYNAMIC DREAMS

1. Your dream should be personal and unique to you. In other words, don't let other people impose their dreams on you. You will own your dream and invest energy into it only if it is *yours*. Far too many goal-setting tools are based on what some "expert" believes you should want instead of what you want. Parents and other family members, too, may have ideas about your purpose and direction. Take in all the counsel and opinions from others—then determine your own dreams.

2. Your dream should tap into your spiritual values. There's nothing wrong with dreaming about owning a red convertible or climbing Mount Everest. But we believe the most powerful dreams are those that have a transcendent quality to them. Dreams that involve changing people's lives, helping the needy, and making the world a better place are those that inspire and motivate us most.

3. Your dream should make you stretch but still be attainable. What's the point of dreaming about something that's easy to achieve? The best marital dreams are those that stretch our ability to plan, activate our imagination, and demand our full talents. Our dream needs to be big enough so that we must work to realize it. At the same time, the dream should be within the scope of reality.

4. Your dream should involve both partners. You may have individual dreams: you want to run a marathon, and your spouse wants to become an expert bridge player. That's fine, but we also encourage you to set some goals that engage and energize both of you.

power to propel you toward your goals. If used wisely, money can help you achieve your ambitions and aspirations.

For the past several chapters we've been discussing key ways that you and your partner can overcome conflicts, develop unity, and enjoy harmony in matters of love and money. The ability to dream together is yet another essential ingredient. After all, our deeply held goals are promises and prizes dangling out in front of us—and the wise handling of money is one of the ways we move toward those sought-after treasures. Here are some of the dreams couples have told us about within the past month.

Rene, age 40: "Ever since I was a little girl playing with dolls, I've dreamed of being a mom and raising a child. I always said that if God blessed me with a child, I'd be a stay-at-home mom at least until he or she was ten years old. (This is because my own parents were busy and gone so much of the time.) My husband and I went through many heartbreaking years when we could not get pregnant. Finally, God provided us with a beautiful baby girl to adopt. Jasmine is the greatest gift we could have imagined, and I'm happy to say I'm able to be home with her full time. Since we make an average income, this required tough financial choices and creative thinking. But it's worked out and I'm living my dream."

> Life is too precious to waste chasing things and pursing goals that don't really matter.

Dean and Jo, ages 43 and 41: "We were deeply in debt from day one of our marriage. (Actually, before that, since we both carried debt *into* the marriage.) Anyone who owes a lot of money knows the heavy burden it is. So our dream has been to get out of debt once and for all—and stay that way. For ten years, we stuck to a very strict payoff plan, and last month our outstanding balance hit zero. We can't adequately express how free we feel! Without that weight constantly holding us back, the future is wide open to us. With one dream accomplished, we can start thinking about the next one."

Jerome, age 38: "Ever since my dad died of cancer twelve years ago, I felt a strong desire to volunteer with cancer patients and their families. I know the heartache involved, and I knew I could offer help, since I've been there. For a long time, this dream seemed impossible as I got lured into the corporate world as a director of marketing for a big software company. This position came with a high salary and huge demands (lots of travel and sixty-plus hours every week). Several years ago, I started thinking strategically and began socking away as much money as I could. Then last year I negotiated with my company to reduce my hours (and salary) to work four days a week and travel no more than once a month. Now, every Friday I volunteer at the local hospice and cancer support group. It's the best thing I've ever done."

> The best relationships involve people who have a clear vision of the life they are pursuing together.

So let us ask you, what do you really want in life? What are your highest priorities? Your dream may be to restore antique cars, take your family on a European vacation, or put your kids through college. You may want to buy a bigger house, start your own business, or give a lot of money to your church or favorite charity. All of those are worthwhile goals. No one can tell you what your dream should be, so long as you have one.

Some couples we work with believe in the importance of setting goals and defining their purpose, and they intend to do it *someday*. Some of these folks yield to the tyranny of the urgent, insisting they're too busy to indulge in dreaming. We understand that. Our typical week is spent taxiing kids to appointments, managing a growing business, standing in line at the grocery store, and responding to dozens of phone calls and emails.

We've noticed that an awful lot of couples spend their lives scurrying around at a dizzying pace without a clear idea of what's important to them. They expend a lot of energy sprinting here and there but with only a vague sense of their true destination. In our view, life is too precious to waste chasing things and pursing goals that don't really matter. So we want to challenge you to identify dreams and goals for your individual lives and your marriage. Become clear about where you want to go and how you'll get there. Dream big, and set about turning those dreams into reality. Let us point out a few reasons why dreams are so valuable to couples.

Dreams Keep You Moving Forward

USE A "DREAM BOARD"

When we work with clients, we suggest they use a "dream board." This is a collage you put together with words, pictures, and articles related to your dreams. It is an excellent visual reminder and a conversation piece for you and your spouse.

Identifying hopes and dreams provides the motivation to press on. As writer Elizabeth Cody Newenhuyse said, "Dreams have the power to drive and animate a marriage. We may nurture some of the same dreams; we may each hold a private fancy. But we need that courage, that hope. Dreams—hope with a blueprint—help construct a meaning for the future. They give us a reason to wake in the morning."2

Sadly, we've worked with many people who seem to go through their daily existence on autopilot. They trudge into the office each morning, fulfill their obligations, and wait for their paycheck. They watch the clock tick down and tear off pages from the calendar while they anticipate retirement. There's got to be more to life than that.

Plenty of other people, thankfully, approach each day with enthusiasm and energy. They go about their lives with a sense of mission. They can echo the words of the apostle Paul: "Forgetting what is behind and straining toward what is ahead, I press on toward the goal to win the prize for which God has called me" (Phil. 3:13–14). We believe that the happiest individuals and the happiest married couples are those who have a clear sense of purpose and direction.

Dreams Bind Partners Together

The great writer Antoine de Saint-Exupéry once said, "Love does not consist in gazing at each other, but in looking outward together in the same direction." Discussing your hopes and dreams develops intimacy, because the information you share is so personal and meaningful. There is something magical about merging our aspirations for the future with someone else's. And working toward the realization of shared dreams bonds a couple together. We believe the best relationships involve people who have a clear vision of the life they are pursuing together.

Among the many excellent psychologists who offer helpful advice, one of our favorites is Dr. Neil Clark Warren. And one reason we appreciate him so much is his emphasis on dreaming together as marriage partners. He said,

> When two people dream together, they merge the resources of their deepest, most powerful centers. They each have tremendous personal power when they access the core emotions and longings in their individual centers. When they pool this power and focus it for the benefit of all three of them—each of them individually and the two of them as a couple—they become significantly stronger than they could be as two separate individuals....
>
> Dreaming and envisioning together are the essence of romance! Show me a couple who dreams about their future together and I will show you a couple who is deeply in love. People who help each other access and focus their individual and corporate dreams are vital to one another. There is nothing in the world so attractive as someone who will dream with us, merge their dreams with our own, clarify the path toward the actualization of the dream, and lock their arms into ours while walking the path.[3]

> Discussing your hopes and dreams develops intimacy, because the information you share is so personal and meaningful.

Dreaming together adds spice and exhilaration to a relationship. When we sense our marriage is growing stagnant, we can focus on our dreams and renew our excitement about the future we're pursuing together.

Dreams Foster Communication

There are few things couples enjoy discussing more than their goals. Partners talk about the direction they're heading, contribute new ideas, and reaffirm their commitment to their objectives.

One couple told us recently, "We've always dreamed of building a cozy log cabin in the woods. We talk about it quite a bit. We cut pictures

DREAMS REQUIRE CONTINUAL NURTURE

¢

Dr. David Niven, pro-
fessor of psychology
at Florida Atlantic
University, encourages
couples to keep their
aspirations fresh and
current. "When a rela-
tionship has a success-
ful history, some may
imagine that the work
has already been
accomplished. But that
is no more true than
imagining that suc-
cessful gardeners can
skip watering and fer-
tilizing this year
because of their good
track record. The fact
that you have experi-
ence and confidence
in your relationship
means that you know
what needs to be
done. It does not
mean that you can
ignore things that
need to be done
because you've done
them before. The task
of a successful rela-
tionship never ends
because the point of a
relationship is to build
toward the future, not
the past."⁴

out of magazines and take day trips into the mountains to look at other people's cabins. We talk about how fun it will be to take weekend get-aways with our family and friends. This is a great connecting point for us, and we feel lots of energy between us as we dream together."

Dreams fuel our imagination and give us something to discuss besides bills and budgets and schedules. Like us, you probably find that conversation easily slips into the mundane and monotonous. Did you remember to pay the phone bill? When is the plumber going to come unclog the sink? What should we make the kids for dinner—mac and cheese or sloppy joes? Having dreams to discuss lifts us out of the hum-drum routine and gets us in touch with the more profound aspects of life.

The Road Map for Realizing Dreams

We've known plenty of people who talk and talk about their dreams but don't do anything about them. You probably know some folks like that, too. They're great at formulating visions and conjuring lofty plans, but they are incapable of implementing a plan of action to bring them to fruition.

We want to encourage you to figure out how to turn your dreams into reality. Don't settle for goals that forever remain hypothetical and spec-ulative. Create a plan and a strategy to reach your goals and fulfill your aspirations. As we talk with couples about how their dreams overlap with their financial situation, we always suggest the following steps:

1. Begin with the end in mind. This means knowing where you want to end up even before thinking about how you'll get there. We've worked with many people who have a hard time breaking out of a short-term perspective. They seem unable to see beyond the immediate circumstances, or perhaps no further than a few years into the future. It's important to take the long view and envision what your lives and marriage will look like when your dream is realized. Once you know where you want to end up, *then* you can begin putting an action plan in place.

2. Define your dream as precisely as possible. Sometimes when we ask our clients about their dreams, they'll say, "I'd like to retire early," or, "I've always wanted to travel the world." Those are good *general* ideas, but those people need to make their dreams much clearer and more precise. More helpful responses would be, "I am going to retire no later than age fifty-eight," and, "By the time I'm sixty-five, I want to visit each country on my top-ten list. Anything after that is a bonus." The more specific your dream is, the better your chances of attaining it.

3. Establish incremental goals and checkpoints. With your exact destination in mind, begin piecing together attainable steps that will advance you toward your ultimate goal. If you have no way of measuring your progress, you'll never know if you're moving in the right direction. Let's suppose your goal is to cut down to part-time work in fifteen years so you can volunteer with underprivileged children. In order to do this, you'll need to save $60,000 to supplement your income (in addition to any retirement savings). It becomes a simple matter of arithmetic: in five years, you'll need $20,000 in the bank; in ten years, you'll need $40,000, and so on. An even better way to segment your goals is into one-year increments, which provides a sense of accomplishment and progress as you move forward. In

FOCUS ON THE FUTURE

Financial consultants Mary Claire Allvine and Christine Larson have found that many money arguments arise because couples are focusing on the wrong things. "For some couples, every money discussion ends in a fight so they just avoid the topic. But the truth is that many of these couples simply haven't started talking about money at the right point. Their money discussions start and end with the bills and the checkbook—not with their dreams and goals. In the end, setting goals together and figuring out how to achieve them in the years ahead can be a deeply romantic, energizing experience."[5]

Dr. Neil Clark
Warren, one of the
nation's foremost
experts on relation-
ships, connects the
quality of your
dreams to the quality
of your marriage.
"Sometimes I wonder
if it is really possible
to dream such a big
dream that it is actu-
ally beyond what we
can finally attain. In
fact, I have begun to
sense that the great-
ness of a marriage is
correlated to the size
and passion of the
dream two lovers
have for their lives
together. Magnificent
marriages involve
two people who
dream magnificently.
The partners encour-
age each other to
dig deeper and
dream bigger, and in
the process they get
in touch with a level
of being and doing
that otherwise would
be far beyond
them."6

this case, you would need to save $4,000 each year. That sounds far less daunting than needing to accumulate $60,000.

4. Review your progress periodically. If you have incremental goals, it is easy to evaluate how you're doing. Compare the current status with the place you should be according to your long-range plan. You may want to establish an annual check-in date (New Year's Day or your wedding anniversary) to monitor your progress.

5. If you get offtrack, make adjustments. Somewhere along the line, you may realize you've veered off course. Perhaps unforeseen expenses or other setbacks have slowed your progress. It may be that your incremental goals were unrealistic to begin with. Instead of allowing obstacles to permanently derail you, make corrections and adjustments in your plans. You may need to extend the time frame or scale back the scope of your ultimate goal—retire at fifty-eight instead of fifty-five, or plan to visit eight foreign countries instead of ten.

6. Include some "stretch" goals along the way. In addition to your incremental goals, try to include a few goals that require extra effort but will help you leap ahead. For instance, if your goal is to save $4,000 per year, you may occasionally say to yourself, *This year, I'm going to really tighten the belt and save $6,000.* Come up with creative ways to stretch yourself. We encourage our staff and clients to include stretch goals every week, month, and year. You'd be surprised how much you can accomplish when you push yourself.

7. Be willing to flex and shift. Our values and priorities have a way of shifting over the years, and some of your dreams may become obsolete. That's fine. Clinging to goals that you're no

longer passionate about makes no sense. For us, having children initi-
ated a major change in priorities. Some of our previous goals involved
things we wanted to accomplish as a couple. But when we welcomed
our boys into the family, we replaced some of our "twosome" goals with
"foursome" goals.

8. Keep each other accountable. As we said in the previous chapter,
it's nearly impossible to achieve your financial goals without accountability within your relationship. Your biggest dreams offer the biggest
opportunity to work together to make them happen. This requires ded-
ication and commitment by both partners, and you'll need to be
answerable to each other all along the way.

Let us tell you about one of our own dreams. Although we have
goals related to our kids' college education, growing our business, and
remaining debt free, we have a dream for the future that we cherish.
One of our favorite things to do is to travel together, and some of our
best memories as a couple have been flying off to far-flung places
around the world. So we came up with this dream. Early in our retirement, we plan to devote one full year to visiting four of our best-loved
places. This means we will spend three months in each place, and both
of us get to choose two locations. At this point, our list includes New
York, California, Switzerland, and Wales.

Writing out these steps has been helpful to us in more ways than
one. It's further clarified our dream and generated lots of enthusiasm.
Even though retirement for us is still a long way off, that travel adventure sounds like a blast, and we can hardly wait. We encourage you and
your partner to go through this process as well. Think through the
steps, and write down your own plan of action.

* * *

Ray and Florence Borquez of Los Angeles have been married since
1946—more than fifty years and going strong! When they were asked
the secret of their marital success, they pointed first to the need for
common goals. Here's what they said.

> What better partnership is there than that of a loving hus-
> band and wife striving together to achieve common objectives?
> And who better to join forces with than the one you love, the per-
> son with whom you've chosen to share your deepest hopes, fond-
> est dreams, your very life?

One of the biggest problems marriages face today is that spouses cling to their own individuality rather than fully entering into their new identity as a couple. They hold on to independence at the expense of the unity God intended, maintaining separate checkbooks, separate pursuits, separate vacations, separate friends. Oftentimes they unknowingly have different visions for their marriage and their future....

God has designed marriage to make the two of you stronger together than you ever were when you were single. As a result, you don't need to be afraid to set big goals.[7]

We can all take a lesson from these wise veterans of marriage. Let's dream big and envision wonderful things for our future together. The quality of our lives and the quality of our relationships are sure to benefit.

PART FOUR

DEVELOPING A POSITIVE, PROSPEROUS PARTNERSHIP

*Five Hot Buttons on Which Couples Need
Compatible Perspectives*

CHAPTER SIXTEEN

A BUDGET IS YOUR FRIEND ... REALLY!

Just say the word *budget* to your spouse, and you're sure to get some sort of reaction. It might be a sigh of relief or an expression of sheer panic, but it will definitely be a response!

Budgeting is simply one of those topics about which everybody has an opinion. It's hard to feel neutral about the topic. Depending on your past experiences with budgets, the word might evoke any combination of emotions: guilt, failure, relief, inadequacy, triumph, confidence, or resignation. Finding out what the word signifies to you and to your spouse is a good place to begin.

Sara had been trying to get her husband to stick to a budget for years. After several years of marriage—and financial tension!—she asked him what came to his mind when she said the word *budget*.

John winced. "Sara, when I was a kid, I wore holes in my jeans long before tattered jeans were in. I heard 'No, we can't afford that' so many times I swore that when I grew up, I'd buy whatever I wanted. I promised myself I'd never feel like a second-class citizen again."

Second-class citizen? Sara was appalled. She had no idea that every time she'd pestered John about sticking to a budget, he was hearing the message "second-class citizen." She was also relieved to realize that, when John resisted her budget, he wasn't fighting Sara but ghosts from his poverty-stricken childhood.

Did these discoveries revolutionize John and Sara's finances overnight? Nope. But they did open the door for the kinds of discussions this couple needed to have in order to begin handling their finances as a team.

Before you and your spouse have your next conversation about the family budget, take this quiz. Each of you answer the question, "When I hear the word *budget*, what thoughts or emotions do I experience?"

Husband	Wife
__ Guilt	__ Guilt
__ Resignation	__ Resignation
__ Relief	__ Relief
__ Anxiety	__ Anxiety
__ Inadequacy	__ Inadequacy
__ Failure	__ Failure
__ Confidence	__ Confidence
__ Dread	__ Dread
__ Anticipation	__ Anticipation
__ Excitement	__ Excitement
__ Pride	__ Pride

Now look at your list compared to your partner's. Do your answers shed any light on why the two of you have either clashed or complemented each other on budget issues in the past? Based on what you've just discovered about your partner, do you have any thoughts on how to better approach the topic of budgeting in the future?

Your Budget: Friend or Foe?

What is the purpose of a budget? For some people, budgets appear to be designed to restrict, limit, and hinder. These people see budgets as a necessary evil, as foe instead of friend. Other people look at the exact same budget and see something completely different. To these folks, the purpose of a budget is not to hinder but to help, direct, and guide, to bring sanity and even freedom. For these folks, a realistic budget is an ally, not an adversary.

How you view the purpose of your budget is pivotal. Your perspective impacts your success because it determines whether you use it or refuse it. If you're still not sure how you feel, consider a few of the ways a budget will benefit you and your spouse.

• Reviewing a budget in a weekly or monthly powwow encourages you and your partner to communicate about the important things in your life together—things such as finances, goals, lifestyle choices, parenting, and so on.

• A budget provides you and your partner with the kind of mutual accountability we discussed in chapter 14. It allows both of you to see in black and white who is spending how much and on what.

• It can be a unifying experience for a couple to create a budget together and then figure out how to stick to it. A budget, in a small way, creates a "we're in this together" attitude, a spirit of teamwork.

• When you regularly review your budget with your spouse, it can help you both focus on your "big picture" goals in life. After all, a budget isn't really about dollars and cents. It's actually about priorities. Working through your financial priorities requires you to grapple with your life priorities at the same time.

• A budget doesn't restrict you from owning good things. On the contrary, a budget actually enables you to purchase the things you really want. How many times have you been unable to afford something you truly wanted or needed because earlier in the month you unthinkingly spent money on things you could have done without? A budget allows you to make an informed choice: Starbucks lattes every morning or cable Internet service? A new bookcase for the den or a weekend getaway with the kids? If you don't have a budget, you don't get to choose—you get whatever you happen to spend your money on first. In contrast, a budget allows you to look at the entire month

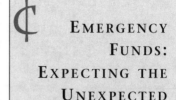

EMERGENCY FUNDS: EXPECTING THE UNEXPECTED

For many people, their budget gets blown apart the moment they have an unexpected expense and no way to pay for it. They're forced to use credit cards or borrow money from another budget category, which throws everything else out of whack. Here's a better solution: from your net income, take at least 5 percent right off the top and put into savings before you pay any other bills. This 5 percent is what we call an emergency fund. If you cannot afford that much at first, at least put something (even 1 or 2 percent) into savings, and increase the amounts as your debts get paid off.

before it begins and make an informed choice. With a budget, you can choose to purchase the things that really matter to you.

• A budget can help you avoid some of the things that couples without a budget experience. For example, a budget can keep you from lying wide eyed in bed at 3 A.M. wondering how on earth you managed to get so far in debt. A budget can keep you from having to check "yes" on every job, loan, or credit application that asks the question, "Have you ever declared bankruptcy?" A budget can even keep you from those month-end marital spats spurred on by one or more unpleasant financial discoveries.

Communication, accountability, team spirit, shared priorities, peace of mind, and marital harmony! If you and your spouse experienced a little more of any of these things, how might your marriage benefit?

It all comes down to attitude. Are you ready to embrace your new budget as the friend that it is? Is your spouse? If so, can each of you agree to the following statements?

- A budget is a good idea.
- Making informed choices about how we spend our resources is a good alternative to simply buying until we run low on money.
- I will track every penny I spend for one month (even those quick trips to the vending machine at work) so that my partner and I can make informed choices about future expenditures.
- I will powwow with my partner either weekly or monthly—whatever we decide—and review our financial successes as well as the areas where we still need to try harder.
- I will come to these discussions with an open mind.

Your Budget: Mastering the Mechanics

Creating a budget is not as complicated as it sounds. You don't need fancy software (unless you'd prefer to use it). Just grab a pen and paper. Here are the steps.

1. Discover Your Monthly Expenses

Do you find yourself at the end of each month looking at the balance in your checkbook, squeezing your head between your hands, and saying, "I don't understand! Where does it all go?!"

Chances are, your best intentions are being sabotaged by hidden spending habits. For example, you might be surprised to discover that your morning latte and muffin are costing you about eighty "unbudgeted" dollars each month. Or that what you're actually spending on gasoline is twice what you had budgeted before oil prices hiked and you agreed to carpool a bunch of kids all over town.

You will never have a good grasp on your finances as long as these sneaky hidden expenditures continue to ambush your budget. In order to successfully manage your money, you've got to tame these seemingly benign saboteurs. But first you've got to catch them.

> You will never have a good grasp on your finances as long as these sneaky hidden expenditures continue to ambush your budget.

Start by keeping a list of everything you spend money on for one month to see where your money is going. Everything means *everything*, including monthly bills and expenses, entertainment, parking—even the change you put in the soda machine. If you pay for the majority of your purchases with a check, credit card, or debit card, you may be able to shorten this timeline by recreating a fairly complete accounting of last month's expenditures by using banking statements.

Keeping a list of *everything* you spend for one month not only helps you identify legitimate monthly expenses, but it's also the best way to catch rogue expenditures beyond your budget. Once these hidden expenditures are known, you can make an informed choice: tame them by giving them a legitimate place in your budget or eliminate them. Teaching rogue expenditures to behave—to stand up and be counted, as it were—will help you take a giant step in the direction of your goals and dreams.

2. Identify Additional Expenses

After tracking your spending habits for one month, you've got a running start on creating a comprehensive list of your expenses. Now complete that list by adding things such as car registration, birthday and Christmas gifts, association dues, semiannual dental checkups, annual eye exams and glasses, insurance premiums, summer vacations, or other expenses that come due on a nonmonthly basis. So that your expenses in any given month are not considerably higher than other months, consider dividing these expenses into twelve equal monthly portions. Each month, add that amount of money to your savings. (For example, save $11 each month toward your $132 registration due each July and so on.)

3. Determine Your Net Spendable Income Per Month

The formula to determine your monthly net spendable income is simple.

Monthly Gross Household Income = $_____
Less Giving/Tithe (10%)
Less Taxes (____%)
Monthly Net Spendable Income = $_____

4. Put Your Budget Together

Now that you have determined what you are spending your money on, it's time to organize it. Put all of your expenditures into categories. Be sure to keep it simple. Here are some suggestions.

Sample Budget Categories

Housing	$_____
Food	$_____
Auto	$_____
Insurance	$_____
Debts	$_____
Entertainment/Recreation	$_____
Clothing	$_____
Savings	$_____
Retirement savings	$_____
Medical expenses	$_____
Miscellaneous	$_____
School expenses	$_____
Child-care expenses	$_____
Total expenses/month	$_____

Remember that you're taking stock of what you spend each month in *general* categories. The "Housing" category, for instance, should include your mortgage or rent, utilities (gas/water/electric), telephone bill, waste removal services, and the like. Next, determine what percent you spend in each category. This will help you see where your money is being spent.

> When you regularly review your budget with your spouse, it can help you both focus on your "big picture" goals in life.

There are various views as to what percentages of your income *should* be spent in each of these categories. For instance, the people we work with who live in states such as California or Florida, where real estate and rent are expensive, often find their housing percentage is much higher then the percentage listed. Remember these are just average guidelines.

Recommended Spending Percentages (Gross Income $5,000)

Gross Household Income = $5,000
Less Giving/Tithe (10%) ($500)
Less Taxes (20%) ($1,000)
Net Spendable Income = $3,500 (per month)

Net Spendable Income
(Percentages below add to 100%)

Housing	33%	($1,155)
Food	12%	($420)
Auto	12%	($420)
Insurance	5%	($175)
Debts	5%	($175)
Entertainment/Recreation	6%	($210)
Clothing	5%	($175)
Savings	5%	($175)
Medical	4%	($140)
Miscellaneous	5%	($175)
Retirement	8%	($280)

BUDGETS AND ¢ THE BUGS BUNNY EFFECT

With tongue in cheek, financial writer Jeff Opdyke explained why it's so hard to stick with a budget. "Basically, a budget is your road map from wherever you are to wherever it is you hope to go. Of course, lots of people read maps about as well as they read Sanskrit. If you reflect back on your knowledge of Bugs Bunny cartoons, you might recall that many a time the wabbit popped up in some unexpected locale only to realize yet again that he should've taken a left at Albuquerque.

"That's exactly how it is with budgets—you hang a right in Wal-Mart instead of left, and soon enough you're spending a couple hundred dollars on that DVD player instead of checking out with just a cheap extension cord in your bag…. One or two similar purchases and suddenly you've blown your budget for the month."2

A quick look at your spending will reveal if you are in the black or the red, the positive or the negative. Is the sum positive? Great. You make more than you spend. Apply the difference to your debt or savings.

If the sum is negative and your expenses exceed your income, you have two choices: make more money or spend less. For example, do you really need to spend $600 a month on groceries, or can you trim it down? Consider shopping for bargains, buying in bulk, and eating out less often. Is there a convenience or service you can do without? How many Netflix movies are you actually watching each month? Are there telephone services you're paying for that you rarely use? If you're paying for an expensive cell phone plan and ending up with unused minutes at the end of each month, switch to a lower-cost plan that better fits your needs.

5. Live Within Your Budget

If you have created a budget on paper that makes sense, you've come a long way. Now you need to use it! Here are some tips.

Make a date with your budget. Like any good relationship, your budget requires regular attention. We meet once a month for a powwow, but others prefer more often. Schedule a regular time (say, once a month or every two weeks) to pay bills and review your checkbook and budget. If you use a computer software program that syncs with your bank account, you may need to set aside ten minutes every couple of days to download and review your expenditures.

Communicate frequently with your spouse. Make sure you and your spouse include time in your powwow to talk about successes, failures, feelings, goals, and improvements associated with your budget.

Spend designated funds only on what they have been allocated for. If your budget calls for $100 to be designated for savings, don't use those dollars for lift tickets to go skiing instead. To help curb rogue spending, some people use the tried-and-true "envelope system." If you would like to try this, cash your paycheck and separate the cash into labeled envelopes. For example, if you have designated $500 per month for groceries, put $500 into an envelope marked "Groceries." When that money is gone, that's it for the month. While you will probably still need to write checks for mortgage and utilities, this system works well for groceries, gas, dry cleaning, entertainment, and similar expenses.

However you manage, refer often to your budget, and strive to spend designated amounts on designated items and nothing else. We have seen high-income couples use this system to get out of debt and get their budget under control.

Curb impulse spending. The next time you see something you just can't live without, ask yourself a few questions. Do you have the extra space in your home to store the item you're about to purchase? Will this item end up in the Goodwill donation box a year from now? Is this a matter of a short-term whim prevailing over a long-term plan? If all else fails, give yourself a twenty-four-hour "cooling-off" period to think about the purchase. Allow at least forty-eight hours for high-ticket items such as cars, home-theater systems, and time-shares.

Continue to increase your financial savvy. While some people seem born frugal, others need time to learn how to negotiate between necessities and luxuries. Continue developing your financial IQ. The following Web sites contain lots of great ideas and resources:

- www.stretcher.com. The Dollar Stretcher Web site is chock-full of articles dedicated to "Living better ... for less."

¢ **MAKING CENTS**

How many people use a budget? Almost half (43 percent) of people surveyed said they stick to a monthly budget most or all of the time. The same percentage confessed that they haven't even established a budget.[3]

"There is no dignity quite so impressive, and no independence quite so important, as living within your means."

—Calvin Coolidge

- www.thefrugalshopper.com. Includes tips on saving money, including deals and coupons designed to make your money go further.
- www.tightwad.com. Contains freebies and money-saving tips.

Finally, realize that the very fact you need a budget is a sign that you have been blessed. After all, a budget means that you have enough financial resources to require wise management! As you begin to see your budget as a reason for gratitude, a key to financial freedom, and a tool to improve communication and harmony in your marriage, we have no doubt that you will experience new levels of success—and lower levels of stress—with your finances and in your relationship with your spouse as well.

CHAPTER SEVENTEEN

FOCUS ON YOUR FUTURE

We frequently meet couples who have differing viewpoints on how to financially prepare for the future. One such couple was Todd and Melissa, and their situation was similar to many others we've seen.

Todd grew up in a family where his dad was a CPA. His dad started talking to him about retirement when Todd got his first job at age sixteen, frying burgers at McDonald's. He knew what a 401(k) was and how it worked before the average college graduate hit the workforce. Todd now appreciates the fact that his mom and dad have the luxury of spending time with their grandchildren and traveling whenever they want to.

Todd wants to put himself and Melissa in the same situation. He believes saving 20 percent of their income is necessary to achieve this goal.

Melissa, on the other hand, grew up in a rather well-to-do family. She has no idea what her parents' retirement resources look like. But she believes that someday she and Todd will receive a fairly large inheritance. Although she agrees that saving for retirement is important, she also believes that just taking advantage of the 401(k) matching programs offered by their employers will be sufficient.

This has become a source of conflict for them. Todd often insists, "We can't count on any inheritance. We need to save as much as we can now."

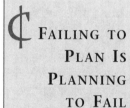

FAILING TO PLAN IS PLANNING TO FAIL

Financial consultant Venita Van Caspel offered wise counsel when she said, "It has been said that if you aim at nothing in life, you are likely to hit nothing! I have never had anyone come to me and say, 'I plan to fail.' Yet I have observed many who failed to plan and who unfortunately met with the same dismal results."[3]

Melissa counters by saying, "We have twenty-five years until retirement, and I would rather enjoy additional income now."

At first glance, it might seem that Melissa and Todd will never find common ground on which to stand together. In reality, they *can* find common ground—and so can you and your spouse.

Agreement, Then Action

We hope that you and your partner aren't as polarized in your viewpoints as Todd and Melissa. It might be that you both agree you need to prepare for retirement, but one of you wants the security of a savings account, while the other wants the potential greater return of stocks. Perhaps one of you is saying, "Retirement? What's that? I love what I do and plan on working till I drop!" And the other is saying, "Are you crazy? We're retiring as early as possible, so we can tour Europe and play golf and volunteer with kids while we're young enough to enjoy those things."

Of course, retirement may not be the only major financial event looming on your horizon. It may be that you want your children to attend college, but you have differing opinions about how to make that happen. Viewpoints can range from "they can work their way through college just like I did" to "let's pay for everything" and anything in between.

As you're reading this, it's possible that you're thinking, *I'm actually not sure how my spouse feels about some of this stuff. We've never actually discussed it!* If this were not a book on how to improve your marriage as well as your finances, we would launch directly into a discussion on how to financially prepare for your future. But as Todd and Melissa's relationship illustrates, when it comes to planning for your future as a couple, *agreement* needs to precede *action*. In fact, *agreement* and *action* are steps two and three. Step one is *disclosure*, and Todd and Melissa have taken that step. They may not agree on how—or even if—to plan for their future, but at least they have discussed the subject with each other.

MAKING CENTS

Who's socking away money? Only 52 percent of us have money saved up outside of a work-related savings or retirement plan. Nearly one-fifth of folks earning more than $50,000 a year have nothing saved.

How much do you contribute to your company's retirement plan? Only 14 percent of participants contribute the maximum amount to employer-sponsored 401(k)s and similar plans.[1]

What kinds of conversations have you had with your partner? If you have yet to really discuss the future together, here are a few questions to get the conversations started.

• "How do we envision our retirement years? What kind of lifestyle will we want, and what kind of retirement income will we need in order to sustain that lifestyle?"

• "Are we willing to consult a financial professional if there are indications that this might be helpful?"

• "When it comes to college for our kids, do we have a plan? What kind of financial responsibility will we assume at that time? Do we want to foot the entire bill? Encourage our child to live at home for free while attending a local college? Apply for grants and scholarships?"

• "To what degree are we willing to help elderly parents, should they need assistance? What plan do we have in place (or should we begin) to free up that money?"

> ¢ **NO END IN SIGHT?**
>
> The ancient sage Seneca could have been speaking about financial planning when he said, "We are always complaining that our days are few and acting as though there will be no end to them."

• "How can discussing our options and planning for our future strengthen our marriage now?"

Talking through issues such as these gets each of you thinking about the practical realities as well as the relational opportunities. These subjects can be divisive or unifying, depending on how they are approached. As we've said in earlier chapters, a teamwork mentality goes a long way toward strengthening your relationship *and* helping you to be wise money managers.

Getting Started: Debunking Common Myths about Retirement

If you think Social Security will get you through your golden years, think again. At best, Social Security may account for a *portion* of your retirement income. According to the US Census Bureau, people age sixty-five and older are getting only 38 percent of their income from Social Security. They are supplementing that income with current earnings (21 percent), income from various assets (19 percent), income from pensions (19 percent), and other sources (3 percent).[2] Some economists believe that Social Security will be even less of a factor in coming years, but even if these statistics hold true during your retirement, you will still need to come up with an estimated 60 percent of your living expenses in addition to whatever Social Security can provide.

Another common myth—particularly among young couples—is the idea that it's too soon to start planning (or saving) for retirement. Trust us, it is never too soon to start saving for retirement. In fact, the impact of beginning *today*—regardless of how young or old you may be—cannot be overstated. For example, if at age forty-five a person begins to save just $50 per month with an 8 percent annual return, by the time he is sixty-five. he will have a little more than $25,000 in principal and compounded interest. However, if a person begins to save that same $50 per month twenty years sooner—at age twenty-five—he will have made an additional two hundred forty payments into his savings account. That comes to an additional investment of about $12,000. Can you guess what his balance will be by the time he turns sixty-five? If you added $12,000 to the $25,000 for a total of $37,000, think again. With the magic of compounded interest, the sixty-five-year-old who began saving $50 a month at the age of twenty-five will not have $25,000 or even $37,000, but $175,000! (A plan of regular investing does not assure a profit or protect against loss in a declining market. An investor should consider his or her financial ability to continue an investment throughout periods of fluctuating price levels.)

WHAT ABOUT SELF-EMPLOYEED PEOPLE

If you are self-employed, you don't have the benefit of an employer who matches your retirement savings, but you still have options. Consider opening an IRA, a Roth IRA, or other plans available for individuals. Be sure to consult with your financial professional to assist you in finding the best option.

Whether you are twenty-five, thirty-five, or forty-five, there is no better time than today to begin saving dollars for your future needs. Even if you can't afford to save much, begin with a small amount and increase it as you are able. Over time, your money should grow. With the power of compounded interest, even modest savings—if made on a regular and ongoing basis—can accumulate into a substantial amount.

Taking Practical Steps

Whatever future event you are saving for—college tuition, retirement income, or anything else—the steps are the same: examine your current situation, determine how much you will need in the future, decide on a strategy, and evaluate your progress. Let's take a closer look.

1. Take Inventory

What resources are currently available to you? Examine your current situation as it pertains to your future financial needs: what do you currently have saved toward future needs and goals? Are you putting money aside every month for either your retirement or your children's educations? If so, how and how much?

What savings instruments or programs are available to you through your employer, and are you taking full advantage of them? For example, does your employer (or your spouse's employer) offer a retirement savings plan such as a 403(b) or 401(k)? Does your employer offer a retirement savings matching program? If so, for every dollar you save, your employer may match those funds up to 100 percent. If you aren't sure, check with your human resources department. When you put money into a traditional IRA, you reduce your current federal—and possibly state—taxable income and defer paying taxes until withdrawal. (For traditional IRAs, withdrawals are taxed as ordinary income for the year in which they are received. Tax penalties and penalties for early withdrawal may apply if funds are withdrawn prior to age 59½.) When you put money into a Roth IRA, your contributions are not tax deductible, but your withdrawals are tax free.

¢ **IF YOUR EMPLOYER OFFERS YOU RETIREMENT MONEY, TAKE IT!** Many employers offer matching-contribution programs to help their employees save for retirement. Frankly, not taking advantage of these programs is like throwing money out the window. This is like receiving "free" money through a bonus, and usually all that is required to sign up is a few forms to fill out.

2. Determine Your Future Needs

When you think of the word *retirement*, what comes to mind? Lying in a hammock on a sandy beach? Playing golf or fishing? Spending time with grandchildren?

What about volunteering with the needy or pursuing a new ministry? After all, retirement can be more than a reward for past service; it can also be a transition to future outreach. Questions to ask yourself might include, "What ministry might God be calling me to in my later years?" and "What financial resources will be available to me as I seek to invest my life in something meaningful?" Bottom line, if we wisely manage the money acquired during our income-producing years, we'll be in a better financial position to take on new challenges in our later years. It's a concept we call "future-funded ministry," and wise planning today can make this a reality tomorrow.

These are important considerations because your view of retirement will determine how you prepare for those years. How much money you'll need during retirement can vary greatly depending on what kind of lifestyle and opportunities you hope to enjoy.

What else should you consider? How about the fact that people are living longer and enjoying more active lifestyles longer into their retirement years, as well as the fact that health care costs continue to rise. All of these factors are important as you answer the question, "How much retirement income will I really need?"

Naturally, your answers to these questions—as well as the number of years until you retire—will provide a good indication of how much you should be saving today. Here's a good rule of thumb: we advise saving 7 to 13 percent of your current monthly income. In addition, many online resources offer cash-flow worksheets to help you determine the rate at which you should be saving in order to help end up with the kind of resources you may need.[3]

Do You Need a Financial Professional?

The reason for an adviser is to provide objective advice about retirement planning. A financial professional's job is help you identify your goals, put together a strategy, and identify investments that will help you accomplish your goals.

3. Decide on a Strategy

The savings and investment strategies to choose from are countless, and we'll be taking a closer look at many of them in chapter 18. As you are considering any investment or savings program, think through the following three questions:

"What is the purpose of this account or program?" For example, are you saving for retirement? College tuition? Purchasing a home? Identifying the purpose of that particular savings instrument can help you stay focused and on track when you are tempted to take that

money and use it for any other reason other than the one for which the account was created.

"How long do I want to save before beginning to use the money in this account?" In other words, is saving for this particular purpose a short-term or long-term goal? Will you dip into this account and begin using these funds in less than five years, more than fifteen years, or something in between? Determining the time frame can help you decide where to place these funds in order to help achieve the highest return. Some savings instruments (such as certificates of deposit) offer higher returns, a guarantee of principal, and FDIC insurance, but assess penalties for early withdrawals.

> Retirement can be more than a reward for past service; it can also be a transition to future outreach.

"With what level of risk am I comfortable?" When it comes to risk, do you consider yourself a conservative, moderate, or aggressive investor? Are you a risk-taker or a security-seeker, as we discussed in chapter 3? Once again, how you answer these questions will play a large role in the kinds of investment or savings programs you choose. That is why it is important for both of you to answer these questions and discuss your answers.

Remember that your finances are to serve your family and your marriage, not the other way around. As you discuss these matters with your spouse, remember that negotiation and compromise are allies that can help you achieve unity.

4. Evaluate Your Progress

Over time, things change: your priorities, your perception of risk, the amount of time left before retirement commences or tuition bills start, the economic marketplace. A good practice is to contact a financial professional once a year to assess your progress and determine whether or not you need to make any small or large adjustments to help stay on track.

* * *

Preparing financially for your future isn't rocket science. The steps are simple. At the same time, by *not* taking them you can be setting yourself up for disastrous results down the line. To enjoy maximum opportunities in your future, take the time today to discuss these matters with your partner. Together, examine your current savings options to see if you are taking full advantage of the kinds of resources available to you. Compare visions of what your retirement and/or your children's college experience will look like, and determine what kind of financial resources will be necessary to make those dreams come true. Finally, decide on a strategy to get you from here to there, and reevaluate your progress frequently.

So much in our lives is uncertain; so much in our future is unknown. Yet when it comes to being financially secure in the years ahead, we don't have to guess and wonder. With a little foresight, we can rest assured that we have been good stewards of the resources entrusted to us and have adequately prepared for much of what tomorrow may bring.

MAKING YOUR MONEY WORK FOR YOU

Investing means different things to different people. For some, investing means real estate and nothing else. For others, stocks, bonds, and mutual funds are the only way to go.

If you're like many people, it may feel natural for you to have the same perspective on investing that your parents did. If your parents owned half a dozen rental houses, you may gravitate toward real estate investments yourself. If your family preferred "no-risk" ventures, such as interest-bearing accounts, you may find yourself doing the same.

This is all well and good, particularly if your spouse has a similar mind-set. Trouble can brew, however, when husband and wife have vastly different viewpoints on what savvy investing looks like. When couples are not "on the same page" when it comes to investing their money, several potential dangers can arise.

The first danger is for the couple to avoid the subject altogether. This is, of course, one way to "keep peace" in the family, but it may come at the cost of unrealized financial resources for your family.

The second danger is for one member of the couple to make all the investment decisions, leaving the other partner in the dark. This can lay the groundwork for marital disharmony if an investment project goes belly-up and money is lost.

Third, couples who cannot see eye to eye regarding investment strategies not only lose financial return, but also miss out on the fun of working together as a team and the excitement of reaping the rewards of their joint labor.

In the process of figuring out your style of investing as a couple and working together as a successful team, ask yourselves the following questions.

What Are Our Investment Options?

Let's take a look at five of the most common investment options.

1. Real estate. This involves purchasing a property with the sole intent of making a profit. Within real estate, there are countless ways to make a profit on your invested dollars. "Fix and flip" investments consist of purchasing a property, sprucing it up, and then selling it for a profit. Residential rentals or commercial leases help you realize a return by renting your property to others. Tenant-in-common investments allow you to own a percentage of a large, professionally managed property, such as an apartment complex, office building, or mall.

2. Annuities. An annuity is a tax-deferred investment product sold by insurers, banks, brokerage firms, and mutual fund companies. Some fixed annuities provide a rate of return for a specific contract period. Others may be fixed for a year or so but can then move up and down. Variable annuities allow investors to allocate their money among a basket of investment subaccounts; the return depends on the performance of the investments selected. Index annuities give guaranteed principal and pay a percentage of the index return to the investor, conditioned on contract provisions.

3. Stocks. These represent a stake in the ownership of a company. In essence, when you buy a share of stock, you become part owner of that company. For example, if a company sold or "floated" 100 shares of stock, and you bought ten shares, you would literally own 10 percent of that company. As a shareholder, or stockholder, you do not get to make decisions about how the company is run, but you do get to elect the board of directors, which makes those decisions for you. In order to keep shareholders happy, the management of the company must make money and give a little back. That return to you is called a "dividend."

4. Bonds. A bond is a loan to a company. In much the same way that consumers go to a bank to borrow money for the purchase of a home, a company might fund an enormous project by selling bonds. The company has now taken on debt, which it must repay to the bondholder, with interest, before profits can be declared.

5. Mutual funds. This is a pool of money from many investors that a professional money manager uses to buy the stocks and bonds of many different companies. The purpose behind a mutual fund is to help control risk and provide professional money management. A mutual fund may hold stocks and/or bonds of hundreds of companies across many different industries or even countries. Within a fund with multiple and diverse holdings, a single company facing struggles would probably not impact the fund, since it would be buoyed by the other holdings. Mutual funds can vary from extremely conservative to extremely aggressive.

Whether you buy stocks, own real estate, or invest in mutual funds, the point is to get your money working hard for you. But be aware that in all of these investment options, except for fixed and indexed annuities, principal is not guaranteed, and you could lose money.

What Kind of Risk Do We Feel Comfortable with as a Couple?

Some investments are riskier than others. Some believe the riskier the investment, the greater the potential return. Together, you and your spouse need to determine the amount of risk with which you feel comfortable. This plays into our discussion in chapter 3: risk-takers versus security-seekers. If both you and your spouse enjoy risk or want security (and to a similar degree), you probably won't encounter problems in this area. We've found that all couples are *not* exactly alike in this area, so they have to negotiate and compromise.

We designed the following questionnaire to help couples identify their investment risk levels. Read the following questions, and circle the number that most closely represents your beliefs and financial situation. Then add your answers to determine your total score. Have your spouse do the same. We suggest you do this separately in order to get a true understanding of where each of you stands.

Investment Risk Questionnaire

A. Of my gross household income, I spend the following percentages on obligations such as credit cards, car payments, rent or mortgage payments, and tithes and offerings:

    1. more than 50 percent.

    2. between 33 percent and 50 percent.

    3. less than 33 percent.

B. For me, setting aside money for anticipated expenses (such as retirement, college

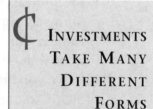

¢ INVESTMENTS TAKE MANY DIFFERENT FORMS

Often people will invest in precious metals, such as gold or silver. We also know people who have art collections, antique collections, and even Beanie Baby collections. As you might expect, values of these investments fluctuate greatly.

funding, and future giving to my church) and for unanticipated expenses (such as emergencies and home or auto repairs) is

    1. ideal, when I am able to do it.

    2. something I simply do.

    3. a priority that I take care of before paying other obligations.

C. In case of a financial crisis, I currently have emergency savings that would allow me to pay for

    1. less than two months of committed monthly expenses.

    2. two to five months of committed monthly expenses.

    3. six months or more of committed monthly expenses.

D. I believe that the chance of my experiencing a dramatic drop in income or increase in expenses in the next two years is

    1. very likely.

    2. possible.

    3. quite unlikely.

E. I would rate my experience as an investor as

    1. beginner.

    2. experienced.

    3. sophisticated.

F. The statement that would best describe my attitude toward volatility is

    1. I feel uneasy knowing that the market is causing fluctuations in my account value.

    2. I understand that the market goes up and down; that's just what it does.

    3. I love volatility, because I believe it helps me buy my investments "on sale."

G. If my investment's value were to decline, I would

    1. sell at the first indication of any drop in value.

    2. sell if the value of my investment drops 25 percent or more in a given year.

    3. consider buying shares at the lower cost per share.

H. The majority of my current investments are in

    1. CDs, savings accounts, money markets, government bonds, and the like.

    2. big-company stocks ("blue chips"), bonds, growth-and-income mutual funds.

3. small-company stocks, aggressive mutual funds, growth positions.

I. My perspective on risk would best be characterized by the statement

1. I don't care what the market is doing. I need to feel that my investment is "safe," or even guaranteed," even if that means I have to pay higher expenses and/or get a lower return.

2. I want a better rate of return that I feel I can sustain over time. I want growth, as well as a degree of stability. I don't need great returns, but I am willing to take risk to try to outpace inflation.

3. I should try to get the highest sustainable return that I am realistically able to get. I know that this means that my portfolio will have quite a bit of fluctuation in value. Yet I believe that temporary downs are the price I will pay for the returns I expect over time.

Add up the numeric value of each of your answers and check your score with the table below.

Your Total Score:	Your Investor Profile:
9–15	Conservative Investor
16–24	Moderate Investor
25–27	Aggressive Investor

How does your profile differ from that of your spouse, if at all? If there is a difference in your preferred investment styles, is there middle ground on which you can both agree?

When Ann and Ben completed the questionnaire, it confirmed what they had known for most of their eight-year marriage: Ben had a much more aggressive investment style than Ann. Throughout their marriage, attempts to talk about their differences had only resulted in arguments. Ben seemed unable to explain why he gravitated toward stock in high-risk companies that sometimes folded, and Ann felt unheard when she argued for a low-risk investment.

As they reviewed their answers to the questionnaire, each gained new insights. Ben said, "I had no idea you thought we could be in financial stress in the next couple of years." And Ann said, "I had no idea you see dips in the market as *opportunity!* They stress me out!"

Being able to talk about some of the feelings, hopes, fears, and beliefs accompanying their differing investment styles gave this couple the motivation they needed to find common ground with which they could both feel comfortable.

As they considered new investment strategies on which they could both agree, one of the questions they asked themselves is a question you and your spouse need to ask as well.

Are We Putting All Our Eggs in One Basket?

As the economy experiences natural highs and lows, investments are affected in different ways. For example, a change in the economy might cause one company's stock to soar, while another bites the dust. Record-low interest rates may mean that bonds are paying very little, while real estate opportunities skyrocket.

WHAT'S THAT MEAN?

One term that is often abused in the investment world is "asset allocation." This term simply means deciding how much money to place in different asset classes or types of investments at any given time. Your investment choices should be taken from different types of asset classes, including stocks, bonds, international, cash, or other short-term investments.

A key to surviving market fluctuations can be found in one word: *diversification*. By investing your money among a variety of investments and projects with varying degrees of risk and rates of return, you help create a level of protection for your assets. This is because conditions that cause a loss in one kind of investment could be the very conditions that create a gain in another. Of course, there is no assurance that a diversified portfolio will perform better than an undiversified portfolio, nor will diversification ensure against market loss.

Various studies have proved that, over a large span of time, no single kind of investment consistently outperforms all the others. One study compared cash, bonds, stocks in large companies, stocks in small companies, and stocks in international companies over a thirty-two-year period. In 2002, for example, bonds performed best, while large-company stocks were the worst performers. In 2002, small-company stocks soared, while international stocks performed badly. In 1998, large-company stocks provided the best performance of all, while small-company stocks provided the greatest loss. You can see how things go up and down, back and forth.

Diversification can help you ride out the lows of any given investment with gains from investments in other categories.

The other benefit of diversification is that it provides for spouses with different investment styles and risk levels. In the case of Ben and Ann, she felt better about some of his more risky ventures when she realized that half their portfolio was devoted to conservative mutual funds.

Putting all the eggs in one basket might work for kids at an Easter egg hunt. But when it comes to protecting and growing your financial portfolio, it may be best to have a variety of baskets. Simply put, diversification is a wise approach.

¢ **MAKE SURE YOUR DIVERSIFICATION IS TRULY DIVERSE**

Some people believe that holding many funds in their mutual fund portfolio means they have proper diversification. Often this isn't true. Remember, many mutual funds hold the same stocks and/or bonds. So you may have several mutual funds all investing in the same stocks. Read your prospectus to make sure this kind of overlap doesn't happen.

What Is the Time Frame in Which We Want to Realize the Greatest Return on This Investment?

Different investments realize their greatest return in different periods of time. When will you see your greatest return?

Bruce and Cheryl own nine rental houses and condos in the Denver area. Their goal is not to generate short-term cash flow but to create long-term security: they finance each rental with a fifteen-year loan, putting enough down payment so that the anticipated rent will just cover their mortgage. It might look like Bruce and Cheryl are just "breaking even" year after year, but fifteen years from now when they are collecting rent from ten mortgage-free properties, their cash flow will be significant! However, keeping the properties rented is the key to success in this situation.

Glenn and Michelle follow a very different strategy. They just purchased a fourplex in Arvada, Colorado, with 15 percent down and an interest-only adjustable rate mortgage. For the next five years, Glenn and Michelle will collect $2,000 in rent while making interest-only payments of $550 per month. Unlike Bruce and Cheryl, Glenn and Michelle have no intention of paying off this property quickly or even at all. Their strategy is to use the fourplex for immediate cash flow and sell the property in five years before their mortgage adjusts and their payments increase.

Understanding your goals for any given investment—short-term profit or long-term gain—can help you make the wisest possible decisions for your family.

Do We Have a Realistic Understanding of the Nature of Investments?

The very nature of investments is to ride the highs and lows created by a changing economy. Investments are often a matter of "two steps forward, one step back." How will you and your spouse handle the disappointment or even stress of an investment that is gaining slower than you expected or is even taking a short-term loss?

¢ CUTTING THROUGH THE CONFUSION

Some people are confused about how an IRA works. An IRA is a vehicle that includes other kinds of investments. What kinds of investments go inside traditional IRAs and Roth IRAs? The most popular are mutual funds, fixed annuities, variable annuities, CDs, and stocks. The point is, the IRA and Roth IRA are not the investment in and of themselves. They are the *holders* of the investment.

Gene and Geri have invested in commercial real estate for about thirty years. As a rule, tenants come and go with little drama, but every now and then a property will sit vacant for months until the right tenant comes along. The positive attitude of this couple helps them weather these seasons.

Gene says, "When things are slow or stressful, I don't say, 'Oh, woe is me!' Instead, I'm still grateful. Occasional losses aren't fun, but they mean I'm in the game. And I trust God that it will all work out just fine. So far it has."

"Strange as it sounds," Geri adds, "vacancies are a good problem to have. It means we own property, something a lot of people only dream about. I'd rather have *this* problem than no investment property at all."

Adopting a positive attitude about your investments can go a long way toward making the experience not only profitable, but also enjoyable for you and your spouse.

Above all, realize that investments are an opportunity for you and your spouse to work together as a team and to have fun watching your assets grow. Like every other aspect of money management, investments can strengthen your relationship or weaken it. The difference is in how you approach the issues, how well you communicate, how well you understand each other, and how well you negotiate. Use your investment to bring unity and joy to your relationship.

CHAPTER NINETEEN

SAFEGUARDING YOUR FAMILY

Their names were Brian and Roberta, but they could have been any number of couples we've worked with who had the same conflict. It was our first meeting with them, and we were going over general information to ascertain where they were at financially. Then our conversation hit a snag.

"What about insurance?" Scott asked. "Are you feeling comfortable with the amount and types of coverage you have?"

Brian and Roberta exchanged meaningful glances. He shifted in his seat while she continued to stare at him. Or maybe *glare* at him would be more accurate.

Bethany tried a different approach. "Well, tell us what insurance you *do* have, and we'll start there."

"We have auto insurance on our two cars," Brian said. He gave a few details, such as the deductible amount. "And our family is covered under the health insurance offered through my company." He paused, so we assumed he was finished.

"You'll notice," Roberta chimed in, "that he didn't mention life insurance. He keeps telling me he's going to look into it, but he hasn't yet. Fact is, we've been talking about it for a couple of years. I think it's downright irresponsible not to have some kind of life insurance, especially since we have a baby now and own a house.

¢ INVESTIGATE GROUP LIFE INSURANCE

Your employer may offer a group life insurance plan. Often, there is a basic plan provided by your employer plus the option to purchase additional insurance. Usually these rates are inexpensive. This is a convenient way to pay for insurance because the premiums are taken directly from your paycheck. A word of caution: when you leave your employer, you may no longer be covered.

Not to mention the fact that I stopped working to stay home with Connor."

Ah, so that was it. She had been after him to get a life insurance policy, and he hadn't come through. Were we surprised that Brian—who was otherwise conscientious and diligent—had dragged his feet in this area? Not in the least. That's because, as we alluded to earlier, we've seen this scenario played out in our office many times over.

Sometimes the circumstance vary slightly, but it is usually the woman who wants the sense of security that insurance provides—whether it be life, health, auto, or disability insurance. She wants to know she'll be taken care of should a crisis occur, and this is especially true if there are children at home. On rare occasions, the roles are reversed, and it's the man who presses for insurance—or more of it.

Most people know insurance is important, and most insist they're going to get it. Why, then, do many fail to follow through? We've seen the same four themes show up consistently.

¢ Caring for your family without health insurance is as precarious as walking a circus tightrope without a net.

1. The "I'll Never Die" Syndrome. Some people seem to believe they're impervious to the laws of nature. You could also call this the Superman complex. Bullets can bounce off their chests, and speeding trains pose no threat. Indeed, many men, especially, have the belief (perhaps more subconscious than conscious) that the angel of death will never catch them—at least not for a long, long time.

2. They think they can't afford it. For couples struggling to pay the rent, buy groceries, make credit-card payments, and keep the car running, insurance seems like a luxury. What they don't realize is that some policies are quite inexpensive, and even a *little* insurance is better than none at all.

3. Some are focused on the immediate future. With busy lives, hectic schedules, and urgent needs to attend to, people sometimes fail to look ahead five, ten, twenty years. When they become so consumed with today, they put off planning for tomorrow.

4. They don't understand it, so they don't get it. The world of insurance can seem bewildering and perplexing. So many varieties and options are available, and some insurance agents speak in a language not understood by the average person. So rather than wade into the murky waters, couples often ignore the matter altogether.

Do any of these rationales ring a bell? Maybe one of these reasons has prevented you from getting insurance. Or perhaps you *do* have insurance but want to take a second look at your coverage. With this is mind, we want to provide a brief summary of options. Keep in mind that the

> If you or your spouse were to lose your income—even just part of it—what kind of position would you be in financially?

information in this chapter is general, and you'll need to consider many specifics for your unique situation.

An Overview of Options

Today, Americans have more options than ever when it comes to purchasing health, life, disability, or long-term care insurance. With so many choices, it can be difficult to decide which plans you really need and how to select the right ones for you and your family. For some families, the dilemma is much more basic than this. Some families—finding themselves in transition or experiencing financial stress—put off purchasing adequate insurance, convinced that, at least for the time being, their money is better spent elsewhere.

How important is it for you to spend money on insurance? To help you decide, ask yourself the following questions:

- What will happen to my family if I am *not healthy?*
- What will happen to my family if I become *disabled?*
- What will happen to my family if I need to be *cared for?*
- What will happen to my family if I die before I've settled my *financial commitments?*

If you're not sure how your family would survive financially in each of the above situations, don't panic. Health insurance, disability insurance, long-term care insurance, and life insurance provide assistance for each of these situations and more. Let's take a look at each of these kinds of insurance.

Health Insurance

Sharon is a forty-five-year-old single mother of two children. Six months after her divorce became final and she was removed from her ex-husband's health insurance, she had yet to research and select a health insurance carrier of her own. She justified her decision by saying, "I don't have time to do the research" and "I don't have the money to pay health insurance premiums at the moment." She even told her best friend, "Even *with* health insurance, the worst thing that has happened to me in ten years is the flu. I'm sure I'll be fine."

One morning while walking from the front door to her car, Sharon decided to take a shortcut through a flowerbed. When she tripped over the sprinkler head and ended up sprawled in her driveway with her foot throbbing and swelling, her first thought was, *It's broken*. Her second thought was, *Health insurance!*

Aided by her teenage daughter, Sharon stabilized her softball-sized ankle under an ice pack, then dialed her former health insurance provider in a panic. She assumed it was too late to get insurance coverage for her current injury, but the experience had brought home a truth Sharon could no longer ignore: health insurance was *not* a luxury. No matter how careful or healthy she tried to be, illness could strike without warning, and injury could lurk as nearby as the flowerbed.

With the cost of doctor bills and hospital care soaring out of control, it is more important than ever to have health insurance coverage. In fact, caring for your family without health insurance is as precarious as walking a circus tightrope without a net. In selecting the right plan, your goal is to insure yourself and your family against serious financial losses that can result from an illness or accident.

FLEX SPENDING ACCOUNTS COME IN HANDY

One vehicle that people do not take full advantage of is their employer's Flex Spending Accounts (Section 125). This program allows you to set aside money, pretax, for out-of-pocket medical expenses, including copayments, prescriptions, and over-the-counter drugs. Contact your human resources department to see if this medical savings plan is available to you.

Many types of health insurance policies are available. Most people think of health insurance as a plan that covers medical bills, hospital expenses, and surgeries. In the past, plans were referred to as "major medical" or "comprehensive" plans. Today, you are more likely to hear about "managed-care plans" like HMOs (health maintenance organizations), PPOs (preferred provider organizations), or POS (point-of-service) plans.

Health insurance is typically obtained through your employer as a group policy or, if you are self-employed, through an insurance agent with an individual policy.

What should you look for in a health insurance plan? Shopping for health insurance involves more than just finding the plan with the lowest cost (called the "premium"). It is important to look at what you are receiving for your annual deductibles, copayments, lifetime maximum amounts, prescription coverage, and network. One way to keep your premium payments lower is by selecting a higher deductible. Here are some things to evaluate as you are comparing health insurance plans.

> Strive to buy the best coverage you can afford, but don't pay for what you don't need.

- What medical services are covered? Possibilities include inpatient hospital services, outpatient surgery, in-hospital physician visit, doctor's office visits, skilled nursing care, medical tests and X-rays, prescription drugs, mental health care, drug and alcohol abuse treatment, home health care visits, rehabilitation facility care, physical therapy, speech therapy, hospice care, maternity care, chiropractic treatment, preventive care and checkups, well-baby care, and dental care.
- Are there exclusions or time tables for preexisting conditions?
- How does the insurance company handle pre-authorizations?
- How much does it cost?
- How much is the annual deductible?
- What coinsurance or copayments apply?

Disability Insurance

Another type of coverage to consider is disability insurance, a type of plan that provides you with income if you can't work for an extended period of time because of illness, injury, or accident. Think about it. If you or your spouse were to lose your income—even just part of it—what kind of position would you be in financially? According to the

Consumer Federation of America (CFA) and the American Council of Life Insurance (ACLI), as many as 82 percent of American workers have no disability coverage or believe that their current coverage is adequate to meet their financial needs.

If you become disabled, it's possible that you may find other sources of income on a limited basis. For example, depending on your circumstances, Social Security may provide some relief. Workers' compensation is another possibility, providing benefits in the event that your illness or injury is work related. Finally, your car insurance may pay some benefits if your disability resulted from an automobile accident.

Still, to adequately provide for your family for the duration of your disability, disability insurance is your safest best. Your employer may offer short- or long-term disability coverage, and your human resources representative can tell you for sure. If you are self-employed, you can purchase an individual disability insurance policy.

What should you look for in a disability insurance policy? Here are a few suggestions.

• Ask your financial professional which kind of disability insurance is best for you: long term or short term. The difference is the length of time you can be covered.

• Make sure you understand the percentage of your income that is guaranteed if you become disabled (for example, 50 percent, 60 percent, etc.).

• Establish the length of time—thirty, sixty, ninety days—you will need to wait before you can begin drawing disability payments. Establish the length of time you can continue receiving benefits (common configurations include two years, five years, or until a specified age such as sixty-five).

• Be sure to find out the conditions under which you are eligible to receive payments. Can you receive payments if you are unable to perform the duties of your current occupation or only if you can

WILL SOCIAL SECURITY HELP?

Many people believe that if they become disabled, Social Security will assist them. Think again! To qualify for Social Security, your disability must prevent you from doing *any* kind of work—not just your usual job. The definition of disability for Social Security states that a person must be completely disabled with no hope of recovery for a period of at least one year or have a disability expected to end in death.

engage in no gainful employment at all? In other words,
clarify your insurance company's definition of "disability."

- Will this policy pay only for accidents, or for illness, too?
- To make the plan you choose more affordable, select a longer
  elimination period (the number of days after you become disabled that you must wait before receiving benefits). Strive to
  buy the best coverage you can afford, but don't pay for what
  you don't need.

Long-term Care Insurance

According to the *New England Journal of Medicine*, 43 percent of people
over age sixty-five will spend some time in a nursing home. The
national average for nursing home costs range from $40,000 to
$100,000 annually. The cost of daily home care is about $36,000 annu-
ally. The average length of stay in a nursing home is about two and one-
half years.

You may be thinking, *But I'm young! I'll think about nursing homes
and long-term care when I'm older.* And yet long-term care is not just for
older people; sometimes events occur that make long-term care an issue
for younger folks as well. We have a friend who was in an accident, and
he is now confined to a wheelchair for life. He is only thirty-five years
old. Thankfully, he had a long-term care policy, and he now receives
$4,000 per month to cover his care needs.

What should you look for in a long-term care policy? First, establish
your long-term care insurance need. When you decide to obtain a long-
term care plan, your first call should be to your employer to see if this
kind of policy is offered. If it is, you may be able to obtain a policy at a
lower rate than you could purchase on your own. It is important to
remember that in most cases a long-term care policy can be taken with
you when you leave your current place of employment. This is important because your rate will be lower and as long as you continue to pay
the premium, you will be insured.

Whether purchasing a group or individual policy, be sure to read the
policy thoroughly before you buy, and be certain that you understand
what is covered and what is not. For an individual policy, compare
plans from at least three companies before you make a decision. Be sure
you are clear on all the terms, benefits, exclusions, limitations, and
waiting periods. For example, does the policy cover nursing home care?

How Much Is Enough? ¢

People often ask, "How much life insurance do I really need?" We advise people to have, at a minimum, enough insurance to

• pay off your home mortgage;

• pay for your children's college education;

• retire all debt, including auto loans, credit cards, and so on;

• pay for burial costs and other current expenses you would like to cover; and

• provide living expenses for your spouse and family for three to seven years. (This allows the freedom for your family to heal and for your spouse to focus solely on your children, if need be.)

Assisted living? Home health care? If so, what is the dollar amount of the maximum daily benefit allowed?

One other important factor: the younger you are when you purchase long-term care insurance, the cheaper your premiums are likely to be. Premiums often remain the same for the duration of the policy. Under normal circumstances, then, the younger you are when you purchase a policy, the less expensive it will be over the long haul.

Life Insurance

While some people use life insurance as a tax shelter and others use it in their estate planning, life insurance is more commonly used to provide financial security for surviving family members in the event of the death of a wage earner.

We recently had the chance to counsel with a young widow from our church. Her husband, Kirk, was killed by a drunk driver while riding his bike home from work. Prior to his death, he had been paying less than $20 a month for a $500,000 life insurance policy. Upon his death, this money allowed Kirk's wife to keep the family home and also guaranteed funding for their children to attend college. Kirk's family was not forced into financial crisis at the same time it was grieving the loss of a beloved husband and dad.

Different types of life insurance are available to help you accomplish different goals. Do you want coverage for a lifetime or for a certain number of years? Do you want to build up a cash value or not?

The two main types of life insurance are *term insurance* and *cash value insurance* or what people used to call "permanent" insurance (which includes whole life, universal life, and variable life).

Term insurance policies provide life insurance for a specified period of time and benefits in the event of death, but they do not generate any "cash value" (the money that grows over the years with taxes deferred). If you need insurance only for a certain period of time—and you don't have a lot of money to spend on insurance—you may be able to get more coverage by buying term insurance.

Like term insurance, *cash value insurance*—also known as permanent insurance—provides benefits to your beneficiaries in the event of your death. In addition, this type of insurance accumulates a dollar value over time. You can access this cash value in the future if you need money or as loan collateral if you want to borrow. Unlike term insurance, cash value insurance is not just for a specific time period. It generally lasts for a lifetime, and as long as you pay your premiums, your coverage will never expire and will never need to be renewed. The three main kinds of cash value insurance are whole life insurance, variable life insurance, and universal life insurance. Each one offers slightly different advantages, and you can learn about the specific benefits of each on the Internet or from your insurance agent or financial professional.

Keep this in mind: while many couples insure only the primary breadwinner, we believe both spouses should be insured to cover debt, child-care needs, and other expenses.

Safeguard Your Future—and Your Marriage

All this money talk is well and good, but how does something as seemingly mundane as insurance help you achieve financial harmony and even provide safeguards for your marriage? Consider these benefits of being adequately insured.

Avert Financial Crisis

The truth is, whenever couples face financial crisis, the potential exists for stress and tension to negatively affect

¢ QUESTIONS
TO ASK
YOUR
INSURANCE
AGENT

When researching a long-term care policy, be sure to ask your insurance agent or financial professional the following questions:

• What is the amount of monthly benefit I would need?

• How many years will it cover me?

• How long is the elimination period?

• Does it cover both home care and nursing home care?

• Is my premium fixed for the benefit duration?

• Do I have inflation protection inside the policy?

their relationship. The number one purpose of insurance—whether it is health, disability, long-term care, or life—is to avert financial crisis. The financial relief that insurance provides in times of chaos or loss can indeed keep your marriage from being wounded, perhaps even fatally so.

Create Security

As we said earlier, women in particular—and men to a lesser degree—crave a sense of security. It is a need, especially if there are children at home. Insurance creates a sense of security. It also answers the questions, "Will I be taken care of in the event of loss of health or income?" and "Will my spouse and family be taken care of in the event of my death?"

Foster Unity

When husbands and wives make joint decisions regarding insurance or any other big-ticket item, it gives them a "we're in this together" sense of unity. They are taking steps to care for each other (and perhaps children) and safeguard their future. In essence, this says, "I care about you so much that I want to make sure you're provided for if something should happen to me."

Insurance remains a powerful tool you can use to not only safeguard your family's financial future but also to communicate volumes to your partner and reduce stress in your marriage as well. Easily overlooked, it is nevertheless one of the best methods of protecting your assets against catastrophic loss at some point in the future.

CHAPTER TWENTY

THE SOURCE OF TRUE RICHES

The animated short film *Gone Nutty* features a neurotic prehistoric squirrel named Scrat, who scurries to store up one more acorn before the Ice Age hits. From all appearances, Scrat has been very busy. As he carries the last acorn to his lair, an old hollow tree, we get a peek at his vast treasure trove of nuts, which completely fills the inner cavity of the tree.

Scrat lugs the acorn to the top of the tree and tries to force it into the middle of the pile. It's a tight squeeze, but Scrat pushes with all his might. When he finally shoves the nut down into the center of the acorns, he looks pleased with himself.

As he walks away, though, the nut pops out of place. Scrat calmly returns and pushes it back in. As he turns to wander off, the nut pops out again. His frustration mounts as he pushes it back down into the hole. After the nut becomes dislodged for a third time, Scrat becomes more aggressive. He jumps up and down on the acorn, trying to squeeze the stubborn nut into place. Finally, the pressure causes the storehouse to explode, sending the acorns and Scrat reeling down an icy incline and off a precipice.

While Scrat free falls down the deep gorge, he desperately reaches to catch some of the acorns tumbling alongside him. He succeeds in grabbing a bunch of acorns, only to slam hard into the canyon's icy floor. As Scrat comes to his senses, he spots an acorn hurtling toward him. He frantically tries to avoid the impact, but to no avail.

What's worse, upon impact, the acorn actually triggers an intercontinental divide and leaves a battered and bruised Scrat on an icy plateau. He reaches down to pull the one remaining acorn out of the ice. When he finally pulls the acorn free, it disintegrates into ashes.[1]

Besides providing some clever fun, this short film offers a thought-provoking moral. It's a precautionary tale about trying to accumulate too much and hoarding riches. The film very well could have ended with the proverb that says, "It is possible to give away and become richer! It is also possible to hold on too tightly and lose everything. Yes, the liberal man shall be rich! By watering others, he waters himself" (11:24–25 TLB).

This may be the last chapter in this book, but it is hardly the least important. In fact, it may be the most important. Our attitudes about sharing versus hoarding, giving versus gathering, speak volumes about the condition of our heart and soul. What's more, giving can be a tremendously positive aspect of your relationship, bringing joy and fulfillment as you demonstrate gratitude to God by helping others.

When Is the Right Time to Give?

Perhaps you have thought, *As soon as I get ahead financially, I'm going to start giving more.* It might be that you would like to tithe more to your church or support a local charity or nonprofit organization whose passion you share. Maybe your alma mater has a scholarship fund to which you'd like to contribute, or perhaps you've always had the good intention of sponsoring a child in an impoverished country.

And yet, if you're like most people, you face the temptation to delay charitable giving until you have a comfortable margin in the bank. Have you had these goals for months, maybe even years? Are you surprised that you never manage to get ahead enough to turn noble intentions into actions? Frankly, we're not surprised when people put off giving until they have a surplus. This is because, typically, charitable giving hinges less on excess than it does on exercise. It hinges less on dreams than it does on decisions.

Charitable giving is not unlike a muscle that needs to be conditioned in small tasks before being able to take on larger endeavors. *What* you give is secondary to *how* you give. Do you give with a grateful heart? Do you give often and freely? Do you make charitable giving a part of your budget, regardless of how small your budget happens to be or how little you can afford to give? Do you experience joy every time you give, regardless of whether the gift is large or small? Have you discovered that the most precious gifts—to the people who receive them as well as to the givers—are not those given out of excess but those that require some level of sacrifice on the part of the provider?

Your answers to these questions are far more important than your answer to the single inquiry, "How large a check can you write?" Consider, for example, the story of the widow's offering found in Mark 12:41–43.

> Jesus sat down opposite the place where the offerings were put and watched the crowd putting their money into the temple treasury. Many rich people threw in large amounts. But a poor widow came and put in two very small copper coins, worth only a fraction of a penny.
>
> Calling his disciples to him, Jesus said, "I tell you the truth, this poor woman has put more into the treasury than all the others."

The good news is that regardless of how large or small your budget happens to be, you can use a portion of your resources to make a positive difference in your church, your community, even the world. In fact, you would be wise to do so. This is because whether you are giving charitably today is the single best indicator as to whether you will give charitably tomorrow or next year, when you may have more resources at your fingertips. Flex your giving muscle today even if the checks you write are small, and you will find yourself far more prepared to write larger checks as your resources grow.

Tell Me Again *Why* I Should Give?

Does the thought of giving make you grin or groan? Does it fill your heart with gladness or guilt? The topic of charitable giving doesn't have to be a source of distress or discomfort. In fact, according to the Bible, giving can be a source of freedom, joy, and blessing in your life. As it says in Acts 20:35, "It is more blessed to give than to receive." In addition, charitable giving says a lot about the condition of your heart. Randy Alcorn, author of *The Treasure Principle,* says that "there's a fundamental connection between our spiritual lives and how we think about and handle money." Jesus himself said, "For where your treasure is, there your heart will be also" (Matt. 6:21).

Still, many people are resistant. Like the squirrel in the film, their attitude is one of *getting* rather than *giving*. Why should you give? Here are some of our thoughts on the matter.

God Is the Owner of Everything—Even Your Paycheck

As we said in chapter 9, we believe God gives us the opportunity to manage his resources. In Deuteronomy 10:14, we read, "To the LORD your God belong the heavens, even the highest heavens, the earth and everything in it." In other words, it's not your money anyway. So have fun spreading it around.

God Is Honored When We Give

Giving shouldn't be an act of duty but of gratitude. As the writer of Proverbs said, "Honor the LORD with your wealth" (3:9). Do you give out of obligation or out of a sincere desire to honor God? Sharing our resources is one way of acknowledging that the Creator of the universe is in charge and sovereign over all the world.

Giving Changes Others

As Randy Alcorn wrote, "Because we give, eternity will be different—for others and for us." When we give money to help others, their lives are changed for the better. What may not be as apparent is the change that occurs within people when they are shown love and mercy.

MAKING CENTS

Percentage of total charitable contributions from individuals: 75 percent.

Average annual amount that contributing households give to charities (which represents about 3 percent of their income): $1,620.[2]

Giving Changes Us

Winston Churchill is quoted as saying, "We make a living by what we get. We make a life by what we give." Giving not only changes others, but it also leaves the giver enriched and enhanced. Generosity is definitely a change agent, quite often for the beneficiary but *always* for the person who practices it on a regular basis.

Attitude Matters

These are just a few of the reasons *why* we should give. Let's also take a look at *how* we should give.

Give as a Priority

We quoted the first part of Proverbs 3:9 ("Honor the LORD with your wealth"), but don't miss the second part of that verse: "with the firstfruits of all your crops." Whatever we give should come right off the top, not what might remain at the bottom of the budget. Recently, we spotted a sign on a church in Colorado Springs that said, "Give to God what is right, not what is left." That's a good motto to live by.

Give Cheerfully

Have you ever received a gift from someone you could tell wasn't thrilled about giving it? The reluctant attitude spoils the very purpose of the gift. Second Corinthians 9:7 says, "Each man should give what he has decided in his heart to give, not reluctantly or under compulsion, for God loves a cheerful giver." In part, giving cheerfully means giving without grumbling, whining, or reluctance. Being cheerful is not an emotion as much as it is a choice, and you can decide to give with a positive attitude.

Give Generously According to How You Have Been Blessed

In Deuteronomy 16:17 we read the following: "Each of you must bring a gift in proportion to the way the LORD your God has blessed you." Charitable giving isn't a competition. Don't despise what you can give because it may be smaller than what your neighbor can give. Consider all of your blessings, then give accordingly.

Give as a Family

One family we know invites its members to put loose change in a "giving jar," and they use that money when they come across a financial need. Getting the entire family involved not only generates a compounded sense of excitement and motivation, but also creates wonderful experiences and memories for your family.

For several years now, we have divided our giving into two categories—a "church fund" and a "special needs" fund. We feel it's important to support the local church we attend, and we give a portion of our income every month. We also set aside money to help meet needs that arise unexpectedly or infrequently. We might hear about an urgent need by a missionary, or we might learn about a neighbor who is struggling. Some money is set aside in advance to help on these occasions. We don't mention this to pat ourselves on the back, but to underscore the point that giving enhances family relationships. We talk through our decisions as a couple, and now that our boys are getting older, we tell them what we're doing with our money and why. This has been a great source of joy for our family.

Charitable Giving and Your Marriage

Above all, don't allow charitable giving to become a source of stress or division in your marriage. If one spouse wants to make a particular donation and the other spouse doesn't agree on the amount or cause, negotiate. Can you agree on a smaller amount or a different organization? If our goals are really to give cheerfully, to honor God with our gifts, and to bless those around us who might be in need, it seems counterproductive to let that same gift serve as a source of tension or resentment at home. What good is it to bless total strangers, while wounding or frustrating those we love the most?

How can you develop unity with your spouse in the area of charitable giving? Here are a few ideas.

Read the Same Books or Literature

Developing a similar mind-set can be aided when both partners are exposed to the same teaching on giving. As we've already mentioned, Randy Alcorn's book *The Treasure Principle* changed our perspective and unified us in the area of giving. We encourage you to read Randy's book, or other books, and discuss them together.

Communicate Freely and Frequently on This Subject

If you find yourself in the middle of a disagreement, ask yourself what's really at the heart of the issue. Is your spouse *really* objecting to contributing to the homeless mission, or is she reacting to the fact that you wrote a $200 check without telling her? Give each other plenty of time to ponder various ideas by communicating on a regular basis. We encourage you to include decisions about giving in your regular financial powwows.

Discover Mutual Passions

Find a connecting point, a mutual passion, with your spouse. It may be that one of you has a heart for the lost tribes of Borneo, while the other feels passionate about caring for unwed mothers. While it's fine to support separate charities, try to find one (or more than one) that you *both* feel strongly about. This shared vision will go a long way toward creating harmony in your gift-giving efforts.

Practice Discipline in Your Finances

Good stewardship and budgetary discipline can mean less financial stress in your life and marriage in general. This can allow you and your spouse to stay open to new ideas and projects related to charitable giving. After all, you may find it difficult to agree on tithing or a charitable donation when you're feeling stressed because your credit cards are maxed out or you're having a difficult time making rent that month.

As with many areas of your finances, tithing and other charitable giving have the potential to enrich your life and your marriage. With good communication and planning, you can experience the joy of giving *and* harmony in your marriage as well. You'll be in a position to bless others around you *and* feel blessed in return.

* * *

Writer Ed Chinn told the story of his friends Bruce and Lenore Mitchell, who felt they should give away all of their possessions. They were newlyweds at the time, and Bruce first felt called to part with their furniture, appliances, wedding gifts—everything. After a few days, he reluctantly shared his feelings with his young wife, only to discover that she had the very same conviction.

Confident that God was directing them, Bruce and Lenore began the process of divestment. Within a few days, everything was gone. Bruce recalled, "Even the original painting my grandmother had painted—a family heirloom—was given away."

Although somewhat perplexed as they slept on the floor in an empty house, they felt peace and the assurance that they had done the right thing.

A few weeks later as they were driving home, they saw smoke rising off in the distance. As they drove closer to their neighborhood, they realized the smoke was billowing up from their property. Their house, consumed by flames, burned to the ground.

One night after the Mitchells had settled into temporary housing, car lights appeared in the

THE GLARING FACTS ABOUT SHARING

Nearly every study indicates that American Christians give an average of 2 to 3 percent of their income to churches and charities. A recent Barna Research report provides even more sobering insight: among people calling themselves born-again believers, giving increased 44 percent in those who gave nothing the previous year.

And there seems to be a lot of self-deception in regard to giving. One-third of born-again adults said they tithed in 2000, but a comparison of giving and household incomes revealed that only one-eighth actually did so.[3]

driveway. A friend walked to the front door carrying the gift Bruce and Lenore had pre-sented to him a few weeks earlier. During the days that followed, a steady stream of cars came to their home, returning nearly every item they had given away.

Forty years later, Bruce reflected on that incident. "We learned at an early age that you can only have what you give away. Today, we once again treasure my grandmother's paint-ing. It hangs in our home only because we once gave it away."4

Not everyone feels called to give away all of his or her possessions, nor do we think that is necessary in order to honor God and demonstrate a generous spirit. However, Bruce's words hit the bull's-eye: "You can only have what you give away." By holding our possessions and money with an open hand, we are freed from the compulsive need to cling tightly and hoard our stuff.

Most often, when we give, we won't receive back as directly as Bruce and Lenore did. But we will undoubtedly receive back in many ways and in greater measure. Surely that's what Jesus meant when he said, "If you give, you will get! Your gift will return to you in full and overflowing measure, pressed down, shaken together to make room for more, and running over. Whatever measure you use to give—large or small—will be used to measure what is given back to you" (Luke 6:38 TLB).

When we view giving for what it is—a privilege and an opportunity—our individual lives and our marriages will be enriched beyond measure.

Conclusion: Your Relationship Can Be Ordinary or Extraordinary

Some wise sayings never become outdated. That's why we love a statement made by Solomon, one of the most insightful and astute people to ever live. This is what he said thousands of years ago: "It's better to have a partner than to go it alone. Share the work, share the wealth" (Eccl. 4:9 MSG).

That's the theme woven throughout this book. You and your partner can choose to work together, strive for unity, and cooperate as teammates—or you can choose to be two distinct and separate individuals. As we've talked with thousands of couples as part of our work as financial counselors—and dozens more during the research for this book—we've become absolutely convinced that spouses who work closely together are *far* better off. They thoroughly enjoy their relationship, and they are more successful in every way. Teamwork, partnership, cooperation—these are the things that enrich our lives and help us achieve our goals.

Money is an important aspect of our lives. There's no doubt about that. Our economic resources allow us to pursue dreams, fulfill responsibilities, care for loved ones, and assist people in need. But money is also a symbol and a symptom within a marriage: it reveals the quality of the relationship and the character of the people in it. We believe strongly that what matter most are integrity, honesty, and morality. Your finances are a means to live out your most cherished beliefs and values.

Our hope for you is that money is a blessing and a benefit to your marriage. If we have helped you along toward that goal, we are sincerely grateful.

READERS' GUIDE

*for Personal Reflection or
Group Discussion*

Readers' Guide

Chapter 1: Savers versus Spenders

1. To what degree is the saver-versus-spender conflict a problem in your relationship? When was the last time you had a disagreement about spending or saving? What were the specifics? How can you better compromise and resolve differences in this area?

2. How do you respond to the pros and cons of spenders and savers presented in the chapter? Do you agree with them? Could you add to the list?

3. What is the balance between prudently planning for the future and living fully in the present moment? Reflect on the following Bible verses.

   • "He who ignores discipline comes to poverty and shame" (Prov. 13:18).

   • "Now listen, you who say, 'Today or tomorrow we will go to this or that city, spend a year there, carry on business and make money.' Why, you do not even know what will happen tomorrow" (James 4:13–14).

Chapter 2: Dueling Over Debt

1. What is your attitude toward debt? Do you despise it, tolerate it, or accept it as a fact of life in the twenty-first century? Is this attitude similar or different within your relationship?

2. If you are currently in debt, how is it affecting your relationship? How do you see your debt affecting your financial future?

3. What do you think is meant by the proverb, "The borrower is servant to the lender" (22:7)? How does that apply to your situation?

Chapter 3: Risk-Takers versus Security-Seekers

1. Do you consider yourself a risk-taker or a security-seeker? How similar or different are you and your partner in this area? How has this issue presented itself in your relationship?

2. What's the balance between being too cautious and too aggressive? What are the dangers for each extreme?

3. The Bible contains plenty of encouragement for both risk-takers and security-seekers. For instance, Proverbs 21:5 (MSG) says, "Careful planning puts you ahead in the long run." But then Jesus' parable about using talents seems to encourage risk-taking. (See Matt. 25) His story ended this way: "Take the thousand [dollars] and give it to the one who risked the most. And get rid of this 'play-it-safe' who won't go out on a limb. Throw him out into utter darkness" (25:28–30 MSG). What do you think is the balance between both admonitions—risking and seeking safety? In what cases might either approach be wise or foolish?

Chapter 4: Exasperating Expectations

1. What expectations did you and your partner bring into your relationship that cause conflicts? How were those expectations formed?

2. Of the eight "provocative presumptions" mentioned in this chapter, which apply to you and your spouse? Can you add any to this list?

3. Reflect on the following proverb in light of our discussion about expectations: "The gullible believe anything they're told; the prudent sift and weigh every word" (14:15 MSG). What assumptions did you have as a young person that you later realized were inaccurate?

Chapter 5: Flying Blind

1. Are you "flying blind" when it comes to your finances? If that term doesn't describe you, then do you know a couple for whom it does apply? Considering your own situation, or the couple you know, why do you think people remain stuck in a flying-blind pattern?

2. What aspects of your household finances are disorganized or perhaps in total disarray? To what degree has this caused tension in your relationship? What will you do to rectify the situation?

3. King Solomon once said, "God made man simple; man's complex problems are of his own devising" (Eccl. 7:30 JB). In what ways does our society make financial management more complicated than it needs to be? How might you make your own personal money management less complex?

Chapter 6: It's All Relative

1. Identify the primary money messages conveyed by your parents. (Use the list provided in the chapter to get you thinking.) How are these messages similar or different for you and your partner? In what ways do they complement each other, and in what ways do they conflict?

2. What beliefs about finances and work from your childhood are worth embracing and maintaining? Which ones would you like to throw overboard? Do you agree with the assertion that we either repeat or reject our parents' money attitudes and habits? If so, which have you done?

3. According to the book of Proverbs, "A greedy man brings trouble to his family" (15:27). This underscores the idea that a parent's actions and beliefs affect his spouse and children. In what ways did your mom and dad's approach to finances—positive or negative—influence you?

Chapter 7: Swayed by Society

1. In what specific ways has our culture influenced your money personality? In what ways would you like *not* to reflect our society's attitudes about money, work, and spending?

2. How has our society's influence regarding money affected the relationship between you and your partner?

3. Reflect on the following encouragement from the apostle Paul in light of our discussion: "Don't become so well-adjusted to your culture that you fit into it without even thinking.... Readily recognize what [God] wants from you, and quickly respond to it. Unlike the culture around you, always dragging you down to its level of immaturity, God brings the best out of you, develops well-formed maturity in you" (Rom. 12:2 MSG). In what ways might you resist cultural misconceptions and develop a more "mature" attitude toward money?

Chapter 8: It's the Way You're Wired

1. Among the money personalities described in this chapter, where do you fit? How does your money personality and your partner's conflict with and complement each other?

2. How can you better maximize the strengths each of you has to offer, while minimizing the weaknesses?

3. Paul, in his letter to the church at Corinth, stressed the importance of developing unity in relationships despite a wide variety of skills, gifts, and functions. (See 1 Cor. 12:12–31.) Are differences in your relationship a roadblock to unity? If so, how can you overcome that obstacle? How might you apply to your situation Paul's encouragement to pursue harmony?

Chapter 9: The Power of Paradigm

1. What's your perspective on the connection between spiritual beliefs and the use of money? How specifically do your convictions and values influence your attitude toward finances?

2. Do you and your partner have different values and spiritual beliefs, especially as they relate to money? How can you better communicate and compromise in order to foster unity?

3. Early in this chapter, there's a quotation that begins, "Money is a mirror." This echoes the proverb that says, "As water reflects a face, so a man's heart reflects the man" (27:19). In what ways does your use of money reflect your values and beliefs? How would you like to change your financial attitudes and decisions to better align with your spiritual convictions?

Chapter 10: The Past Informs the Present

1. What is the biggest financial setback you've experienced as an adult? What is the most positive experience? How have these events changed your attitude toward money?

2. Think about the significant financial experiences both you *and* your partner have had. Are any of these similar? Based on these events, what can you learn from each other?

3. The book of Proverbs says, "Of what use is money in the hand of a fool, since he has no desire to get wisdom?" (17:16). How can you benefit even more by

exploring your past experiences? In what other ways can your gain wisdom about yourself and your money personality?

Chapter 11: Take Time to Talk

1. How would you rate the communication within your relationship (poor, fair, excellent)? What ideas from this chapter will you apply to improve your communication?

2. Are money matters easy or difficult for you and your partner to discuss? Why do you think so many couples struggle to communicate openly about money?

3. In light of our discussion in this chapter, reflect on this proverb: "A word aptly spoken is like apples of gold in settings of silver" (25:11). How can you apply that intriguing imagery to your relationship?

Chapter 12: We Can Work It Out

1. How often do you and your partner argue about money (once a week, once a month, every six months)? Do you usually settle the issue or leave it unresolved?

2. What ideas do you have to make conflict constructive in your relationship? How can you start implementing those ideas?

3. The apostle Paul wrote, "Each of you should look not only to your own interests, but also to the interests of others" (Phil. 2:4). How does that statement relate to the issue of conflict resolution? How can you apply this idea to your own relationship?

Chapter 13: The Case for Creative Compromise

1. Why is compromise in relationships so difficult to achieve? How do you and your partner rate in the area of compromise (excellent, fair, poor)?

2. What are some common roadblocks couples face when trying to work as a team? How can these be overcome?

3. Reflect on the following biblical passage in light of our discussion about compromise: "What causes fights and quarrels among you? Don't they come from your desires that battle within you? You want something but don't get it" (James 4:1–2). In what ways do our selfish desires harm our closest relationships?

Chapter 14: Accentuate Accountability

1. Why are so many people resistant to accountability?

2. How can you and your partner use accountability in a positive, productive way?

3. Think back to the 1 Thessalonians passage we quoted in the chapter. How can you and your partner better "speak encouraging words" and "build up hope" within your relationship?

Chapter 15: Dare to Dream

1. Have you and your partner discussed the direction your lives are heading, perhaps even identifying specific dreams and goals? If not, when will you do so?

2. What potential obstacles might stand between you and your dreams? How can you make sure they don't impede your progress?

3. The Old Testament prophet Amos makes this intriguing statement: "Do two people walk hand in hand if they aren't going to the same place?" (3:3 MSG). Reflect on that question in light of the discussion about goals and dreams. How does that verse apply to your relationship? Do you have the sense of moving forward together hand in hand? If not, how can you make that happen?

Chapter 16: A Budget Is Your Friend ... Really!

1. What's your reaction to the word *budget*? Do you view a budget as your friend or a foe? Are you and your partner similar or different in this area?

2. Do you find a budget difficult to use? If so, why? How can you and your partner better utilize a budget in order to move toward your goals and dreams?

3. Reflect on the following proverb: "The wisdom of the wise keeps life on track; the foolishness of fools lands them in the ditch" (14:8 MSG). How might this proverb be applied to money management and budgeting?

Chapter 17: Focus on Your Future

1. What major events are looming ahead for you and your partner (retirement, college education for kids, assistance for elderly parents, and so on)? Have you discussed your goals and dreams for each of these events?

2. Do you and your partner feel a sense of unity and harmony in regard to planning for future events? What are some areas of disagreement? How can you compromise and negotiate to be more aligned on these issues?

3. The Old Testament prophet Isaiah said, "The noble man makes noble plans, and by noble deeds he stands" (32:8). What do you think that statement means? How does it apply to you and your future?

Chapter 18: Making Your Money Work for You

1. How well do you understand each other's risk tolerance and investment preferences? Is this an area you've discussed thoroughly, a little, or not at all? If you'd like to increase your level of understanding, how will you do that?

2. Is investing a source of tension within your relationship? How can this be a fun, enriching endeavor rather than a stressful, divisive one?

3. In light of the discussion about investments, reflect on the following words of Solomon: "Be sure to stay busy and plant a variety of crops, for you never know which will grow—perhaps they all will" (Eccl. 11:6 NLT). Are you and your partner being wise in setting aside money for the future and helping to safeguard your investments by spreading them around? What changes could you make?

Chapter 19: Safeguarding Your Family

1. How can insurance—which we typically think of in strictly financial terms—be a source of unity for couples?

2. Has the issue of insurance been a sore spot in your relationship? If it still is, how can you resolve it?

3. Jesus once said, "Do not worry about tomorrow, for tomorrow will worry about itself. Each day has enough trouble of its own" (Matt. 6:34). What is the balance between safeguarding ourselves and our families with insurance and trusting God to meet our future needs?

Chapter 20: The Source of True Riches

1. Why are some people reluctant to share their resources with others? Is giving something that is easy or hard for you to do? How could it become a more joyful experience for you?

2. In what ways does giving benefit marriages and families? Why do some spouses become divided over giving, while others are united by it?

3. Paul wrote, "He who supplies seed to the sower and bread for food will also supply and increase your store of seed and will enlarge the harvest of your righteousness. You will be made rich in every way so that you can be generous on every occasion, and through us your generosity will result in thanksgiving to God" (2 Cor. 9:10–11). Reflect on your own financial situation in light on those verses. What does it mean that "you will be made rich in every way"? Does the encouragement to "be generous on every occasion" mean we should respond to *all* the requests that come our way?

Notes

Introduction: The Clash over Cash
1. Scott Stanley and Howard Markman, "Marriage in the '90s: A Nationwide Survey," 1997. Prep, Inc.
2. *Parent Life* magazine, March 2003.
3. Olivia Mellan, "Men, Women, and Money," *Psychology Today*, January 1999, 36.
4. William Fleeson, Ph.D., "How Healthy Are We?: A National Study of Well-Being at Midlife," eds., O. G. Brim, C. D. Ryff, and R. C. Kessler. (Chicago: University of Chicago Press, 2004). Quotations cited in Melissa Stoppler, "Marriage and Money Most Closely Linked to Quality of Life," *Newswise*, February 18, 2004.

Chapter 1: Savers versus Spenders
1. Olivia Mellan, "Men, Women, and Money," *Psychology Today*, January 1999.
2. Betsy Stone, *Happily Ever After* (New York: Doubleday, 1997), 110.
3. Bernice Kanner, *Are You Normal about Money?* (Princeton, N.J.: Bloomberg Press, 2001), 5–6.

Chapter 2: Dueling Over Debt
1. From the newsletter of Richard Stearns, president of World Vision, www.preachingtoday.com.
2. These statistics according to a survey conducted by the Jumpstart Coalition, which promotes financial literacy.
3. Liz Pulliam Weston, "Teach Your Teen How to Handle Credit Cards," www.msn.com, June 23, 2002.
4. Stacy Teicher, "King Kong Debt Meets Middle-class Life," *Christian Science Monitor*, August 16, 2004.
5. Bernice Kanner, *Are You Normal about Money?*, 88.

Chapter 3: Risk-Takers versus Security-Seekers
1. Sherman Hanna and Rui Yao, "The Effect of Gender and Marital Status on Financial Risk Tolerance," *Consumer Interests Annual*, vol. 50, 2004.
2. "Financial Practicality vs. Risk: The Battle of the Sexes Continues." Source: "A Study about Money," March 31, 2001, conducted by Yankelovich Partners, Inc. Accessed at www.microsoft.com/presspass.
3. Bernice Kanner, *Are You Normal about Money?*, 75, 77.
4. Judith Briles, "Face Your Financial Fears," www.msmoney.com.

Chapter 4: Exasperating Expectations
1. Judith Wallerstein and Sandra Blakeslee, *The Good Marriage* (New York: Houghton Mifflin, 1995), 21–22.
2. Kim Clark, "Women, Men, and Money," *Fortune*, August 5, 1996.
3. Bernice Kanner, *Are You Normal About Money?*, 93, 90.
4. C. S. Lewis, *A Grief Observed* (San Francisco: HarperSanFrancisco, 2001), 81–82.
5. Olivia Mellan, "Men, Women, and Money," *Psychology Today*, January 1999.

Chapter 5: Flying Blind
1. These statistics are taken from Bernice Kanner, *Are You Normal about Money?* (Princeton, N.J.: Bloomberg Press, 2001), 128, 138, 154.
2. "Miles to Go: A Status Report on Americans' Plans for Retirement" (1997) www.publicagenda.org/research.
3. Bernice Kanner, *Are You Normal about Money?*, 53, 71
4. Quoted in an article by Laura Lee, *The Futurist* magazine, September/October, 2000, 20–25.

5. These statistics come from the US Postal Service and were cited on the Web site www.newdream.org/junkmail.
6. Juliet Schor, *The Overspent American* (New York: Basic Books, 1998), 83.

Chapter 6: It's All Relative
1. Bernice Kanner, *Are You Normal about Money?*, 14.
2. "Cat on a Hot Tin Roof," MGM 1958. Screenplay by Richard Brooks and James Poe, based on the play by Tennessee Williams.
3. Olivia Mellan, *Psychology Today*, January 1999.
4. Jeff D. Opdyke, *Love and Money* (Hoboken, N.J.: John Wiley & Sons, 2004), 127.
5. Judith Viorst, *Grown-Up Marriage* (New York: Free Press, 2003), 53.

Chapter 7: Swayed by Society
1. Lynne Twist, *The Soul of Money* (New York: W. W. Norton, 2003), 10–11.
2. Ruth Benedict quoted in *The New Beacon Book of Quotations by Women*, ed. Rosalie Maggio (Boston: Beacon Press, 1996), 155.
3. Juliet Schor, *Born to Buy* (New York: Scribner, 2004), 9.
4. Juliet Schor, *Born to Buy*, 171.
5. Victor Strasburger, "Children and TV Advertising: Nowhere to Run, Nowhere to Hide," *Journal of Developmental and Behavioral Pediatrics*, June 2001, 185.
6. James McNeal, *Kids as Customers* (New York: Lexington Books, 1992).
7. George Comstock, *Television and the American Child* (New York: Academic Press, Inc., 1991).
8. Dr. David Walsh with the National Institute on Media and the Family has provided outstanding research and commentary. We highly recommend his material, which can be accessed at www.mediafamily.org.
9. Lynne Twist, *The Soul of Money*, 10–11.
10. This documentary—along with much other insightful information—is described on the Web site www.globalissues.org.
11. Haddon Robinson, "A Good Lesson from a Bad Example," www.preachingtoday.com.
12. David Boyle and Anita Roddick, *Numbers* (West Sussex, UK: Anita Roddick Publications, 2004), 6, 47.
13. Joe Dominguez and Vicki Robin, *Your Money or Your Life* (New York: Viking, 1992), 13.
14. Jim Auchmutey, "Our Overflowing Lives," *Atlanta Journal Constitution*, January 20, 2002.

Chapter 8: It's the Way You're Wired
1. Judith Viorst, *Grown-up Marriage* (New York: The Free Press, 2003), 39–40.
2. Gary Smalley and John Trent, *The Two Sides of Love* (Colorado Springs: Focus on the Family, 1990).
3. The Myers-Briggs Type Indictor is one of the best tools available for understanding your personality type. For more information, visit www.myersbriggs.org.
4. We are grateful to Matt Bell, whose column "Maximizing Your Inner Money Manager" inspired the section on the four temperament types and how they affect money management. His regular column, carried under the banner "The Steward's Wallet," can be found at www.supermarketguru.com.
5. Ray Linder, *What Will I Do with My Money?* (Chicago: Northfield Publishing, 2000), 96.

Chapter 9: The Power of Paradigm

1. Rosalie Maggio, *Money Talks* (Paramus, N.J.: Prentice Hall, 1998), viii.
2. Michael Phillips quoted in Rosalie Maggio, *Money Talks* (Paramus, N.J.: Prentice Hall, 1998), 206.
3. Stephen Covey, *The Seven Habits of Highly Effective People* (New York: Simon & Schuster, 1989), 24, 32.
4. John Ortberg quoted in "Who Do You Believe Really Owns It All?" by Brad Hulse, www.moneyandfaith.net.
5. For more information, visit www.pallotticenter.org.
6. Gordon Kirk, *An Examination of the Biblical Principles of Financial Stewardship: A Thesis Presented to the Department of Systematic Theology, Talbot Theological Seminary,* June 1974.
7. See www.barnaresearch.com.
8. Bella English, "The Richest Man in Town," *Boston Globe,* March 23, 2004.

Chapter 10: The Past Informs the Present

1. Stephen King, "Scaring You to Action," www.beliefnet.com.
2. This survey was conducted by Visa USA, and the results were accessed at www.preachingtoday.com.
3. Terry Savage, *The Savage Truth on Money* (New York: John Wiley, 1999), xiii.
4. Peter Lynch, *Beating the Street* (New York: Simon & Schuster, 1993), 11.

Chapter 11: Take Time to Talk

1. Jeff Opdyke, *Love and Money* (Hoboken, N.J.: John Wiley & Sons, 2004), 235.
2. Bernice Kanner, *Are You Normal about Sex, Love, and Relationships?* (New York: St. Martin's, 2004), 128–29.
3. H. Norman Wright, "Communication: Key to Your Marriage," *Marriage Partnership,* vol. 12, no. 2.
4. For an in-depth look at this study and many other helpful ideas, see John Gottman, *The Seven Principles for Making Marriage Work* (New York: Crown Publishers, 1999).
5. Mary Loftus, "Till Debt Do Us Part," *Psychology Today,* November/December 2004, 44.
6. Olivia Mellan, "Men, Women, and Money," *Psychology Today,* January 1999.
7. Survey conducted by *Reader's Digest* and reported in Jennifer Harper, "Some Things Are Secret, and That's No White Lie," *Insight on the News,* September 3, 2001.

Chapter 12: We Can Work It Out

1. Dr. Scott Stanley quoted in Mary Loftus, "Till Debt Do Us Part," *Psychology Today,* November/December 2004, 46.
2. Mary Loftus, "Till Debt Do Us Part," *Psychology Today,* November/December 2004, 46.
3. John Gottman, *Why Marriages Succeed or Fail* (New York: Simon & Schuster, 1994), 28.
4. Neil Clark Warren, *Catching the Rhythm of Love* (Nashville: Thomas Nelson, 2000), 167–168.
5. Bernice Kanner, *Are You Normal about Sex, Love, and Relationships?* (New York: St. Martin's Press, 2004), 126, 128.
6. David Niven, *The 100 Simple Secrets of Great Relationships* (San Francisco: HarperSanFrancisco, 2003), 27.

Chapter 13: The Case for Creative Compromise

1. Stephen Covey, *The Seven Habits of Highly Effective People,* 207.
2. Dr. Allan Cordova quoted in Natalie Jenkins, Scott Stanley, William Bailey, and

Howard Markman, *You Paid How Much for That?!* (San Francisco: Jossey-Bass, 2002), 157.
3. David Boyle and Anita Roddick, *Numbers* (West Sussex, England: Anita Roddick Books, 2004), 42.
4. This story originally appeared in Sherri Dalphonse, "Love and Money," *Washingtonian*, February 2000.

Chapter 14: Accentuate Accountability
1. Linda Waite and Maggie Gallagher, *The Case for Marriage* (New York: Doubleday, 2000), 40–41.
2. Archibald Hart, *Leadership*, vol. 9, no. 2.
3. John Maxwell, *Leadership Wired*, June 2003.

Chapter 15: Dare to Dream
1. *About Schmidt*, written by Alexander Payne. New Line Cinema, 2002.
2. Elizabeth Cody Newenhuyse, "The Power of Dreams," *Marriage Partnership*, vol. 7, no. 3.
3. Neil Clark Warren, *The Triumphant Marriage* (Colorado Springs: Focus on the Family, 1995), 12–13.
4. David Niven, *The 100 Simple Secrets of Great Relationships* (San Francisco: HarperSanFrancisco, 2003).
5. Mary Claire Allvine and Christine Larson, *The Family CFO* (New York: Rodale, 2004), 108.
6. Neil Clark Warren, *The Triumphant Marriage*, 18.
7. Ray and Florence Borquez quoted in Bill Morelan, *Married for Life* (Colorado Springs: Honor Books, 2004), 22–23.

Chapter 16: A Budget Is Your Friend ... Really!
1. James Dobson and Ron Blue, "Four Guidelines for Money Management," www.family.org.
2. Jeff Opdyke, *Love and Money* (Hoboken, N.J.: John Wiley, 2004), 134.
3. Bernice Kanner, *Are You Normal about Money?* (Princeton, N.J.: Bloomberg Press, 2001), 5–6.

Chapter 17: Focus on Your Future
1. These statistics are taken from Bernice Kanner, *Are You Normal about Money?*, 65.
2. One helpful online resource is the Web site www.oppenheimerfunds.com. Click on "Explore Investment Options," "Retirement Planning," and finally "Getting Started."
3. Venita Van Caspel quoted in *Money Talks*, ed. Rosalie Maggio (Paramus, N.J.: Prentice Hall Press, 1998), 31.
4. Bernice Kanner, *Are You Normal about Money?*, 58.

Chapter 20: The Source of True Riches
1. *Gone Nutty*, written by William Frake and Dan Shefelman. Twentieth Century Fox, 2002.
2. From the "Monitor" column, *Kiplinger's* magazine, October 2004, 32.
To read the complete study results, visit www.barnaresearch.com.
3. Update, June 5, 2001.
4. Ed Chinn, "You Can Only Have What You Give Away," posted on the Web site www.family.org/focusoverfifty.
5. www.businessday.com, August 26, 2003.